SECRETS
OF A
PIVOT BOSS

SECRETS
OF A
PIVOT BOSS
REVEALING PROVEN METHODS FOR
PROFITING IN THE MARKET

FRANKLIN O. OCHOA, JR.

PUBLISHING

SECRETS OF A PIVOT BOSS
ISBN-10 0615391273
ISBN-13 9780615391274

Library of Congress Cataloging-in-Publication Data

Ochoa, Franklin O.
Secrets of a pivot boss: proven methods for profiting in the market / by Franklin O. Ochoa, Jr.
1.   Stocks—Charts, diagrams, etc.   2.   Futures market—Charts, diagrams, etc.
            3.   Investment analysis.   I. Title
LCCN 2010907089

Printed in the United States of America.

To the women who inspire me: my wife Claudia, daughter Olivia, and mother Maria.

CONTENTS

ACKNOWLEDGMENTS

Anyone that has attempted to tackle a project of this magnitude knows the task is nearly insurmountable without an incredible supporting cast. I'd like to thank the entire Nirvana Systems family for supporting me during this project and throughout my professional career. Special thanks go to Ed Downs for giving me my start in this exciting industry. His vision and leadership have been amazing to watch over the years. Thanks to Steve Belknap for being the captain of the ship. Thanks also go to Jeff Drake, Matthew Greenslet, and Gianluca Paganoni, whose development and coding efforts led to my discovering the amazing relationships these powerful indicators have to offer. I would also like to thank Kevin Gallagher for his contagious enthusiasm for trading. Bouncing trading ideas off each other over the last several years has been instrumental in my development as a trader and analyst. Thank you, Melissa Drake, for creating the wonderful cover art for the book.

Behind every man is an amazing woman. In my case, I have three amazing ladies in my corner. I'd like to thank my mother Maria for being my number one fan. She inspired me at an early age, and has never stopped. Everything I am is a testament to her. I'd like to thank my beautiful and talented wife Claudia for her unwavering support, inspiration, and everlasting patience through this long and trying process. She is the pulse of my family, without whom, I would be lost. Lastly, I'd like to thank my daughter Olivia for being the ultimate inspiration for writing this book. I want you to know that through hard work and dedication anything is possible. The sky is the limit for you, baby doll.

Thanks to the memory of my father Franklin, who passed too soon, but remains an important part of who I am.

INTRODUCTION

"Fear and hope remain the same; therefore the study of the psychology of speculators remains as valuable as it ever was."
- Jesse Livermore (1877– 1940), Legendary Trader

The Dow Jones Industrial Average closed the day at 11,842.69 on June 20, 2008. After the session closed, I scrawled *"Target 8385"* in my notebook, along with extremely bearish targets of the other major market indexes. This came six months after I called for a drop back to the 10,000 level despite the Dow reaching an all-time high at 14,198.10 on October 8, 2007. Needless to say, I received a lot of flak from traders and investors from around the world, claiming I was purposely pumping fear into the market. This was not my intention. I was merely translating what the charts were telling me, and I reported my findings to the public through my daily market newsletter. In the months that followed, the market experienced a major collapse, with the Dow eventually finding a bottom at 6,469.95 on March 6, 2009—a whopping 45 percent nosedive from my June 20 prediction.

How was I able to forecast this move? The concepts and techniques in this book helped me with the prediction. Every now and again, a book is published that offers incredible insight into professional trading. My friend, you are holding that book in your hands right now.

This book offers a road map to the market that can be so unbelievably accurate it's like trader voodoo.

For every trade, there is a good price, a bad price, and a fair price. The techniques and concepts in this book will help you find the best price. Professional traders use tools that are based purely on price, which is a leading indicator in its own class. In this book, you will discover the best leading indicators available to traders: The Money Zone, Floor Pivots, and the Camarilla Equation. Some of these tools have been around for decades, but many traders do not know they exist or how to use them properly to profit in the market. In fact, the traders that do use these tools are typically the ones that drive better cars and have bigger homes. Traders like Larry Williams, Mark Fisher, John Person, and John Carter all use pivots in their trading. These are distinguished traders, educators, and authors that have seen the road map and can no longer look at charts the same without these powerful tools plotted in some form or fashion.

Independently, the Money Zone, Floor Pivots, and the Camarilla Equation offer road maps to trading virtually any chart you can plot. But when used in combination, these tools create the GPS navigation system to trading the market. While you may have studied forms of pivots in the past, I am providing a fresh perspective that can only be described as a truly unique approach to playing these amazing levels for profit. Concepts like two-day pivot relationships, pivot width forecasting, pivot trend analysis, and multiple pivot hot zones can improve your analysis and trading by leaps and bounds.

Not only will I teach you incredible pivot relationships, but I will also divulge my best trading secrets, including powerful candlestick setups and proprietary indicators that I have created to both trade and analyze the market in a highly accurate and profitable manner. Taking this a step farther, I have also provided the actual code to each of the scripts that I've written in Appendix B to help you find the same amazing setups that I will teach.

The market revolves around repetition due to human nature—namely fear, greed, and uncertainty. This truism is why the Money Zone, Floor Pivots, and the Camarilla Equation work and will continue to work in the future.

Secrets of a Pivot Boss offers the most comprehensive collection of pivot-related trading ideas and concepts available to traders. Whether you are a real-time trader, swing trader, position trader, or investor, you will find great value in this book, both as a teaching tool and as a reference, regardless of the markets you trade or your level of experience. I have analyzed the market every day for the past twelve years and have cultivated the techniques in this book into a fine art using the best leading indicators available to traders. I truly believe the concepts in this book will help to guide you to a higher level of trading success.

CHAPTER 1

UNDERSTANDING MARKETS

"Nowhere does history indulge in repetitions so often or so uniformly as in Wall Street."

- Jesse Livermore

About a month ago, I woke up filled with excitement about the upcoming trading day. I had a feeling that a huge breakout was going to be seen in the market and I wanted to be sure that I profited from the move. This type of move only occurs two or three times a month, but the amount of money you can make during these few days can be incredible. Using the techniques that I will teach in this book, I was able to pinpoint the explosive breakout that occurred on this day *before* the opening print was even recorded. How did I do this? By having a keen understanding of market dynamics and pivot point concepts. Needless to say, the market experienced a major rally on this day, allowing me to capture a healthy five-figure gain in just one session! The trades I took on this day, like the one shown in Figure 1.1, were easily identifiable using the concepts in this book, and I will show you exactly how to find them.

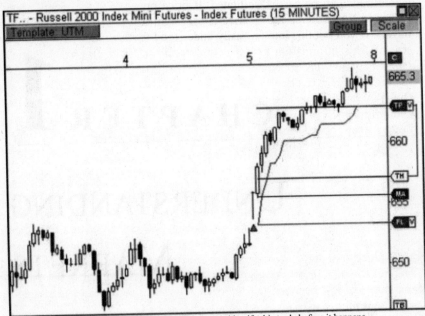

FIGURE 1.1: The concepts in this book will help you identify this trade before it happens.

However, before an aspiring trader can learn to make money in this game, he or she must first obtain a proper understanding of the market. Too often, novice traders race out of the gate in search of sizzling setups and black box mechanical trading systems, without ever understanding fully the role of the marketplace and its buyers and sellers. To have a chance at profiting from the market, you must have a firm understanding of market dynamics. Understanding, after all, is the operative word. As you make your way through this book, you will learn many definitions, concepts, and setups as they pertain to the market. However, your ability to gain the most out of the information will come from the evolution of your learning into true understanding. The ability to understand why the market is behaving the way that it is will allow you to innately anticipate market behavior and pinpoint entries and exits using the tools and techniques in this book. In many cases, to begin to understand the market is to first understand the auction process.

THE AUCTION PROCESS

The role of the marketplace is to facilitate trade between buyers and sellers. Price will auction higher and lower as it attempts to find an area where trade can be easily facilitated. If price opens too low, it will auction higher to find sellers, and if price is too high, it will auction lower to find buyers. If you put this into an easily understood framework, you will come to see that this information makes complete sense. If an original painting by Pablo Picasso were to be auctioned for a starting bid of $10 on the open market, buyers would enter the market en masse because price is too low. Buyers would drive price higher until the last buyer stood alone, essentially ending the auction with the sale, likely for a price in the tens of millions of dollars. However, what would happen if I were to auction off a painting by my one-year-old daughter with a starting bid of $1 million dollars? Obviously, the starting bid is too high; the price would begin to auction lower in search of buyers. Eventually, price would auction low enough to find a buyer, perhaps her loving grandmother, for a mere $10.

Price continually moves higher and lower in search of the best value to both buyers and sellers. Buyers will enter the market when they feel price is below value, while sellers will enter the market when they believe price is overvalued. This will be a consistent theme over the course of the book. It boggles my mind how a novice trader can be a smart shopper in the everyday marketplace, but become a completely different person when engaging the stock and futures markets.

Meet Novice Joe, who is a fantastic shopper when it comes to food, clothes, and even cars, but throws all of his instincts out of the window when it comes to trading. Joe loves to eat lobster, but he knows that this can be an expensive habit, so he must buy when the price of lobster is below value. He keenly observes the price of lobster regularly and knows that the average price per pound is about $10.99. As you can expect, when the price per pound drops to $6.99 he pounces on the offer and buys several pounds.

The very next morning, however, Joe engages the stock or futures market in a completely different manner. Instead of waiting on value, as he did with the lobster, he hastily pulls the trigger at the most inopportune times, buying when the market is overvalued, and selling when the market is undervalued. Essentially, his trading behaviors would translate into his buying lobster at $15.99 per pound, which he would never do. The concept of value is easily understood, but consistently applying it to the market occurs with experience, which can only be obtained through vigorous study and practice.

Sometimes, price needs to probe higher in order to find a compromise between buyers and sellers, while other times price needs to probe lower before finding an agreeable price. Imagine a local cake baker that has just opened her bakery and is currently in the price discovery phase. Jennifer, owner of Just Baked Cakes, is unsure of the market value of her cakes and initially lists her cakes to sell at $20 apiece. The market clearly sees this price as below value, as evidenced by the boom of orders she receives. She sold 100 cakes in her first week and is extremely excited. However, she decides to raise the price to $30 to see how the market will respond. She is delighted to see that her orders remained constant at 100 cakes per week, meaning that buyers still feel that her cakes are a value at the current price. She feels the need to probe even higher in order to maximize her profit potential, therefore, she raises the price of her cakes to $35 apiece. This time, however, the market responded with fewer orders to buy, as she only received 75 orders. She quickly reinstates the $30 price tag and feels confident that she has reached a fair facilitation of trade between buyer and seller.

This example paints a vivid picture of why you will see price rally through resistance only to sell off sharply, or drop through support only to rally with conviction. Sometimes the market must break to rally, and break out to sell off. The market is constantly searching for the best area for trade facilitation, and usually needs confirmation at an extreme before it can proceed on its merry way. To understand the auction process further, let's understand its participants: buyers and sellers.

THE TYPES OF BUYERS AND SELLERS

The role of the marketplace is to facilitate trade between buyers and sellers. However, every buyer is not the same, nor is every seller. There are two types of buyers and two types of sellers. The ability to distinguish between these categories will allow you to anticipate upcoming price movement and behavior. That is, understanding whether price is moving due to a responsive reaction on the part of a buyer or seller, versus price movement caused by initiative participation, goes a long way toward understanding how price will react.

Your ability to determine which market participants are influencing price will allow you to judge the conviction and behavior of price movement.

A buyer that enters the market when price is *below value* is considered a *responsive buyer*. In essence, Novice Joe was a responsive buyer when he waited until the price of lobster dropped to $6.99 per pound before entering the market. Likewise, a *responsive seller* waits until price is *above value* before entering the market with sell orders. Responsive buying and selling will typically drive price back toward the mean, sending price toward an area that is considered fair value by the market. Therefore, price movement is short-term oriented and lacks true conviction.

An *initiative buyer* enters the market when price is *at or above value*. This type of buyer is taking the initiative to push price to a higher area of value. If there was a shortage of lobster in Novice Joe's area and additional lobster would not enter the market for another year, you may see Joe become an initiative buyer. In this case, Joe would aggressively look to buy all the lobster he could find, which would push price to a higher level of value. This type of buying would cause other buyers to enter the market en masse, causing price to explode to new heights. Along the same lines, an *initiative seller* is enters the market when price is *at or below value*. This seller is taking the initiative to push price to a lower area of value. Initiative participants have greater conviction behind their behaviors, which has a greater influence on price. These types of moves indicate a more confident buyer or seller, which is then reflected in aggressive price movement.

As you learn the concepts behind the book, begin to associate certain price behaviors or setups to initiative or responsive participation. This will allow you to continue to evolve in your understanding of the market and its tendencies.

RECYCLING MARKET DAYS

I was teaching a trader boot camp recently when a trader asked how I would have traded the prior day. I responded that the prior session was one of the easiest days to trade. The market gapped up at the open and trended higher throughout the session, making it easy to buy and hold throughout the day, or buy the pull-backs along the way. He wasn't so impressed with my answer.

"That's easy to say now, since you have hindsight," he fired back.

The response I gave him is the same that I will share with you right now. Every market day is unique, but it is a clone of a prior day in history. Technical analysis works because trader psychology, and human psychology for that matter, never changes. It has been the same since the first exchange opened its doors. However, most novice traders, and even experienced traders, do not make the correlation that every market day is a version of one that occurred in the past. As a matter of fact, many traders do not make this discovery for quite some time into their trading careers. But once they do, they begin to understand the market on an entirely different level, which allows them to anticipate market movement.

Think about the first time you heard a new song. You like the beat and you relate to the lyrics, but they are completely new to you. However, once you've heard this song five or six times, or even one hundred times, every lyric, beat, and drum solo has become engrained in your brain. You can anticipate the chorus and the upcoming instrumental solo. You can even identify the song by hearing a two-second snippet. Trading is no different. Once you've mastered the types of trading days that occur in the market, you will be able to anticipate reversals, breakouts, and even stalled markets with a high level of accuracy and authority.

Trading is a game of repetitions. Traders that can consistently trade the best repetitions are those that have mastered the markets.

Some highly successful traders will exclusively trade one or two setups, but they will continuously pound these setups with big volume and make a killing in the market. Trading doesn't have to be difficult. Like most things in life, trading can be as easy or as difficult as you make it. It can be as stressful or stress free as you make it. I know I just dropped a bombshell on you, but think about it for a moment. All trading requires is a focused trader who is disciplined and knows his/her bread and butter setups. If you are disciplined enough to adhere to a proper trade management approach, and play only the best setups time and again, you will become a successful trader. Many novice traders focus on the money too early in their trading career, which is a mistake. Focus on playing the best setups at the right times while using prudent money management techniques and the money will come. As you will come to see, proper preparation also plays a major role in successful trading.

The best traders are those that can quickly discern the pattern of the market and successfully deploy their capital at the best price.

The first step in identifying your bread and butter setups is identifying the types of market days that you will see time and again. Once you quickly and accurately can identify the type of market day that is developing, you can then identify which of your setups to deploy. Trading has always been about pattern recognition. The best traders can quickly diagnose and identify the pattern of the market, which allows them to visualize where price is headed and the level of conviction behind the move. This upcoming section may be one of the most important facets of this book, as learning and understanding the material will be paramount to building the foundation to the rest of the book.

THE TYPES OF MARKET DAYS

There are six types of market days that we will cover. These types of days are repeatedly seen in the market, but no two days are ever identical. As such, these categories should be used more as guidelines, rather than seeing them as etched in stone. Again, your ability to recognize the pattern of the day accurately will be a huge step toward successfully engaging the market.

The first type of market day that we will cover is called the *Trend Day*. The Trend Day is the most aggressive type of market day. On a bullish Trend Day, the open usually marks the day's low, while the close usually marks the day's high, with a few ticks of tolerance in either direction. On a bearish Trend Day, the open will usually mark the day's high, while the market will usually close near the session's low. The market will typically start fast on this type of day and the farther price moves away from value, the more participants will enter the market, creating sustained price movement on increased volume. Initiative buying or selling is the culprit on this type of market day, as these participants are confident they can move price to a new area of established value. Price conviction is strongest during a Trend Day.

Imagine a sprinter lined up at the starting blocks of a one hundred-meter dash. As soon as the gun is fired to begin the race, the sprinter accelerates out of the blocks and eventually hits his full stride. The sprinter will maintain a high level of speed throughout the race until he ultimately reaches the finish line. Likewise, the market will start strong right out of the gate and will usually maintain a unidirectional stance throughout the day, never calling into question the day's direction or conviction. This type of day has the highest price range (high price minus low price), meaning it can be quite costly if you are positioned against the market or if you fail to recognize the pattern early enough to enter alongside the market. These types of days only occur a few times a month, but catching these moves can certainly make your month, in terms of profits. The Trend Day is usually preceded by a quiet day of market activity, which is usually a day with a small range of movement. Coincidentally, this type of market behavior will usually follow a Trend Day as well.

Take a look at Figure 1.2, which is a fifteen-minute chart of the Mini-Sized Dow Jones futures contract, also called the YM. This chart clearly illustrates the Trend Day and its basic characteristics. Notice the YM opened the day with a gap to the upside, which is a common trait of a bullish Trend Day. The low of the day was established within mere ticks of the opening print, and the session's close price fell within two ticks of the high. Clearly, the day's direction was never called into question, as initiative buying pressure sparked steady strength throughout the session. This initiative buying pressure led to the recruitment of additional market participants, which boosted price even higher. Lastly, the prior day's range was relatively smaller than usual, especially in the latter half of the day where the YM basically traded in a 49-tick range in the last five hours of the session. This type of quiet trading behavior can usually tip you off to a potential Trend Day in the upcoming session. Remember, keeping your ear to the ground would have easily allowed you to sense that a big day could be had in the following session. Trading is about reading the cues the market constantly feeds you.

The ability to read the market's cues quickly and accurately will set you apart as a trader.

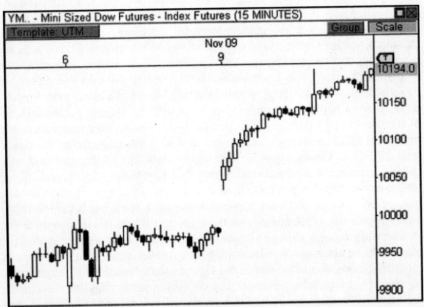

FIGURE 1.2: The Trend Day

The second type of market day is called the *Double-Distribution Trend Day*. While this day is a trending day, it in no way has the confidence or conviction of a Trend Day. Instead, this type of day is characterized by its indecisive nature at the outset of the session. During this type of day, the market will usually open the session in a quiet manner, trading within a fairly tight range for the first hour or two of the session, thereby creating an initial balance that is narrow. The *initial balance* is traditionally defined as the price range of the first hour of the day, which is extremely important to professionals on the floors of the exchanges. They use the *initial balance high (IBH)* and the *initial balance low (IBL)* as important points of reference in order to facilitate trade between buyers and sellers. If the initial balance is too narrow, price will break free from the range and auction toward new value, creating *range extension*, which is any movement outside the initial balance. After the initial balance of the Double-Distribution Trend Day has been defined, price will break out from the range and auction toward new value, where it will form a second distribution of price. This is the market's attempt at confirming whether new value has indeed been established.

If the Trend Day is akin to a sprinter, then the Double-Distribution Trend Day is more like a jogger. The jogger will take his time to properly stretch and warm up before actually beginning his run. Once the "warm up" phase is complete, the jogger runs at a moderate pace toward his destination. Once he has finished his run, he will begin the "cooling down" phase of his exercise. Along the same lines, the Double-Distribution Trend Day opens the session quietly, trading within a tight range that can be viewed as the day's "warm up" period. Eventually, price breaks free of the range and begins trending toward new value, igniting initiative buying or selling. Once the market finds new value, it then builds out another range before ending the day. The ranges formed at both the beginning and end of the day is where the term "double-distribution" comes from, as the bulk of the day's volume resides at one of these extremes, essentially forming a double distribution of trading activity.

Take a look at Figure 1.3, which is a five-minute chart of the E-Mini NASDAQ 100 futures contract, also called the NQ. This chart shows a classic Double-Distribution Trend Day, as price basically traded within a fairly narrow range during the first two hours of the day. Since the initial balance was narrow, it became evident that either buyers or sellers would eventually overwhelm the range and push price toward a new area of value. In this case, initiative selling pressure extended the day's range to the downside and pushed price to lower value, where it eventually ended the day within the boundaries of a second range, thereby forming a second distribution of the day's trading activity.

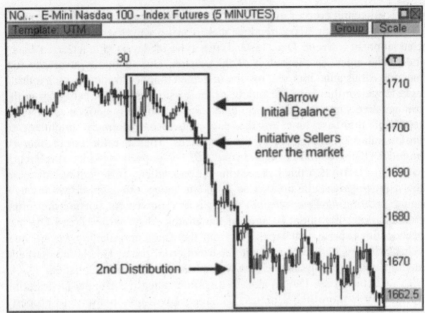

FIGURE 1.3: The Double-Distribution Trend Day

The initial balance is the base for any day's trading and is extremely important to the Double-Distribution Trend Day. A narrow initial balance is easily broken, while a wide initial balance is harder to break. The fact that the initial balance is narrow on this type of day indicates that there is a good possibility of a breakout from the initial range, indicating that you will likely see a move toward new value. Think about it like this, if you were designing a coffee table, one of the biggest areas of focus would be the base of the table. If the base is wide, you will be confident that the table will remain upright, regardless of any pressure or weight added to the table. However, if the base of the coffee table were made too narrow, it is only a matter of time before the table topples over or crumbles beneath its weight. Similarly, the narrow initial balance at the beginning of the Double-Distribution Trend Day indicates that either buyers or sellers will eventually overwhelm one side or the other. Once direction is decided, price will freely move toward a new area of value since it is being driven by initiative market participants.

The third type of market day is called the *Typical Day*. The Typical Day is characterized by a wide initial balance that is established at the outset of the day. On this type of day, price rallies or drops sharply to begin the session and moves far enough away from value to entice responsive participants to enter the market. The responsive players push price back in the opposite direction, essentially establishing the day's trading extremes. The market then trades quietly within the day's extremes the remainder of the session.

The opening rally or sell-off is usually sparked by reactions to economic news that hits the market early in the day. This opening push creates a wide initial balance, which means the day's "base" is wide and will likely go unbroken. Remember, if the base of the coffee table is wide, it will likely remain upright regardless of any added pressure or weight. Likewise, a wide base during the first hour of the market will likely mean that the day's extremes will also remain intact, or unbroken.

Figure 1.4 is a five-minute chart of the Dow futures contract, which clearly illustrates the classic Typical Day. The YM opened the day with early strength in the first hour of the session, establishing a 117-point range, or initial balance. After the wide initial balance was established, the battle lines had clearly been drawn between buyers and sellers. During this type of day, you will usually see price trade back and forth within the boundaries of the opening range, as fair trade is easily being facilitated.

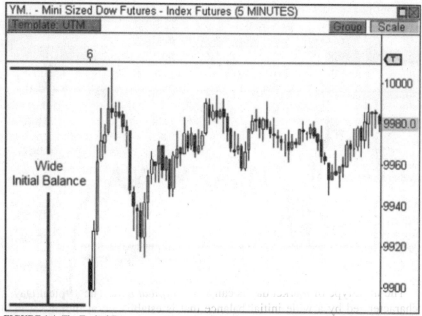

FIGURE 1.4: The Typical Day

The fourth type of market day is the *Expanded Typical Day*. This type of day is similar to the Typical Day in that it usually begins the session with early directional conviction. However, price movement at the open is not as strong as that seen during a Typical Day. Therefore, the initial balance, while wider than that of a Double-Distribution Trend Day, is not as wide as that of the Typical Day, which leaves it susceptible to a violation later in the session. Eventually, one of the day's extremes is violated and price movement is seen in the direction of the break, which is usually caused by initiative buying or selling behavior.

Take a look at Figure 1.5, which is a five-minute chart illustrating a common Expanded Typical Day in the YM. Notice the initial balance was wider than that of a Double-Distribution Trend Day, but not so wide as to challenge the width of the Typical Day. When the base of the day is neither wide nor narrow, it can be a coin flip whether a breakout will occur. The fact that the initial balance is not wide introduces the potential for failure at some point during the day at one of the extremes. In this particular case, initiative sellers overwhelmed the bottom of the day's initial balance and extended price movement to the downside. Selling pressure essentially expanded the day's range, thereby introducing the namesake for this type of day. The initiative selling pressure led to continued weakness the rest of the day, as price moved to establish lower value.

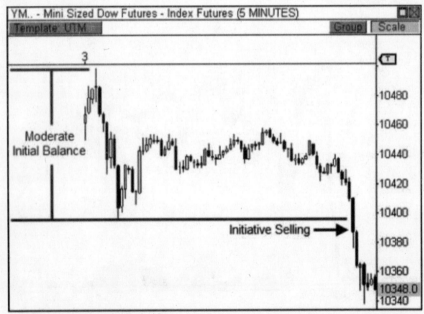

FIGURE 1.5: The Expanded Typical Day

Keep in mind that during an Expanded Typical Day, both the upper and lower boundaries of the initial balance are susceptible to violations. On any given day, you will see one, or both, of the boundaries violated, as buyers and sellers attempt to push price toward their own perceived levels of value.

The last two types of days seem similar, but they have distinct differences that set them apart from each other. The Trading Range Day and the Sideways Day even sound similar, but the difference lies within the participation levels of both buyers and sellers. The *Trading Range Day* occurs when both buyers and sellers are actively auctioning price back and forth within the day's range, which is usually established by the day's initial balance. On this day, the initial balance is about as wide as that of a Typical Day, but instead of quietly trading within these two extremes throughout the day, buyers and sellers are actively pushing price back and forth.

This type of day is basically like a game of tennis. The players stand on opposite sides of the court and take turns volleying the ball to one another throughout the match. As the ball is in flight, a player will wait for the best opportunity to strike the ball, essentially returning the ball to the other side of the court. Likewise, buyers and sellers will stand at the extremes of the day and will enter the market in a responsive manner when price reaches the outer limits of the day's range. Responsive sellers will enter shorts at the top of the range, which essentially pushes price back toward the day's lows, while responsive buyers will enter longs at the bottom of the range, which pushes price back toward the day's highs. This pattern will continue until the closing bell sounds.

Figure 1.6 shows a five-minute chart of the YM during a classic Trading Range Day. Notice that the initial balance was fairly wide to begin the session, which meant that the base for the day would likely support the session's trading activity. As price rose toward the top of the range at around 9,740, responsive sellers saw price as overvalued and entered the market with sell orders, essentially pushing price back toward the day's low. As price approached the bottom of the range at around 9,660, responsive buyers saw value and entered the market with buy orders, which pushed price toward the opposite extreme. This type of market day offers easy facilitation of trade and gives traders amazing opportunities to time their entries.

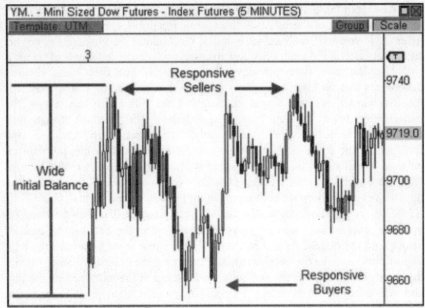

FIGURE 1.6: The Trading Range Day

During a *Sideways Day*, however, there is no volleying of the proverbial tennis ball between buyers and sellers. As a matter of fact, there isn't even a game being played. On this type of day, price is stagnant, as both buyers and sellers refrain from trading. This type of session usually occurs ahead of the release of a major economic report or news event, or in advance of a trading holiday. There is no trade facilitation and no directional conviction. The initial balance is rather narrow, which at first indicates the potential for a Double-Distribution Trend Day. However, the initiative buying or selling required for a Double-Distribution Trend Day never enters the fray, which leaves the market terribly quiet the rest of the session.

Figure 1.7 shows a five-minute chart of a typical Sideways Day, which occurred the day before the Thanksgiving holiday. The YM opened the day with a narrow initial balance and range extension was seen to the upside for a brief period of time. However, initiative buyers did not enter the market en force, which essentially caused price to reverse from the session's high to settle within an extremely tight range that spanned about 25 ticks over the final four hours. The range actually narrowed to a 14-tick spread in the final hour of the day, indicating that market participants had either fallen asleep or had hit the pub early.

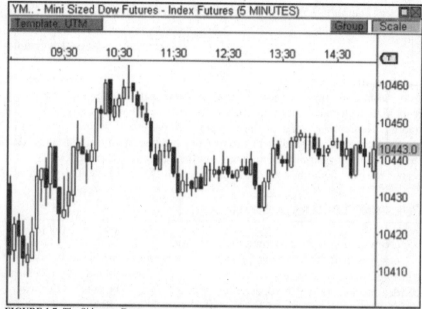

FIGURE 1.7: The Sideways Day

It is my firm belief that *not* every trading day should be a trading day. Many traders believe that since they are traders, they must be in a trade at all times. These traders feel like it's a badge of honor to tell their trader buddies that they traded forty-two round trips today...*before* lunch. As such, they force themselves to trade in the most unfriendly markets, usually to their own detriment. I am on the opposite extreme.

You should only trade when the circumstances are the most favorable for a profitable outcome.

Great quarterbacks always reserve the right to punt the football instead of forcing a turnover. Likewise, traders should always reserve the right to stand on the sidelines. Those traders that can learn to sit on their hands will profit by not losing. This is something that cannot be overstated. The difference between profitable traders and losing traders can usually be summed up by the number of unprofitable days and the severity of unprofitability on these days. Learn to eliminate those unprofitable days by only trading in the most favorable market conditions, and you will prosper in this game.

"The only thing to do when a man is wrong is to be right by ceasing to be wrong."

- Jesse Livermore

It is my hope that you will continue to study the six types of market days with each new session. The faster you can quickly and accurately recognize each market day, the faster you will be on your way to profitable trading. Remember, each of these types of days is not set in stone. While every market day is similar to a day from the past, similar does not mean "exactly." You must be able to snuff out the subtleties of each new day as it relates to a day from the past. Steadfast practice creates valuable experience.

PURSUING UNDERSTANDING

Now that you have learned the basic framework of market dynamics, it is your job to transition from learning to understanding. Instead of simply learning a new concept or idea, make it a habit to understand why a concept or idea works the way it does. Why does a Trend Day behave the way it does? Why does the initial balance of a Typical Day hold throughout the session? Why do responsive buyers and sellers provide less punch than their initiative counterparts? Understanding the answers to these questions will allow you to progress as a trader.

As you progress through the text, you will encounter powerful material that could revolutionize the way you trade. The material contained herein has been paramount to my success as both a trader and market analyst. However, the degree to which this book can help you will be dependent upon your ability to learn, understand, and apply the concepts to your trading. Each new piece of information is interrelated to the next. Each concept is a mere building block for the next piece of information. Continue to relate prior information to newly received inputs as you make your way through this reading, as this process will certainly benefit you in the end.

CHAPTER 2

ENGAGING
THE SETUP

*"I may plunge or I may buy one hundred shares. But in either case I
must have a reason for what I do."*

- Jesse Livermore

Market professionals rely solely on price behavior to cue entries into the
market. Having a keen understanding of market dynamics, the types of
market days, and the ability to recognize early market tendencies are usually
enough to trigger a well-informed entry into the market for this group of
traders. However, having clearly-defined setups at the ready can prove to be
quite helpful when prospecting entry opportunities. In the following sections,
I will uncover some of my favorite technical candlestick setups that have

proven to be extremely powerful during my trading career. Each setup represents certain market behaviors and psychologies that, when paired with clearly established overvalued or undervalued areas, can prove to be quite powerful. As you proceed throughout the rest of the text, you will see exactly how I use each of these setups to confirm entry points at important pivot levels, which include the Money Zone, Floor Pivots, and the Camarilla Equation. Before we begin, however, let's take a look at the basics of a candlestick.

THE ANATOMY OF A CANDLESTICK

Imagine someone is trying to describe to you the brilliance and energy that is New York City's Times Square through the use of hand drawn, black and white stick figures. It goes without saying that the inability to capture the essence of Times Square using this method is quite an understatement. Now imagine the same person hands you a photograph of Times Square. This full color snapshot immediately conveys the energy and vividness that Times Square embodies. This is the difference between a standard bar chart and a candlestick chart.

Candlestick charting was pioneered by the Japanese centuries ago, but it only recently became popular to Western traders due, in part, to the work by Steve Nison, whose book, *Japanese Candlestick Charting Techniques*, helped introduce the power of candlesticks to the masses. This is one of the first books I read on technical analysis, and it immediately became one of my favorites. Another book, *Candlestick Charting Explained* by Greg Morris, has also been a favorite in my library. Both of these comprehensive resources have been paramount to my understanding and use of candlestick techniques.

A *candlestick chart* displays the same data as a typical bar chart (open, high, low, and close), but conveys the information in a more visually appealing manner. This allows for quick and effective judgment of price relationships and the inherent market psychology contained within each candle.

Trading is a game of recognition. The traders that consistently recognize profitable patterns in the market ahead of the crowd will be those that prosper in this game. Candlestick charting allows you to quickly gauge current market sentiment and anticipate potential price movement, which is essential to profitable trading. Once you become familiar with candlesticks, there is no way you will turn back to a boring bar chart.

Take a look at Figure 2.1, which illustrates the anatomy of a bullish and bearish candlestick. The portion of the candle that spans from the open price to the close price is called the *body*. If the close price is *above* the open price

(C > O), the candle is typically colored white or green to denote a bullish sentiment. If the close price is *below* the open price (C < O), the candle is typically colored black or red to denote a bearish sentiment. The top and bottom of the candle denote the high price and low price of the bar, respectively. If the high or low is beyond the limits of the body of the candle, then a *wick* is present, which is also called a shadow or tail. The distance between the low and the high of the candle is called the *range*.

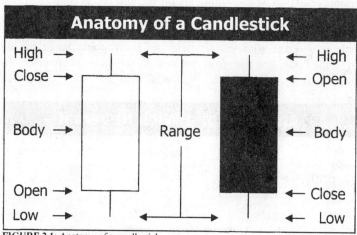

FIGURE 2.1: Anatomy of a candlestick

Candlesticks come in all shapes, sizes, and combinations. Your ability to quickly piece together the market's puzzle using this vital information will be extremely beneficial to your trading success. Now that we have covered the basics of a candlestick, let's proceed to the meat of the chapter.

THE WICK REVERSAL SETUP

The first candlestick pattern that I will discuss is the *wick reversal setup*, which is a pattern that can spotlight some of the best reversal opportunities in the market. If you have ever studied market tops, bottoms, and reversals, you'll notice that in a high percentage of these cases, the charts are peppered with wick reversal candlesticks at these integral points in the charts. A single reversal wick may highlight an opportunity, while other times, a gang of reversal wicks in succession will be screaming reversal. When properly qualified, there is no doubt that this pattern can be a powerful tool in your trading arsenal.

The wick reversal setup is one of the most visually compelling candlestick patterns due to its long price tail, which helps to highlight major reversal opportunities in the market.

PATTERN STRUCTURE

While this candle pattern is well known and seemingly elementary, I feel it is necessary to identify and explain the key components that make for a successful wick reversal opportunity, as these factors can be easily overlooked. In my opinion, there are three factors to consider when reviewing a reversal wick candlestick: the body, the size of the wick in relation to the body, and the *close percentage*, which is where price closes in relation to the range of the candle. Figure 2.2 illustrates these components.

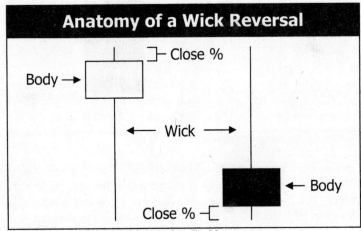

FIGURE 2.2: Anatomy of a wick reversal candlestick

As you recall, the body of the candlestick is the portion of the bar that spans from the open price to closing price. The body of the candle is used to calculate the size of the wick. Traditionally, you would like to see a wick that is at least two times the size of the body. Therefore, if the range of the body of a candlestick is 10 ticks, then the wick has to be at least 20 ticks to arrive at the traditional 2:1 ratio. While technically you only need a 2:1 ratio for a candle to be considered a reversal wick, I usually like to see a higher ratio from 2.5:1 to 3.5:1. This allows you to eliminate some of the weaker reversal candles, but doesn't limit you by being too rigid, thereby reducing the number of trading opportunities. In other words, if you only choose to find candles that have a 5:1 wick-to-body ratio, then you are significantly reducing the number of opportunities for trading because you are eliminating many lower ratio candlesticks, while only trading from a ratio (5:1) that doesn't appear in the market very often.

The last component of a reversal wick candlestick is the close percentage. While the length of the wick is the first part to determining the strength of a reversal candlestick, the second part of the equation is determined upon where the bar closes in relation to the overall high and low of the candle. Therefore, if the bar closes in the top 5 percent of the candle, the chances are greater for a bullish reversal than if the bar closes in the top 35 percent of the candle (see Figure 2.3).

If a candlestick closes in the top 5 percent of the bar with the wick on the south side of the candle, this means the bulls were able to rally the market from the low of the candle and close price near the top of the bar, taking complete control from the bears in this one timeframe. However, if the market closes in the top 35 percent of the candle, this means the bulls were still able to take control from the bears, but only marginally since the close of the bar barely made it above the midpoint of the range. This is still a bullish scenario, but not as bullish as the 5 percent scenario.

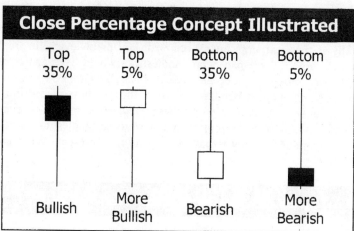

FIGURE 2.3: The close percentage concept illustrated

It is important to emphasize the different components of the reversal wick candlestick, as varying conditions will lead to varying levels of success with this pattern. As I mentioned before, this pattern may seem elementary at face value, but it is actually quite complex when you begin to work with the interrelated components of its structure. Prospecting for a reversal wick that has a 2:1 wick-to-body ratio and a close percentage of 45 percent is going to give you vastly different results from a reversal wick that has a 3.5:1 ratio and a close percentage of 10 percent. Understanding this concept will allow you to focus your energies on the right mix of component variables that make for a profitable outcome. Moreover, finding the best reversal wicks at important undervalued or overvalued areas will be vital to your success with this pattern, which will be a theme throughout the remainder of the text.

PATTERN SUMMARY

1. The body is used to determine the size of the reversal wick. A wick that is between 2.5 to 3.5 times larger than the size of the body is ideal.
2. For a bullish reversal wick to exist, the close of the bar should fall within the top 35 percent of the overall range of the candle.
3. For a bearish reversal wick to exist, the close of the bar should fall within the bottom 35 percent of the overall range of the candle.

PATTERN PSYCHOLOGY

Figure 2.4 shows several types of bullish and bearish reversal wick candlesticks that can all signal profitable reversal opportunities in the market, especially if these patterns are paired with key pivot levels. In traditional candlestick jargon, these particular candlesticks would have names ranging from *hammer, hanging man, inverted hammer, shooting star, gravestone doji,* or *dragonfly doji,* depending on where the candle is placed in a trend. Now you can see why I simply call these candlesticks wicks, or even tails. Instead of fumbling over the proper naming of these candlesticks, I believe it is more important to know what these patterns represent. What are they telling you?

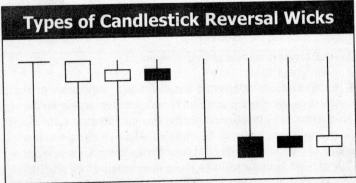

FIGURE 2.4: Types of candlestick reversal wicks

When the market has been trending lower then suddenly forms a reversal wick candlestick, the likelihood of a reversal increases since buyers have finally begun to overwhelm the sellers. Selling pressure rules the decline, but responsive buyers entered the market due to perceived undervaluation. For the reversal wick to open near the high of the candle, sell off sharply intra-bar, and then rally back toward the open of the candle is bullish, as it signifies that the bears no longer have control since they were not able to extend the decline of the candle, or the trend. Instead, the bulls were able to rally price from the lows of the candle and close the bar near the top of its range, which is bullish – at least for one bar, which hadn't been the case during the bearish trend (see Figure 2.5).

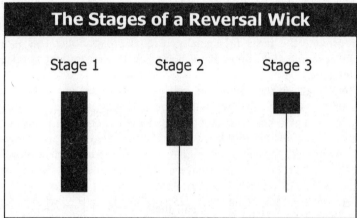

FIGURE 2.5: The developmental stages of a bullish reversal wick

Essentially, when a reversal wick forms at the extreme of a trend, the market is telling you that the trend either has stalled or is on the verge of a reversal. Remember, the market auctions higher in search of sellers, and lower in search of buyers. When the market over-extends itself in search of market participants, it will find itself out of value, which means responsive market participants will look to enter the market to push price back toward an area of perceived value. This will help price find a value area for two-sided trade to take place. When the market finds itself too far out of value, responsive market participants will sometimes enter the market with force, which aggressively pushes price in the opposite direction, essentially forming reversal wick candlesticks. This pattern is perhaps the most telling and common reversal setup, but requires steadfast confirmation in order to capitalize on its power. Understanding the psychology behind these formations and learning to identify them quickly will allow you to enter positions well ahead of the crowd, especially if you've spotted these patterns at potentially overvalued or undervalued areas.

WICK REVERSAL EXAMPLES

Before we move ahead, I would like to mention a tremendous resource that I have provided for you in Appendix B. In this section you will find the code that I have written for the wick reversal system (file name: sysWickRev), so you can quickly and easily find and trade these reversal opportunities. Along with the wick reversal system, I have also included the code for many of the systems, indicators, and stops that I have created and use in my trading. I will discuss each of these snippets of code in greater detail as we progress through the book and as it pertains to the material. Each of these scripts can be used to create fully mechanical trading systems, or simply provide the basis for signal-generated prospecting. This is a truly powerful resource and I hope that it helps you in your trading as much as it has helped me.

The signals on the charts (red and green triangles) are from the actual scripts of the systems that we will discuss, which provide us with visual confirmation that a specific setup has met our criteria for a long or short opportunity. However, just because a signal has fired does not mean that a trade is warranted. Instead, every signal should be scrutinized and confirmed by additional factors, which we have already been begun to learn and will continue to learn as we move forward in the text.

Let's take a look at our first example in Figure 2.6, which is a five-minute chart of the Natural Gas futures contract. In this example, we are looking for a 3:1 wick-to-body ratio and a close percentage of 15 percent. That is, we are looking for a wick that is three times larger than the size of the body and we also want the close of the bar to be in the top (or bottom) 15 percent of the candle. In this example, there are five candles that meet these criteria, which are highlighted by the signals on the charts.

Instantly, I am drawn to the first long signal and the third short signal. Why? These signals formed while testing the outer boundaries of the day's initial balance. As you recall, on four of the six types of trading days (Typical Day, Trading Range Day, Sideways Day, and Expanded Typical Day), the initial balance will hold the entire day, or at least throughout much of the day. Therefore, when these two wick reversal opportunities formed, there was typical market behavioral confirmation behind the tests, which paved the way for nice entry opportunities.

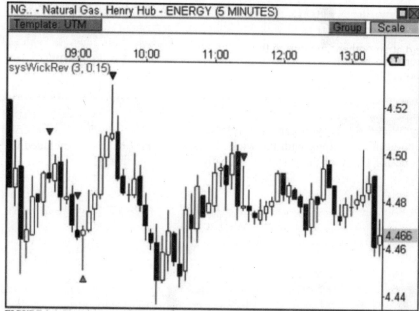

FIGURE 2.6: The wick reversal setup marks several opportunities in Natural Gas futures.

While the other three wick reversal signals passed our setup criteria, some fared better than others. This is due to many different factors, including whether price is above or below value. With at least two of the three signals, this seemed to be the case, which could have caused us to stay away from these signals. One easy method to help further confirmation for this type of setup, which may be a necessity in your early trials with this pattern, is requiring the close price of the bar following the reversal wick candlestick to be lower than the low of the wicking candle (reverse for longs). In each of the three signals that were not ideal, this simple criterion would have kept you out of the trade, as the bar following the reversal wick did not confirm the move. Coincidentally, the two wick reversal patterns that worked out perfectly had the close confirmation of the second bar.

Our second example is a five-minute chart of Research in Motion, Ltd. (ticker: RIMM). Figure 2.7 shows that the high and low during this day was highlighted by the wick reversal setup. Moreover, each of the four wick reversal candlesticks that fired signals helped to identify moves at key points in the chart. As I mentioned before, the trick to this setup is to understand the interrelated components of the candlestick, while also having the ability to decipher when to trust what the pattern is telling you. For this example, I used a 3.5:1 wick-to-body ratio with a 25 percent close percentage, which brought these opportunities to the forefront. If I were to loosen the parameters to a 2:1 ratio with and a close percentage of 40 percent, my chart would become littered with meaningless signals. You must be able to identify the right setup at the right point in the chart to maximize your potential with this setup.

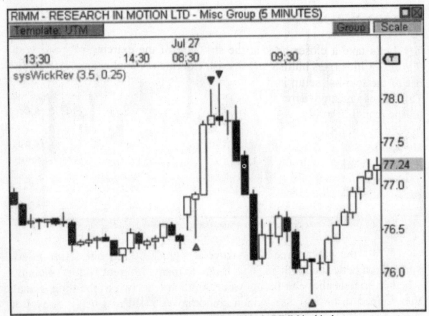

FIGURE 2.7: The wick reversal setup marks the high and low in RIMM in this day.

THE EXTREME REVERSAL SETUP

The *extreme reversal setup* is a fabulous signal that I've back tested over countless years of data on many instruments, different timeframes, and using various trade management methodologies. The results have always been highly favorable. Needless to say, this setup remains a key staple of my trading arsenal. The extreme reversal setup is a classic "rubber band" trade. When a rubber band is stretched to its limits and then released, it snaps back in the direction from whence it came. We are looking to trade the snapback reversal with this setup. The basic setup occurs when an extremely large candle forms that is about twice the size of the average candlestick. While this candle may indicate that a continuation will be seen, the second bar of the pattern does not confirm a continuation and, instead, is an opposing candle that signals an upcoming reversal. When this occurs, you have a fantastic opportunity to buy below value, or sell at a premium.

The extreme reversal setup looks to capitalize on over-extended situations in the market, as responsive buyers and sellers will enter the market to push price back in the opposite direction.

PATTERN STRUCTURE

Let's take a closer look at the structure of the extreme reversal setup. Figure 2.8 illustrates bullish and bearish extreme reversal examples. The first bar of the two-bar setup is the extreme bar, which is the basis for the setup. This bar can be anywhere from 50 to 100 percent larger than the average size of the candles in the lookback period. This figure will vary, however, depending on the volatility of the given market that you are trading. If you are trading a market with extremely low volatility, then you will likely need to see a larger extreme candlestick to properly qualify this candle. Conversely, in markets with high volatility, you may need to downward adjust the size of the extreme bar.

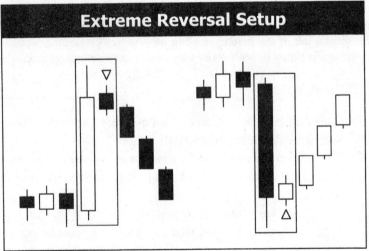

FIGURE 2.8: Diagram of the extreme reversal setup

The second characteristic to consider when judging the extreme bar of the pattern is the percentage of the total bar that is the body of the candlestick. That is, what percentage of the total range of the bar does the body of the candle encompass? This is a little tricky because you would like to see a high percentage of the candle covered by the body, but not so high as to discourage a potential reversal. I will typically allow any signal to pass that has a simple majority of coverage by the body. In other words, any percentage over 50 percent will usually suffice, but I will keep a close eye on any percentage that is above 85 percent. Why? Think about it for a moment, if the extreme bar has a close percentage of over 90 percent, there is a good chance that this bar could indeed lead to a continuation in the current direction. Therefore, you may be entering the market during a "resting" period ahead of a continuation. However, if the extreme bar has 60 percent coverage by the body, this is a better indication that a reversal may indeed occur, as a reversal may have already begun intrabar, especially if the wick portion of the candlestick has formed at the end of the candle where the reversal is to occur.

The second bar of the extreme reversal setup should be the opposite color of the first candle of the pattern. That is, if the first bar of the pattern is bullish (green or white), then the second bar of the pattern should be bearish (red or black). Obviously, the colors of the bars will depend on the charting software you use, but you get the point. The second candle of the setup is just as important as the first, as this candle will either lead to a continuation or signal a reversal. Many times, this candle will be rather small compared to prior price activity, however, this is not always the case. As a matter of fact, if the bar strongly opposes the first, the odds of a reversal increase. That is, if the second bar of the pattern is a big, full-bodied candle that opposes the first, the market may be well on its way to a clear reversal opportunity.

PATTERN SUMMARY

1. The first bar of the pattern is about two times larger than the average size of the candles in the lookback period.
2. The body of the first bar of the pattern should encompass more than 50 percent of the bar's total range, but usually not more than 85 percent.
3. The second bar of the pattern opposes the first. If the first bar of the pattern is bullish ($C > O$), then the second bar must be bearish ($C < O$). If the first bar is bearish ($C < O$), then the second bar must be bullish ($C > O$).

PATTERN PSYCHOLOGY

The extreme reversal setup is a clever pattern that capitalizes on the ongoing psychological patterns of investors, traders, and institutions. Basically, the setup looks for an extreme pattern of selling pressure and then looks to fade this behavior to capture a bullish move higher (reverse for shorts). In essence, this setup is visually pointing out oversold and overbought scenarios that forces responsive buyers and sellers to come out of the dark and put their money to work—price has been over-extended and must be pushed back toward a fair area of value so two-sided trade can take place.

This setup works because many normal investors, or casual traders, head for the exits once their trade begins to move sharply against them. When this happens, price becomes extremely overbought or oversold, creating value for responsive buyers and sellers. Therefore, savvy professionals will see that price is above or below value and will seize the opportunity. When the scared money is selling, the smart money begins to buy, and vice versa.

Look at it this way, when the market sells off sharply in one giant candlestick, traders that were short during the drop begin to cover their profitable positions by buying. Likewise, the traders that were on the sidelines during the sell-off now see value in lower prices and begin to buy, thus doubling up on the buying pressure. This helps to spark a sharp v-bottom reversal that pushes price in the opposite direction back toward fair value.

EXTREME REVERSAL EXAMPLES

The extreme reversal setup is a very powerful pattern that recurs in the market due to basic trader psychology. As such, it is extremely important to know when this pattern is developing. I've written code to help me quickly identify this pattern in the market, which I have included for you in Appendix B. Let's take a look at how the extreme reversal system (file name: sysExtremeRev) helped to highlight key reversal opportunities in the market.

Figure 2.9 shows a fifteen-minute chart of Sears Holdings Corporation (ticker: SHLD). The stock opened the day with a gap up, but quickly filled the gap in the first fifteen-minute bar of the day, forming a giant bar that is easily two to three times larger than the average size of the bars that preceded it. However, despite the bearish nature of this candlestick, the second fifteen-minute bar does not confirm a continuation lower. Instead, this candle is bullish (C > O) and eventually leads the stock higher the rest of the day.

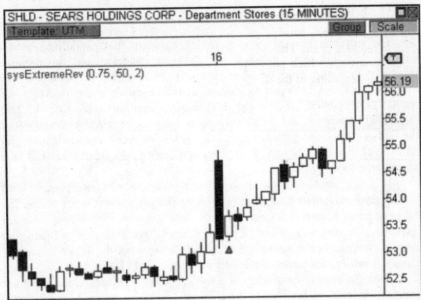

FIGURE 2.9: The extreme reversal setup leads to a rally.

In this example, Sears Holdings opened the day with early weakness, as responsive sellers pushed price back toward a perceived area of fair value. However, once price reached the $53.25 zone, responsive buyers entered the market, which pushed price back toward the top of the day's initial balance. When the upper boundary of the initial balance was broken, initiative buyers entered the market and continued to push price higher. This entire process was sparked by the extreme reversal setup that formed in the first thirty minutes of the day.

One interesting fact about this pattern is the way that it consistently forms at the beginning of the day, especially in the first thirty minutes of the session. Many times, the market will open the day with a great deal of energy, but the move fizzles within thirty minutes, creating a reversal opportunity. As you recall, the first thirty to sixty minutes of the day is when the market establishes the session's initial boundaries. Part of this process may involve developing an extreme reversal pattern that shoots price in the opposite direction. It is no surprise that major economic reports are oftentimes released at 10:00 A.M. ET, which coincides perfectly with the development of this pattern.

Take a look at Figure 2.10, which shows a fifteen-minute chart of Amazon.com (ticker: AMZN). In this example, you see that the extreme reversal setup occurred three days in a row, with two of those instances occurring within the first thirty minutes of the session. In each instance, price over-extended itself, causing responsive participants to enter the market in order to regulate price. This setup was not found at any other time during this three-day stretch, which paves the way to the theory of trading this pattern *only* at the beginning of the day.

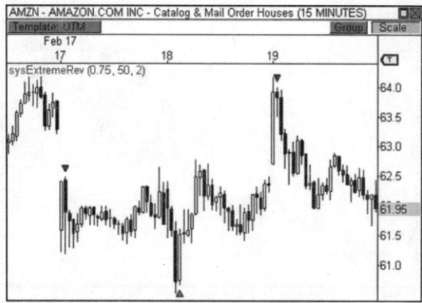

FIGURE 2.10: The extreme reversal setup developed three consecutive sessions.

The extreme reversal setup shines when it has developed in the direction of an existing trend. When a market is trending, this pattern can form during the "pull-back phase" of a trend, thereby allowing you to enter the market at a better value alongside the smart money. To illustrate this point, take a look at Figure 2.11, which is a fifteen-minute chart of Avalonbay Communities, Inc. (ticker: AVB). The extreme reversal setup formed two consecutive days during the retracement phase of a bullish trend. Each pull-back was highlighted by the extreme reversal pattern, which allowed us to easily enter the market in the direction of the existing trend at a better value. The important part of this scenario is the fact that the pattern was able to signal us to a profitable entry point that was *below* value, thus allowing us to enter the market alongside responsive buyers. When a stock is in a clear trend, responsive participants will be looking to enter the market at a favorable entry point. Using this pattern to buy the dips in an uptrend and sell the rips in a downtrend will allow you to align your position with the right side of the market. It is important to note, however, that while trading this pattern can be highly advantageous within a trend, it can also lead to false signals when it fires against an aggressive trend. Be smart and trade when the right circumstances present themselves.

FIGURE 2.11: The extreme reversal setup shines within a trends.

THE OUTSIDE REVERSAL SETUP

Out of all the setups in this chapter, the *outside reversal* setup is probably the most fun to trade. When I see this setup developing, I envision a child on a trampoline, which is probably the reason I associate fun with this setup. For a child to spring high into the air, he must first force the trampoline's bounce mat to go down. The farther the child forces the mat to go down, the higher he will spring into the air. This analogy perfectly embodies the outside reversal setup. Essentially, the market will push price lower before shooting higher, and will push price higher before selling off.

The outside reversal setup takes advantage of the market's tendency to test price levels beyond current value before a reversal can occur.

PATTERN STRUCTURE

The outside reversal setup is basically a hybrid between the engulfing pattern and the traditional outside day pattern. However, unlike the engulfing and outside day patterns, I am not concerned about the current candle's body engulfing the prior candle's body. Instead, I am more concerned with the highs, lows, and closes of the two-bar setup. More precisely, for a bullish outside reversal condition to exist, the current bar's low must be lower than the prior bar's low *and* the current bar's close must be higher than the prior bar's high (L < L[1] *and* C > H[1]). Along the same lines, for a bearish outside reversal setup to exist, the current bar's high must be greater than the prior bar's high *and* the current bar's close must be lower than the prior bar's low (H > H[1] *and* C < L[1]). There are several variations of this type of setup, but this is the one that I find to be particularly useful and predictive when playing key reversal situations. Figure 2.12 illustrates the outside reversal setup.

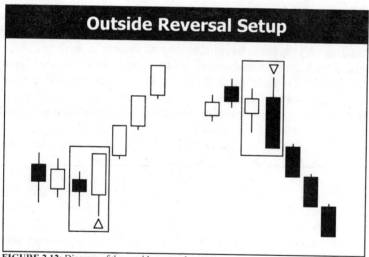

FIGURE 2.12: Diagram of the outside reversal setup

An additional requirement I like to include is a bar size qualifier, which requires the engulfing bar be a certain percentage larger than the average size of the bars in the lookback period. This criterion allows me to further qualify the pattern as a viable reversal candidate. Depending on the volatility of the market I am trading, I like the engulfing bar to be between 5 and 25 percent larger than the average size of the bars in the lookback period. Additional criteria can be added to this setup to qualify its validity further, but I find that this usually dilutes my field of candidates. A qualifier that takes into account increased volume, while powerful, would fall under this category.

PATTERN SUMMARY

1. The engulfing bar of a bullish outside reversal setup has a low that is below the prior bar's low (L < L[1]) and a close that is above the prior bar's high (C > H[1]).
2. The engulfing bar of a bearish outside reversal setup has a high that is above the prior bar's high (H > H[1]) and a close that is below the prior bar's low (C < L[1]).
3. The engulfing bar is usually 5 to 25 percent larger than the size of the average bar in the lookback period.

PATTERN PSYCHOLOGY

The power behind this pattern lies in the psychology behind the traders involved in this setup. If you have ever participated in a breakout at support or resistance only to have the market reverse sharply against you, then you are familiar with the market dynamics of this setup. What exactly is going on at these levels? To understand this concept is to understand the outside reversal pattern. Basically, market participants are testing the waters above resistance or below support to make sure there is no new business to be done at these levels. When no initiative buyers or sellers participate in range extension, responsive participants have all the information they need to reverse price back toward a new area of perceived value.

As you look at a bullish outside reversal pattern, you will notice that the current bar's low is lower than the prior bar's low. Essentially, the market is testing the waters below recently established lows to see if a downside follow-through will occur. When no additional selling pressure enters the market, the result is a flood of buying pressure that causes a springboard effect, thereby shooting price above the prior bar's highs and creating the beginning of a bullish advance.

If you recall the child on the trampoline for a moment, you'll realize that the child had to force the bounce mat down before he could spring into the air. Also, remember Jennifer the cake baker? She initially pushed price to $20 per cake, which sent a flood of orders into her shop. The flood of buying pressure eventually sent the price of her cakes to $35 apiece. Basically, price had to test the $20 level before it could rise to $35.

Let's analyze the outside reversal setup in a different light for a moment. One of the reasons I like this setup is because the two-bar pattern reduces into the wick reversal setup, which we covered earlier in the chapter. If you are not familiar with candlestick reduction, the idea is simple. You are taking the price data over two or more candlesticks and combining them to create a single candlestick. Therefore, you will be taking the open, high, low, and close prices of the bars in question to create a single composite candlestick.

Take a look at Figure 2.13, which illustrates the candlestick reduction of the outside reversal setup. Essentially, taking the highest high and the lowest low over the two-bar period gives you the range of the composite candlestick. Then, taking the opening price of the first candle and the closing price of the last candle will finish off the composite candlestick. Depending on the structure of the bars of the outside reversal setup, the result of the candlestick reduction will usually be the transformation into a wick reversal setup, which we know to be quite powerful. Therefore, in many cases the physiology of the outside reversal pattern basically demonstrates the inherent psychological traits of the wick reversal pattern. This is just another level of analysis that reinforces my belief in the outside reversal setup.

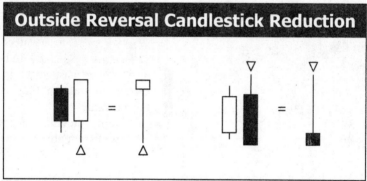

FIGURE 2.13: Diagram of the outside reversal setup's candlestick reduction

OUTSIDE REVERSAL EXAMPLES

As with the wick and extreme reversal setups, I have also included the code for the outside reversal setup in Appendix B. I have used the outside reversal system (file name: sysOutsideRev) to help me easily and quickly identify this pattern for the following examples.

Take a look at Figure 2.14, which is a five-minute chart of the Mini-Sized Dow futures contract. The Dow opened the day lower and held the first ten minutes of the session. The third candle of the day briefly tested new lows for the session and immediately reversed to close above the prior bar's high price, thereby forming a bullish outside reversal setup. This development triggered a steady advance during the first hour of the day. Remember, what makes this pattern so powerful is the behavior of the market participants behind the move. Before responsive buyers enter the market, they first test the waters below the day's low price to see if initiative sellers will enter the market. When initiative sellers remain on the sideline, responsive buyers are able to push price in the opposite direction confidently.

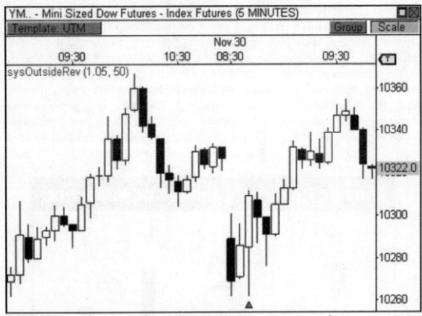

FIGURE 2.14: The outside reversal setup found the bottom in the YM.

Take a look at Figure 2.15, which is a fifteen-minute chart of Research in Motion, Ltd. Price pushed steadily higher from $58.50 to $61.50 over the course of two days, but eventually formed a bearish outside reversal pattern at the top of the move. This setup paved the way for a steady sell-off back to the $58.50 level. In this example, price pushed steadily higher, but ran into a solid wall of responsive selling pressure. However, before responsive market participants could push price back toward fair value, they first had to test new highs to see if additional buyers would enter the market. When initiative buyers sat on their collective hands, responsive sellers were able to push price back toward prior value confidently.

FIGURE 2.15: The outside reversal setup marks the top in RIMM.

THE DOJI REVERSAL SETUP

The *doji* candlestick is one of the most easily recognizable candlestick patterns in the market. This candlestick embodies indecision, which can help to predict an upcoming reversal in price, especially when the pattern forms above or below value. This pattern has been widely documented by many prominent traders and authors and remains a powerful method for spotting important reversal opportunities.

The doji reversal setup pinpoints indecision in the market, which can highlight profitable reversal opportunities.

PATTERN STRUCTURE

The doji is traditionally defined as any candlestick that has an opening price that is equal to the closing price. Traditionally speaking, the range of the doji, from low to high, should be smaller than the average range of the bars in the lookback period *and* the close price (or open price) of the bar must be at or near the center of the bar's range, indicating complete neutrality or indecision.

Figure 2.16 illustrates several types of doji that can be found in the market. The first example illustrates the traditional doji, which has an opening price that is equal to the closing price, a range that is smaller than the average bar in the lookback period, and a close price that is at the center of the range. However, this criterion can be rigid, which severely limits the amount of qualified doji that you will find in the market. With trading instruments moving in minimum tick increments between one and four decimals, it can be tough to find a true doji in the market using this criterion. As such, I am more lenient with the "rules" of the doji, as are many trading professionals. Instead of requiring the closing price to equal the opening price, it is satisfactory to let these two prices fall within a few ticks of each other. Some technicians will even allow anywhere from 5 to 10 percent leniency, as measured by the day's range. That is, if the Dow Jones has a daily range of fifty points, the bar can be classified a doji if is the closing price and opening price are between 2.5 to five points apart. This point is illustrated by the second and third doji in Figure 2.16.

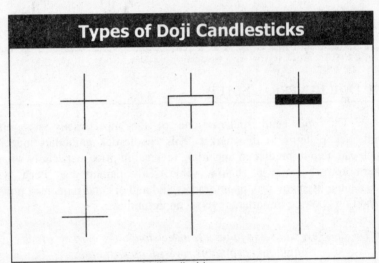

FIGURE 2.16: Different types of doji candlesticks

You will also see leniency in where the close price can fall within the overall range of the candlestick, and in the overall size of the candlestick itself, which does not require the overall range of the doji to be smaller than average. As a matter of fact, many "long-legged" doji are seen across the market and have colorful names like *dragonfly doji, gravestone doji, and rickshaw doji*. When doji are paired with other candlesticks, you will get patterns like *morning star doji, evening star doji*, and the *harami doji cross*.

Again, it is not my concern to name each of these patterns. My concern is to know what these patterns represent and what they tell me about the current market and upcoming price direction. Therefore, I will simply call each of the different classifications of this pattern a doji.

While a doji can provide a powerful indication of an upcoming price reversal, it must be used within proper context. A doji by itself cannot tell you the whole story about what the market is doing or where price is headed. However, if a doji has formed above value and is holding at a pronounced resistance level (either visual or pivot-based), this can be a powerful indication of a downside reversal. Conversely, if a doji has formed below value and is currently sitting on support, you have the makings for a bullish reversal.

There are two important factors to consider when judging the makings of a doji reversal setup. The first factor to consider is the current trend. For a bearish doji reversal to occur, the market must have been moving higher prior to the formation of the doji. On the flip side, price should have been moving lower prior to the formation of a bullish doji. There are many ways to judge this criterion. You can use a simple moving average and require that a bearish doji reversal candidate be above the average, and the bullish doji reversal candidate below it. Or, you can judge current direction by maintaining that a bullish move must have bars with a series of higher closes, and a bearish move a series of lower closes. There are various metrics that can be employed to qualify this criterion. For me, as long as the doji forms above a ten-period moving average for a bearish candidate or below the ten-period average for a bullish candidate, I'm a satisfied customer.

The second criterion that I use to confirm the setup is the closing price of the bars that follow the doji candlestick formation. For a bullish signal, I like the closing price of the bar that follows the doji to be above the high of the doji candlestick. For a bearish reversal, I want the closing price of the next bar to be below the low of the doji candlestick. Generally speaking, I allow a two-bar window for this criterion to be fulfilled. A three- or four-bar window can also be used, but not usually more than that. If the market has formed a doji candlestick and the additional criteria are fulfilled, you have the makings for a solid reversal setup (see Figure 2.17).

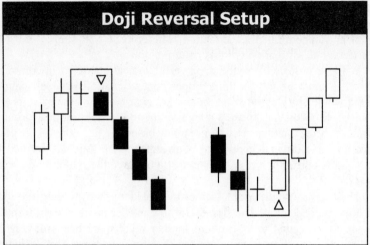

FIGURE 2.17: Diagram of the doji reversal setup

PATTERN SUMMARY

1. The open and close price of the doji should fall within 10 percent of each other, as measured by the total range of the candlestick.
2. For a bullish doji, the high of the doji candlestick should be below the ten-period simple moving average (H < SMA(10)).
3. For a bearish doji, the low of the doji candlestick should be above the ten-period simple moving average (L > SMA(10)).
4. For a bearish doji, one of the two bars following the doji must close beneath the low of the doji (C < L[1] *or* C < L[2]).
5. For a bullish doji setup, one of the two bars following the doji must close above the high of the doji (C > H[1]) *or* C > H[2])

PATTERN PSYCHOLOGY

The doji candlestick is the epitome of indecision. The pattern illustrates a virtual stalemate between buyers and sellers, which means the existing trend may be on the verge of a reversal. If buyers have been controlling a bullish advance over a period of time, you will typically see full-bodied candlesticks that personify the bullish nature of the move. However, if a doji candlestick suddenly appears, the indication is that buyers are suddenly not as confident in upside price potential as they once were. This is clearly a point of indecision, as buyers are no longer pushing price to higher valuation, and have allowed sellers to battle them to a draw—at least for this one candlestick. This leads to profit taking, as buyers begin to sell their profitable long positions, which is heightened by responsive sellers entering the market due to perceived overvaluation. This "double whammy" of selling pressure essentially pushes price lower, as responsive sellers take control of the market and push price back toward fair value.

DOJI REVERSAL EXAMPLES

Like the other setups, I have also included the code for the doji reversal setup in Appendix B. I have used the doji reversal system (file name: sysDojiRev) to help me easily and quickly identify this pattern for the following examples. Let's walk through a couple of examples of the doji reversal setup to register this pattern in our minds visually.

Take a look at Figure 2.18, which is a sixty-minute chart of the Heating Oil futures contract. There are four doji reversal setups in this chart, with each highlighting significant opportunities in this market. As I stated before, the doji candlestick is a sign of major indecision, especially if the pattern forms after a period of trending behavior. Therefore, if a market has been trending in a certain direction over a period of time and then suddenly develops a doji candlestick, price could be on the verge of a reversal. While there are other doji in this chart, only those that passed all three requirements have generated a signal. Remember, for a signal to appear, three factors must be present: a doji candlestick, trend confirmation, and close price confirmation. Each of the signals in this chart highlighted great reversal opportunities, as each was able to forecast an upcoming change in trend.

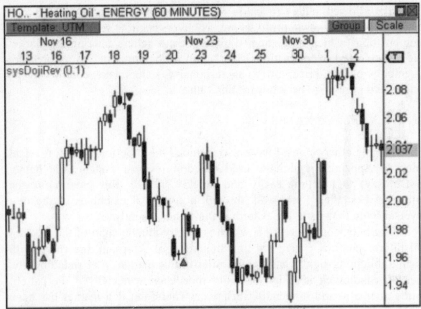

FIGURE 2.18: The doji reversal setup found solid reversals in Heating Oil futures.

With the doji reversal setup, I typically prefer to use a higher timeframe chart. In the prior example, I used a sixty-minute chart instead of a five-minute timeframe. Research has demonstrated that the longer a candlestick setup takes to develop, the more accurate it is in predicting price movement. The doji reversal setup relies on market psychology. With this pattern, a five-minute doji does not have the same psychological power of a sixty-minute doji. That is not to say that this setup should not be used in a five-minute timeframe, I am merely stating my preference. In my opinion, any timeframe above, and including, the fifteen-minute chart will greatly improve the accuracy of this signal.

Figure 2.19 shows a sixty-minute chart of the Mini-Sized Dow futures contract with the doji reversal system plotted. There are four doji in this chart, with each signaling reversals to varying degrees of success. The first signal is the only one that is confirmed by the close price of the second bar *following* the actual doji candlestick, which has been built into the script of the setup. Again, this setup offers a highly confirmed reversal opportunity, but your ability to discern whether this pattern is forming at the right time and at the best value will determine your success with this pattern, which we will continue to explore throughout the text.

SECRETS OF A PIVOT BOSS

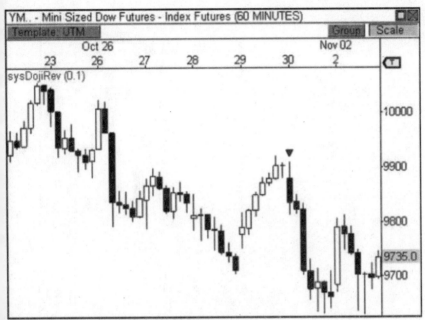

FIGURE 2.19: The doji reversal setup highlights reversals in the YM.

UNDERSTANDING THE SETUP

The best traders in the world use pure price behavior to trigger an entry. They have a keen understanding of markets and market behavior, which allows them to anticipate and visualize future price behavior. They allow intuition and preparedness to trigger entries and will confirm along the way. The key is to understand what price is telling you and having the ability to act on this information quickly and intelligently.

The beauty of the setups that I have outlined is they each have inherent market psychologies that complement the behaviors of successful traders. Understanding these patterns helps you listen to the market, thereby allowing you to position yourself with the proper market participants. It is up to you to properly engage the setups at the appropriate action zones in order to profit in this game. As we move forward, I will illustrate how I identify major action zones in the market using the aforementioned setups to trigger profitable entries in the market at confirmed pivot levels.

CHAPTER 3

INTRODUCING THE
MONEY ZONE

*"I always made money when I was sure I was right before I began.
What beat me was not having brains enough to stick to my own
game—that is, to play the market only when I was satisfied that
precedents favored my play."*

- Jesse Livermore

Thus far, we have covered concepts relating to market dynamics,
creating a solid foundation for the meat of the book, which begins with this
chapter. From this point forward, we will now begin to relate these concepts
to actionable points on the chart. The goal is to highlight the best entry and
exit scenarios using powerful priced-based, market-generated support and

resistance levels. Our first stop on this pivot-based tour is an introduction to the Money Zone.

The Money Zone offers market-generated levels that are based on the time and price relationship.

The Money Zone was created by Nirvana Systems, Inc. to easily display the most important levels that Market Profile™ has to offer. The Market Profile was created by J. Peter Steidlmayer in the early 1980s in a joint effort with the Chicago Board of Trade in order to display the time and price relationship as it unfolded in the market. The result was a revolutionary way of viewing the market's activity using a visual "profile" representing time and price. This breakthrough paved the way for a whole new realm of market understanding, as it created a level of transparency between buyers and sellers that had never been seen before.

The Market Profile structure provides an in depth look at market participation at specific price points, which allows us to use the information to identify areas where price is overvalued, undervalued, and fair valued. This market-generated information is the essence of the Money Zone. However, interpreting these levels is where the money is made. I will soon reveal extremely powerful pivot-based relationships using the information derived from the Money Zone, which can truly change the way you trade. But first, we need a primer of these powerful levels.

ABOUT THE MARKET PROFILE

There are entire books dedicated to the Market Profile, which go way beyond the brief introduction that I will share with you here. In fact, Steidlmayer wrote *Markets and Market Logic* in 1986 to help introduce the concept to the masses, and has since published an additional work on the topic. To date, my favorite book on the Market Profile, and my favorite trading book in general, is Jim Dalton's *Mind over Markets*. This book clearly and effectively explains the Market Profile, and market dynamics, in a manner that is both insightful and delightful to read. Coincidentally, Dalton sponsored Steidlmayer's original work *Markets and Market Logic*.

Before we can understand the Money Zone, we must first understand the basic components of the Market Profile. Let's take a closer look at how the Market Profile is structured.

The Market Profile Structure

1100.00	B	
1099.75	B	
1099.50	ABM	
1099.25	ABCM	
1099.00	ABCLMN	
1098.75	ABCDLMN	
1098.50	ABCDJKLMN	
1098.25	ABCDEJKLMN	
1098.00	ABCDEFJKLMN ◄—	Point of Control
1097.75	ABCDEFJK	
1097.50	ABCDEFGHIJ	
1097.50	ADEFGHI	
1097.25	DEFGHI	◄— Value Area
1097.00	DEFGHI	
1096.75	DEFGHI	
1096.50	EFGH	
1096.25	EH	
1096.00	H	

FIGURE 3.1: Diagram of the Market Profile structure

Figure 3.1 illustrates the basic structure of the Market Profile, with price represented on the vertical axis and time represented on the horizontal axis. The structure uses letters of the alphabet to categorize segments of time next to price, which are technically called *Time Price Opportunities* (TPOs). The first letter of the alphabet represents the first segment of time, which is usually the first thirty minutes of the day. The second letter will correspond to the second segment of the time, which is the next thirty minutes of the day, and so forth. Each new segment of time will correspond to a new letter until trading is done for the day.

During the first segment of time, a letter "A" will be placed next to every price level that was reached during the first thirty minutes of trading. In the illustration, the market traded between 1097.50 and 1099.50 in the opening thirty minutes of trading, therefore, the letter "A" was placed next to each price interval in this range. During the second thirty minutes of trading, the market traded from 1097.50 to 1100.00, therefore, the letter "B" was placed next to each price interval in this range. The profile will continue to build out as the day progresses, providing you with a real-time account of market activity as it unfolds. The resulting bell-shaped profile will give you an accurate picture of the day's time and price relationship, providing you will key levels of interest for the current session and future sessions.

While the structure offers an abundance of information, the two areas that stand out are the Point of Control and the Value Area. The *Point of Control (POC)* is the price where the most trading activity occurred during the day, as represented by the longest line of TPOs nearest to the center of the entire structure. This price is significant because it represents the fairest price to both buyers and sellers. The *Value Area* is important because it illustrates where 70 percent of the trading activity occurred during the day. The top and bottom of the value area range can tell you where buyers and sellers entered the market when they perceived price to be away from fair value. We will delve into these topics in much more detail ahead.

Now that we have covered the basics of the Market Profile structure, let's take a look at how the Money Zone interprets this information.

THE MONEY ZONE LEVELS

The Market Profile structure offers an amazing array of information, from market psychology to price behavior. However, reading and deciphering the information in its current format falls somewhere between complex and dense for the uninitiated trader. Unless you have studied Market Profile, it can be quite difficult to discern quickly what the information is telling you. Learning the nuances of using the structure for trading, while quite powerful, can be a daunting task for traders that are new to the concept. Remember, whole books are devoted to this art.

Alas, the Money Zone takes the most valuable information from the Market Profile structure and presents it in a manner that is both powerful and easy to understand. Essentially, the Money Zone uses the three most powerful levels of the Market Profile and displays the information as horizontal price levels on your charts, without the alphabet soup.

Take a look at Figure 3.2, which illustrates how the Money Zone translates the Market Profile structure into visual price levels. The Money Zone takes the point of control derived from the Market Profile and extends it as a horizontal price level for the following session. In Money Zone lingo, the point of control would also be called the *Value Line (VL)*. These are interchangeable terms as far as I'm concerned. The Money Zone also extends the upper and lower boundaries of the value area for use in the following session as support and resistance levels. Traditionally, the upper boundary of the value area is called the *Value Area High (VAH)*, and the lower boundary is called the *Value Area Low (VAL)*. These levels can also be called the *Money Zone High (MZH)* and the *Money Zone Low (MZL)*. Throughout the remainder of the text, I will use the traditional Market Profile lingo so as not to confuse anyone. Either way, these terms refer to the same levels.

The Money Zone Levels

1100.00	B	
1099.75	B	
1099.50	ABM	
1099.25	ABCM	
1099.00	ABCLMN	
1098.75	ABCDLMN	—— VAH ——
1098.50	ABCDJKLMN	
1098.25	ABCDEJKLMN	
1098.00	ABCDEFJKLMN	—— POC ——
1097.75	ABCDEFJK	
1097.50	ABCDEFGHIJ	
1097.50	ADEFGHI	
1097.25	DEFGHI	
1097.00	DEFGHI	
1096.75	DEFGHI	—— VAL ——
1096.50	EFGH	
1096.25	EH	
1096.00	H	

FIGURE 3.2: Diagram of the Money Zone levels

Now that we have an understanding of how the Money Zone interprets the data from the Market Profile structure, let's proceed to a more in depth discussion of these powerful levels.

THE POINT OF CONTROL

If you had to choose only one price point that you could use as a reference for the day's trading activity, it should be the point of control. As you recall, the point of control is where the most trading activity occurred on any given day. As such, this price is considered to be the fairest value between buyers and sellers. Having the point of control plotted on your charts gives you the pulse of the market as it pertains to valuation. If price extends too far above the point of control, you may see responsive sellers enter the market to push price back toward fair value, which is inherently represented through the point of control. Likewise, if price moves too far below the point of control, responsive buyers will enter the market to push price back toward fair value.

Take a look at Figure 3.3, which shows a two-day view of the Mini-Sized Dow futures contract. The point of control is clearly plotted for the December 3 trading session. Remember, the Money Zone uses the prior day's trading information to forecast pertinent price levels for the following day. Therefore, the trading activity from December 2 dictated where the point of control would be located for the following day.

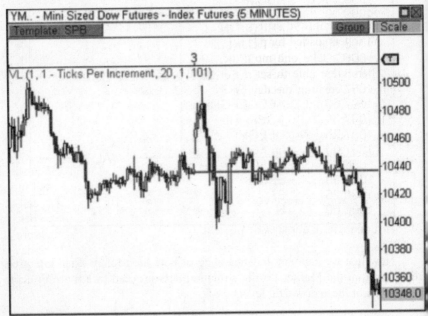

FIGURE 3.3: The point of control shows the fairest price in the chart.

In this example, the point of control is 10,437, which represents the fairest value between buyers and sellers from the prior day. Just by looking at the prior day, you can see that most of the day's trading activity did indeed occur around the 10,437 level. Why do we want to use a prior day's information for the following session? Isn't the information old news by then? By understanding where the market perceived value to be fairest in the prior session, we are able to use this information to help us determine price valuation for the current session.

Notice how the market opened the session with early strength on December 3. Price rallied to 10,499, but immediately began to reverse from that level. As I mentioned earlier, responsive sellers are looking to enter the market with sell orders when they perceive price to be overvalued. In this instance, price was indeed overvalued and responsive sellers were able to push price back toward the point of control, which was the fairest price from the prior session. Therefore, responsive sellers were able to move price from 10,499 back to fair value at 10,437.

Later in the session, price moved too far below the point of control, which triggered responsive buying activity. Responsive buyers entered the market when they perceived price to be undervalued and eventually pushed price from 10,396 back to fair value at 10,437. Essentially, using the prior day's information to generate the point of control for the next day gave us a way to measure when price was over and undervalued. In essence, the point of control allowed us to keep our finger on the pulse of the market, as buyers and sellers jostled for position.

Let's take one more look at Figure 3.3. After responsive buyers and sellers were able to set the day's extremes in the first hour of the session, thereby creating the day's initial balance, price basically hugged fair value for most of the day. However, the market's perception of value clearly changed later in the session, as initiative sellers overwhelmed the IBL and took control of the close. The late-day decline essentially led to an Expanded Typical Day scenario.

The difference between responsive and initiative behavior is clearly evident in this example. As you recall, responsive behavior will move price back toward a perceived area of value, but does not have the conviction to influence price on a larger scale. On the other hand, initiative behavior has much more conviction and confidence behind its actions, which provides the ability to influence price movement significantly. The late-day sell-off clearly had more conviction behind its movement than the day's early responsive behaviors. Your ability to determine who is influencing the market will allow you to judge the strength and conviction of price movement.

THE DEVELOPING POINT OF CONTROL

Many traders find great value in using the Market Profile structure as it develops in real time. As such, the Money Zone has the ability to plot the pertinent levels of the MP structure as they develop in real time. The *Developing Point of Control (DPOC)* indicator dynamically updates as new data enters the market, calculating fair value bar by bar. The Money Zone calls this feature the *Developing Value Line (DVL)*. This process is identical to the way that the Market Profile calculates its point of control throughout the day as the bell-curved structure develops in real time. Essentially, the DPOC allows you to keep your finger on the pulse of the market's perception of fair value as it dynamically changes throughout the day.

What's great about this indicator is that it allows you to see where the static point of control will be located in the upcoming session. Essentially, the level at which the DPOC closes the current session will become the static POC for the upcoming day. Take a look at Figure 3.4, which is the same chart of the YM we studied moments ago. On December 2nd, the DPOC actually began the day with a higher level of perceived value. However, as the day progressed, more and more trading activity occurred at lower price levels, which essentially shifted the DPOC lower. Eventually, the DPOC closed December 2nd at 10,437, which then became the static POC for December 3rd. As you will soon see, this little trick will become an integral part of how I approach the market.

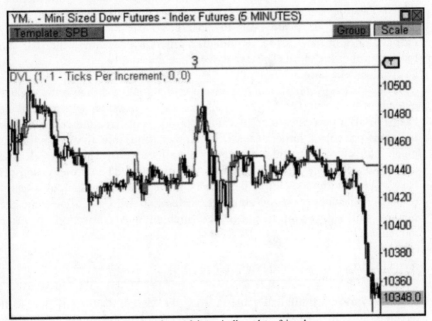

FIGURE 3.4: The developing point of control dynamically updates fair value.

THE VALUE AREA

When price moves away from the point of control, market participants will enter the market when they perceive price to be over or undervalued. Technically, responsive buying and initiative selling occur below value, while responsive selling and initiative buying occur above value. The value area helps to determine when price is above or below value. Remember, the value area is where 70 percent of the trading activity occurred for a given period of time. Therefore, most of the day's trading activity occurred within this range, thereby establishing this area as a zone that easily facilitates trade. Any movement outside of this range will trigger the actions of responsive and initiative participants.

The outer limits of the value area are actually quite important, as they basically draw the battle lines between buyers and sellers. The upper boundary of the value area (VAH) is where responsive sellers and initiative buyers hang out. These groups of market participants will look to begin putting money to work as price moves above this zone. On the flip side, the bottom of the value area (VAL) is where responsive buyers and initiative sellers will look to put money to work.

Take a look at Figure 3.5, which is the same chart of the YM that we have been dissecting. The Money Zone plots the value area for December 3 using the information derived from the prior day's trading activity. Therefore, the current day's value area is where 70 percent of the trading activity occurred in the prior session, thereby establishing this area as a zone that easily facilitates trade. As soon as price moves above or below the value area, key market participants will enter the market.

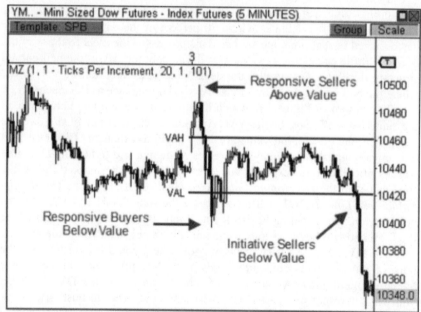

FIGURE 3.5: The value area shows where 70% of the prior day's trading occurred.

On this day, we were easily able to identify the actions of both responsive and initiative participants. Early in the session, price rallied away from the day's point of control (10,437) and through the top of the value area. When this occurs, one of two things will happen: responsive sellers will push price back toward fair value, or initiative buyers will step in and advance price toward a higher area of value. In this case, responsive sellers took over and easily pushed price back toward fair value. Later that morning, price fell through the bottom of the value area, which was a call to action for responsive buyers. However, it was initiative sellers that controlled the close after price testing the waters below the VAL for a second time.

As you continue to make your way through the material it is important to continue to connect the dots regarding responsive and initiative actions and the price levels at which these participants are looking to make a move. If price rallies early in the session and begins to show signs of weakness at or above the VAH, the market is likely to see a surge of responsive selling pressure. Knowing this vital information, along with the actions of other market participants, will allow you to better time your moves in the market.

THE DEVELOPING VALUE AREA

Like the developing point of control, the Money Zone also plots the developing value area as it dynamically updates in real time. The *Developing Value Area (DVA)* calculates where 70 percent of the day's trading activity has occurred in real time, bar by bar. This process is identical to the way the Market Profile calculates its value area throughout the day as the bell-curved structure develops. Essentially, the developing value area allows you to see where the bulk of the day's trading activity is taking place as it happens.

Take a look at Figure 3.6, which illustrates the developing value area on the same two-day view of the YM. As soon as the first bar of the day has completed, the developing value area will begin to calculate. The DVA will dynamically update as the day progresses, widening and tightening along the way as price behavior expands and contracts. When the market closes, the final values of the *Developing Value Area High (DVAH)* and the *Developing Value Area Low (DVAL)* will then become the static VAH and VAL for the next session. Once trading begins the next day, the DVA will pick up where it left off and will begin to update dynamically as new data enters the market.

The DVA can be a very powerful tool to help you distinguish where the bulk of the money is changing hands and when price may be ripe for a breakout opportunity. As price moves above and below the DVA's range, you will see responsive parties enter the market in order to push price back toward fair value. However, the longer the DVA remains in the same general vicinity, and the tighter the range becomes, thereby introducing a breakout opportunity that is fueled by initiative parties.

Perhaps the biggest advantage that a developing indicator gives you is the ability to plan your trading for the following session, which we will explore in various forms throughout the book. The fact that this indicator allows you to visualize exactly where the VAL and the VAH will be located in the following day allows you to analyze important price-to-pivot relationships and plan your trading accordingly. This will be a vital theme the remainder of the text.

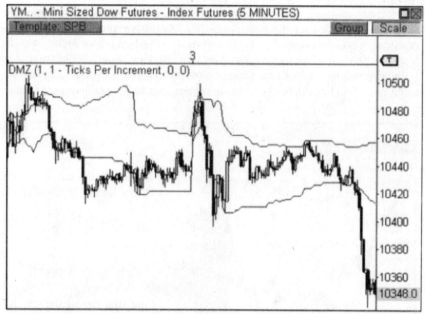

FIGURE 3.6: The DVA indicator dynamically calculates the value area in real time.

VOLUME AT PRICE

The Money Zone is derived solely from price-based, market-generated information. However, volume can play a huge role in determining the market's conviction and overall confidence. The *Volume at Price (VAP)* indicator plots virtually the same type of information as the Market Profile, but does so using volume instead. Similar to the structure of the Market Profile, the volume at price indicator divides volume equally across all of the price points that were reached during a specific period of time and then plots the information using a horizontal histogram directly on the price chart. The display of information is actually quite attractive and allows you to assess major points of interest quickly, thereby highlighting potential areas of support and resistance. Displaying volume at a price in this manner is not a new concept, as this indicator has been around for a while, but the way that it complements the Money Zone makes it a mainstay in my trading arsenal.

Let's take a closer look at the volume at price indicator. Figure 3.7 shows a five-minute chart of the YM during the same two-day stretch that we have been analyzing. The VAP indicator uses the volume activity at a price from the prior session and overlays the histogram over price in the current session. Therefore, yesterday's volume activity at a price is shown on today's chart. The *volume point of control (VPOC)* is the price where the most volume was traded during yesterday's market, thus representing the fairest price as seen through the eyes volume. VPOC is represented on the histogram as the longest horizontal line that stretches across the session. The volume point of control and the price-based POC will usually identify the same price level as the fairest value to traders, but this is not always the case.

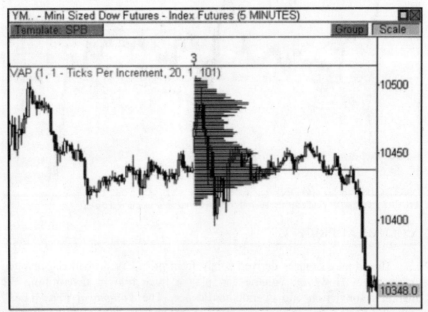

FIGURE 3.7: The VAP indicator plots a horizontal histogram of the volume traded at a price.

You may be asking yourself why this information is important, or even helpful. Why do we need to know where volume was traded yesterday in order to trade today? The answer is simple. In order to anticipate how the market will respond to a certain price level in the current session, you must understand how price reacted to that level in the recent past. Looking back at Figure 3.7, the YM opened the day with early strength, but ran into clear resistance at 10,500, which sent price back toward the volume point of the control. Let's examine the VAP indicator to understand why price was smacked down so easily at the top of the histogram.

The farther price moves away from the VPOC toward the outer extremes of the VAP histogram, the less volume interest price will encounter. For example, when price becomes overvalued, buying interest will dry up because price becomes too expensive. When buying ceases to exist, lower volume is taking place and improper trade facilitation is occurring. The market operates solely to facilitate trade. If prices are too high and volume is not flowing, the price will shift back toward an area that will easily accommodate the proper facilitation of trade.

As the YM approached 10,500, the upper extreme of the histogram showed drastically decreased buying interest, which indicated less buying interest and overvaluation. This led to responsive selling pressure, which pushed price back toward fair value at the VPOC. While both of the outer extremes of the VAP histogram were able to contain price early in the session, the lower extreme was eventually overwhelmed with initiative selling pressure, which caused a significant move away from the VPOC in search of lower value.

While this is an introductory look at how price can react to the volume at price indicator, it's easy to tell that it can be a powerful complement to the way you trade and analyze the market. This indicator is truly one of my favorite trading tools. Like the kid on the trampoline, this indicator triggers thoughts of fun and excitement when I use it to engage the market. As we move forward, I will reveal powerful nuances behind the indicator that will help you trade in a more knowledgeable and profitable manner.

ENGAGING THE MONEY ZONE

The Money Zone has allowed me to enjoy a whole new level of market understanding and trading success. The importance and significance behind these levels plays directly into the hands of how the market operates. To understand these levels is to understand market dynamics. Now that I have laid the foundation of what the Money Zone encompasses, we can now begin to attack these levels from other angles. As you plow your way through this information, continue to transition from a state of learning and absorbing to a state of understanding and engaging. Properly understanding these concepts will allow you to engage the market in a much more knowledgeable and confident manner when we begin to learn advanced trading concepts using these powerful levels.

CHAPTER 4

ADVANCED MONEY ZONE CONCEPTS

"A trader gets to play the game as a professional billiards player does—that is, he looks far ahead instead of considering the particular shot before him. It gets to be an instinct to play for position."

- Jesse Livermore

The Money Zone is an extremely powerful tool because the levels are based purely on market-generated information. The levels show you where real money has changed hands, which is extremely valuable information when trading. The use of the value area or the point of control as support and resistance is significant because these levels are based on the actions of actual market participants. There is nothing about the Money Zone that does or does not work. The Money Zone simply relays real marketplace information on your charts in a manner that is both easily understood and highly powerful. However, it is up to you to properly analyze and engage the information.

While the Money Zone is a simple tool, there is an extraordinary amount of depth behind the information being presented.

The goal of this chapter is to acquire an acute understanding of the Money Zone levels. I will discuss how to use the information to analyze the market in many different ways, which will then allow you to engage the market in a more confident and knowledgeable manner.

THE OPEN IN RELATION TO VALUE AND RANGE

The market's open can have a significant influence on the day's outcome. Specifically, the open in relation to range and value can help you forecast potential price behavior for the session. Understanding the different types of opening relationships can help you prepare for the day's trading activity by proving, or disproving, your price forecast. For example, a day that opens within value and within the prior day's price range will have a markedly different conviction and result than a day that opens out of value and out of the prior day's price range. Quick recognition of the pattern du jour will allow you to identify early market conviction effectively.

The Three Opening Relationships	
In Range and In Value	Acceptance/Rejection
In Range and Out of Value	Acceptance/Rejection
Out of Range and Out of Value	Acceptance/Rejection

TABLE 4.1: The three types of opening relationships

There are three types of opening relationships to consider when contemplating a day's potential outcome (see Table 4.1). With each relationship, you must also factor in acceptance or rejection of value. The first type of opening relationship is an open that occurs within the prior day's price range and within the prior day's value area. An open that occurs in range and in value indicates market sentiment from the prior day has not changed and the market is currently in balance. When this occurs, the day's risk and opportunity are both low, which usually leads to a quiet trading range session. A Typical Day, Trading Range Day, or Sideways Day will usually develop from this type of opening relationship.

Figure 4.1 shows a typical open that occurs within the prior day's range and value in a five-minute chart of the E-Mini Russell 2000. Notice that the market briefly tested price levels above the prior day's range and value area, but responsive sellers entered the market and pushed price back toward accepted value. Price then traded back and forth within the day's initial balance, creating a clear Trading Range Day. Remember, if price opens within range and value, market sentiment has not changed from the prior session. As such, the market is content to trade quietly in a range, as buyers and sellers find easy facilitation of trade, thereby accepting the opening relationship. If the market had rejected the initial relationship, initiative parties would have extended the day's range beyond the prior day's extremes, and a bigger move would have resulted.

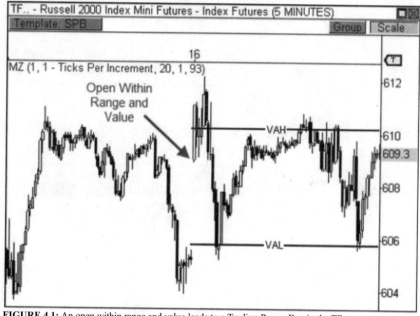

FIGURE 4.1: An open within range and value leads to a Trading Range Day in the TF.

The second type of opening relationship is an open that occurs outside of the prior day's value area, but within the prior day's range. An open that occurs in range, but out of value, indicates that market sentiment has changed slightly, which offers more risk and opportunity. However, in order for greater directional conviction to be seen, the market must break free from the prior day's range and accept new value. If this occurs, a Trend Day, Double-

Distribution Trend Day, or Expanded Typical Day scenario will likely develop. If the market does not break free from the prior day's range, however, further range activity will be seen, paving the way for a Typical Day, Trading Range Day, or Sideways Day scenario.

Figure 4.2 shows a five-minute chart of Crude Oil futures during a day that opened out of value, but in range. Initially, price pushed back into the day's value area, but was met with selling pressure. The rejection at the value area eventually led to the acceptance of slightly lower value. If price had accepted value within the day's value area, the result would have been quiet trading range behavior. Instead, the fact that the market opened out of value indicated the potential for increased directional conviction or, at the very least, active price discovery. While price did not aggressively seek new value, this type of day usually introduces much more active price activity than the prior opening relationship.

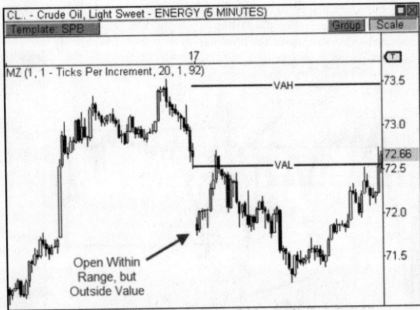

FIGURE 4.2: An open in range and out of value leads to slightly more volatility in Crude Oil.

The last type of opening relationship is an open that occurs out of the prior day's range and out of the prior day's value area. On this type of day, the market has opened out of balance, indicating that market sentiment has clearly changed from the prior day. If the market does not fall back within the prior day's range, this means the market is likely accepting new value and further range extension will be seen, as additional initiative participants will enter the market. A Trend Day or Double-Distribution Trend Day usually arises from this relationship. However, if price pushes back within the prior day's range, this means that responsive market participants were able to push price back toward prior value, indicating a failed breakout attempt, thereby leading to a Typical Day, Expanded Typical Day, or Trading Range Day. If new value is rejected in strong fashion, a Trend Day in the opposite direction could also be seen.

An open that occurs out of range and value offers the most risk and opportunity, paving the way for greater directional conviction. This opening relationship offers the most aggressive price discovery.

Figure 4.3 shows a five-minute chart of the Mini-Sized Dow futures contract during a day that opened out of range and value. The fact that the YM gapped above the prior day's range and out of the Money Zone's value area indicated that market sentiment had clearly changed and initiative buyers were attempting to push price to new value. Since the market accepted new value above the prior day's range, the market trended steadily higher throughout the session, leading to a Trend Day scenario. If price had reversed back into the prior day's range, a rejection of the breakout would have been seen.

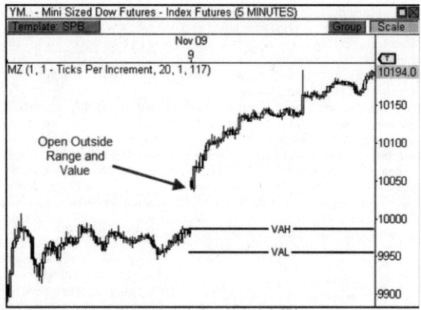

FIGURE 4.3: An open out of range and value leads to a big day in the YM.

This opening relationship helps to confirm one of my favorite trade setups, which helps me trigger entries into moves that usually deliver the biggest rewards. Later in the chapter, and throughout the book, I will show different ways to spot this breakout opportunity before the open of the market even occurs, which gives you advanced warning of a potentially big day ahead.

Like many of the concepts we have learned thus far, the three opening relationships are meant as a guide to help you decipher potential market behavior and conviction. Simply understanding that the market has opened out of range and value will allow you to prepare for a potentially big day payday. Conversely, an opening print that occurs within range and value will allow you to play reversals at the extremes of the day's trading range, or cause you to sit out the session entirely. Simply paying attention to important price-to-pivot relationships can immensely improve your trading.

VALUE AREA RELATIONSHIPS

The value area is important because it represents where 70 percent of the trading activity occurred in a day. The market identified this area as a zone for fair trade facilitation between buyers and sellers; therefore, most of the day's trades occurred within this range. The ability to understand the relationships between current and prior value areas is extremely important market-generated information. Unlike other indicators, a prior day's Money Zone levels are still very relevant in the marketplace for several days, and even weeks. Understanding how current Money Zone levels relate to a prior day's levels will go a long way toward understanding current market behavior and future price movement.

Knowing the type of value area relationship the market is currently operating from allows you to gauge current market strength and prepare for specific types of setups during the day. There are seven types of value area relationships that should be considered when analyzing the current strength and attempted direction of the market: *Higher Value, Overlapping Higher Value, Lower Value, Overlapping Lower Value, Unchanged Value, Outside Value,* and *Inside Value.* Each value area relationship brings with it a directional bias or expected outcome, which can prepare you for certain types of trading scenarios in the following session (see Table 4.2).

Two-Day Value Area Relationships	
Higher Value	Bullish
Overlapping Higher Value	Moderately Bullish
Lower Value	Bearish
Overlapping Lower Value	Moderately Bearish
Unchanged Value	Sideways/Breakout
Outside Value	Sideways
Inside Value	Breakout

TABLE 4.2: Value area relationships

The value area relationships and their respective directional biases should not be viewed as written in stone or used in a rigid manner. Instead, these are guidelines that will help you diagnose current market direction and conviction. The act of noting which type of value area relationship the market is currently exhibiting will give you early directional bias, which you should then analyze for effectiveness of directional conviction, or for failing to realize its directional bias. Both following through and failing to follow through on its directional bias can tell you a lot about the market's current state, which then helps you determine which types of trades are likely to present themselves.

The first value area relationship that I will discuss is the Higher Value relationship, which occurs when the current day's value area is completely higher than the prior day's value area. Therefore, today's value area low is *higher* than yesterday's value area high. This is the most bullish value area relationship, as it indicates the market was effectively able to push price to a higher area of value in a convincing manner. When this occurs, you will typically look to align yourself on the long side of the market. Any pull-back should be viewed as a buying opportunity, especially if a string of higher value days have occurred in a row. This would indicate the market is successfully pushing price to higher value day over day, which is outwardly shown as a bullish trend. However, if the day's open does not coincide with typical higher value behavior, a failure to achieve the day's directional bias could be seen, which would then shift your focus to a bearish scenario. For example, if the market has formed several Higher Value relationships in a row, but opens the day with a bearish gap that sends price below the day's value area and below the prior day's range, this could be a very bearish scenario, as the market has clearly shifted its sentiment. Therefore, when this relationship occurs, the market should open the session anywhere above the value area low in order to remain bullishly optimistic.

Let's take a look at a typical Higher Value relationship in the five-minute timeframe of Amazon.com in Figure 4.4. Notice that the current value area is completely higher than the prior day's value area, which is typically indicative of continued strength. Just knowing this simple fact can help you prepare for the day's potential direction. In this particular case, price opened at the value area high and aggressively pushed through this level, which is behavior that is typically associated with continued strength. Anytime price opens within or above the value area on this type of day, a bullish bias should be expected. However, if price had opened the day with a gap below the day's value area low, a completely different outcome would have occurred. This is the difference between understanding the market's intended directional bias and the direction that actually occurs. To every scenario, there is acceptance or rejection. You must prepare for both scenarios and trade at your earliest inclination of what is likely to occur.

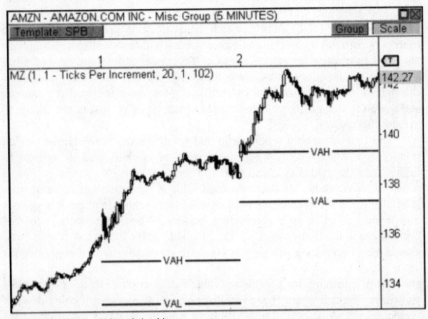

FIGURE 4.4: Higher Value relationship

At times, it becomes quite clear that despite the formation of certain value area relationships, price can take a different path. Figure 4.5 shows a fifteen-minute chart of Research in Motion, Ltd. that illustrates this case perfectly. The market developed a bullish two-day Higher Value relationship, but price ultimately experienced selling pressure throughout the day. Let's understand why this happened.

It's clear that a Higher Value relationship has formed, but two important elements tip you off that price was likely headed lower. First, the fact that price sold off late in the session on January 21, closing beneath the next day's value area, indicated that a rejection of the current value area relationship could be seen in the following session. Essentially, the market is giving you an advanced warning that the following day could turn bearish despite the market successfully advancing to higher value. When this occurs, I watch the opening print closely the next day. If the market opens the session below the day's value area, I will be inclined to sell any rally to the VAL or POC. In this case, RIMM opened the session below the value area and briefly rallied into VAL before forming a bearish extreme reversal pattern, which was all the confirmation needed to enter a short play. As it turns out, RIMM dropped sharply the rest of the session.

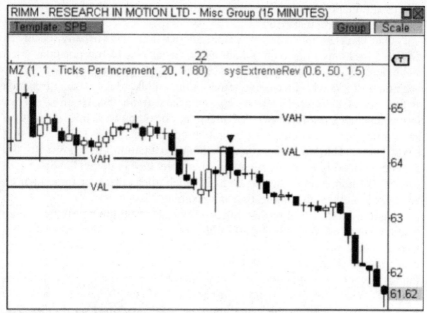

FIGURE 4.5: A failed Higher Value relationship leads to heavy selling pressure.

This is a great example that illustrates a failed value area relationship and reinforces the concept that, while powerful, these relationships offer guidelines that should be proved or disproved by the market's actions. It is your job to formulate a plan for trading each day using the information you have. Once you have formulated a plan, you then allow the market to prove or disprove the plan, which allows you to take the proper course of action. It is this type of preparedness that leads to successful trading. We will continue to explore this concept throughout the text.

Plan the trade. Trade the plan.

The second type of value area relationship is the Overlapping Higher Value relationship, which occurs when the current day's value area is higher than the prior day's value area, but today's value area low is *lower* than yesterday's value area high. This is a moderately bullish scenario, which is a step below the Higher Value relationship. An overlapping higher value day indicates market participants were able to push price to higher valuation, but only marginally. This relationship suggests a bullish bias, but indicates that strength is beginning to waver and leaves the door open for a potential decline. On this type of session, you will typically align yourself on the long side of the market, but will also take into consideration short opportunities given the right circumstances.

The Overlapping Higher Value relationship will usually occur at different locations in a trend, which can then tip you off on potential price movement. This relationship can occur in a trading range market, in the beginning of a newly-developing trend, in the middle of an existing trend, or at the end of a trend. Determining where in a trend this relationship has formed can help you forecast price direction. For example, if this relationship has formed at the extreme of a bullish trend, the market is telling you that buyers were able to push price to higher valuation, but not with the conviction of a higher value situation. Therefore, buyers do not have as much control of the market as they once had, which opens the door to a potential takeover by sellers, thus indicating an upcoming change in trend.

Take a look at Figure 4.6, which shows an Overlapping Higher Value relationship in a five-minute chart of Natural Gas futures. This type of value area relationship typically implies strength, but the outcome will vary depending on how the market opens the session. In this case, Natural Gas futures opened the day with a gap above the value area high, which indicates strength. When this occurs, any pull-back to a Money Zone level should be seen as a buying opportunity. Anytime price opens within or above the value area when this relationship is present, a bullish outcome should be expected. However, if price had opened the session below the day's VAL and below the prior day's range, a bearish scenario would have been the result.

When an Overlapping Higher Value relationship develops, the opening price becomes an integral part of how price movement will play out. You typically want to see price open above the day's value area high for a bullish outcome, or below the day's value area low for a bearish outcome. If the market gaps above VAH to begin the day, I will look to buy any pull-back to the VAH or the day's POC, with my target set to a new high within the current trend.

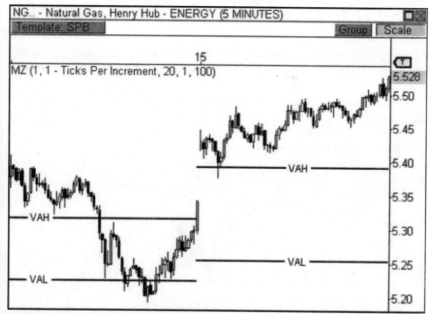

FIGURE 4.6: Overlapping Higher Value relationship.

The third value area relationship is the Lower Value relationship, which offers the most bearish directional bias that you will come across. This relationship is characterized by the current day's value area being completely lower than the prior day's value area. Therefore, today's value area high is lower than yesterday's value area low. Sellers were able to push price to lower valuation successfully, and take control of the market. When this occurs, you will look to position yourself on the short side of the market, especially if a string of lower value days has occurred in a row. This would indicate that the market is currently in a downtrend, which means every pull-back should be viewed as a selling opportunity. Depending on how price opens the session, you will look to sell a pull-back at a Money Zone level.

Figure 4.7 shows a two-day Lower Value relationship in a five-minute chart of E-Mini S&P 400 futures contract. Notice that the current day's value area is completely lower than the prior day's value area, which immediately paints a bearish picture of the day's directional bias. Depending on how price opens the session, you will be looking to take short opportunities in the early part of the session. Since the market opened the day right at the day's value area low, any pull-back to a Money Zone level should be a selling opportunity. In this example, price initially pushed lower from the day's VAL, but pulled back briefly to retest this level twice more before experiencing heavy selling pressure. If price had opened the day above VAH, however, a different outcome may have been seen.

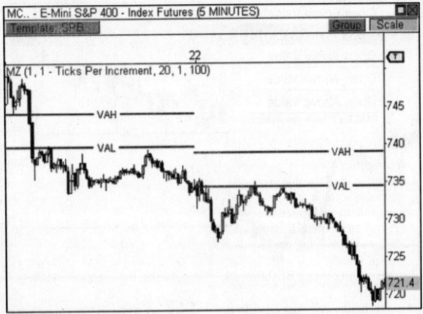

FIGURE 4.7: Lower Value relationship.

When the market successfully pushes the value area completely lower, this is an outward confirmation that the market is seeking new value and is currently accomplishing its goal. Therefore, when I see this relationship form, my bias will be squarely bearish. If the market opens the session below the VAL, I will look to sell any pull-back to the value area or the point of control, especially if the market is in an established downtrend. Keep in mind that even if this relationship develops, I will allow the market to prove or disprove the directional bias. If the market opens the session with a gap above VAH, look to buy a pull-back to the value area or the point of control with your sights set on a bullish session, as this type of behavior indicates the market is ready to buck the trend.

Table 4.3 shows a quick rundown of the various actions to be taken at key Money Zone levels during trending markets. The open in relation to value will help you determine if the market is rejecting or accepting the anticipated directional bias.

Entry Options in a Bullish Trend	
Open Above Value	Buy at VAH and POC
Open Within Value	Buy at POC and VAL
Open Below Value	Sell at VAL and POC
Entry Options in a Bearish Trend	
Open Below Value	Sell at VAL and POC
Open Within Value	Sell at POC and VAH
Open Above Value	Buy at VAH and POC

TABLE 4.3: Entry options during trending markets.

The next value area relationship is the Overlapping Lower Value relationship, which occurs when the current day's value area is lower than the prior day's value area, but today's value area high is *higher* than yesterday's value area low. This value area relationship indicates that sellers were able to push price to lower valuation, but only marginally, which paves the way to a potential buyer takeover. Sellers were able to push price lower, but do not have the conviction of a Lower Value relationship day. On this type of session, you will typically look to position yourself on the short side of the market, but will also take longs if the right opportunities present themselves.

Like the Overlapping Higher Value day, the Overlapping Lower Value day can occur at different spots on the chart, each of which can give you a certain bias about future price direction. If this type of value area day occurs at the end of a downtrend; for example, sellers may have exhausted their power to push price lower, which sets the stage for a potential buyer takeover and a likely change in trend.

Figure 4.8 shows a typical Overlapping Lower Value scenario in the five-minute chart of the E-Mini S&P 400 futures contract. Again, since the value area is overlapping to the downside, a bearish directional bias is present in the market. Any open within or below the day's value area should be seen as an opportunity to sell the market on a pull-back, which was the case in this instance. If the market had opened the day above the value area, the day's initial directional bias may have failed.

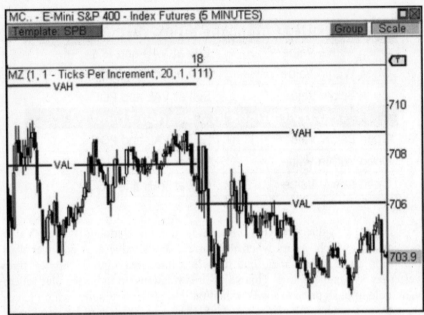

FIGURE 4.8: Overlapping Lower Value relationship

An Unchanged Value relationship occurs when the current day's value area is virtually unchanged from the prior session. One of the extremes of the value area may overlap to one side, but on the whole, the area is virtually the same as it was before. This type of day indicates that buyers and sellers are happy with the trade facilitation being conducted in this area and are satisfied with current price and value. When this type of value area relationship occurs two or three days in a row, the implication is the market is on the verge of a big breakout opportunity. Typically, you will see continued trading range behavior on the second day of an unchanged or neutral relationship. A Trading Range Day will usually arise out of this value area relationship. However, be prepared to play a breakout from the range on the third day of this relationship.

Let's take a look at Figure 4.9, which shows an Unchanged Value relationship in the five-minute chart of the Mini-Sized Dow futures contract. The current day's value area is virtually unchanged from the prior session, which means the market has found common ground between buyers and sellers. In this example, the market is in balance and will likely continue to trade within the current range. Therefore, you will look to trade the extremes of the day's initial balance.

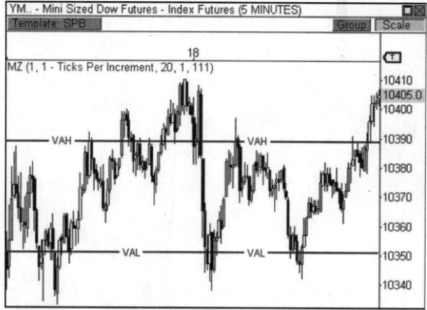

FIGURE 4.9: Unchanged Value relationship

While the second day of an Unchanged Value relationship usually leads to trading range behavior, three consecutive days of this behavior will usually result in a breakout opportunity, as shown in Figure 4.10. This chart shows the following day from the previous example and illustrates a clear breakout right at the open of the session. In this case, the YM opened the day beyond the session's Money Zone levels, which is the first major indication that a true breakout will occur. Secondly, the YM never reversed to "test" the lower Money Zone level, choosing instead to head straight to lower value, which offers further insight into the conviction of the initiative participants pushing the market lower.

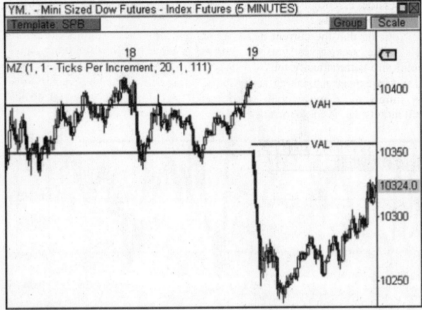

FIGURE 4.10: Three days of an Unchanged Value relationship usually leads to a breakout.

An Outside Value relationship occurs when the current day's value area completely engulfs the prior day's value area. Essentially, buyers and sellers are happy with the trade facilitation in this area, but expanded the range for better trade in the prior session. When an outside day relationship occurs, you are more likely to see a Trading Range, Typical, or Sideways Day, as the market will likely bat the ball back and forth within a given range. Typically, this type of relationship day has unbiased directional conviction, but where the market closes the prior session can tip you off to future price movement. For example, if price closes at the upper extreme of this day, a hypothetical victory has been achieved by buyers, which could lead to a bullish outcome in the upcoming session.

Figure 4.11 shows an example of an Outside Value relationship in the five-minute chart of the YM. Notice that the prior day's closing price occurred near the top of the day's range, which indicated a potentially bullish session for the upcoming day. The fact that the value area relationship was an outside value scenario indicated that price could be range-bound throughout the session, leading to either a Trading Range or Sideways Day, which was indeed the case. Take note, however, that just because the day turned out to be a Trading Range Day did not mean that the day was not bullish. The bulls were successfully able to keep trading activity above the day's value area the entire session, essentially advancing price to a higher area of value, which is a victory for the bulls.

Noticing that the current day's value area completely engulfs the prior day's value area gives you a significant edge in your trading. This relationship automatically tells you to prepare for a Trading Range session, and not to expect a breakout scenario. In terms of trading philosophy, this may simply mean exchanging your 2 ATR trailing profit stops for fixed profit targets. Or, it could mean switching from market to limit orders.

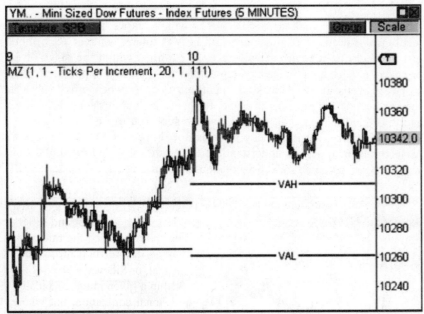

FIGURE 4.11: Outside Value relationship

An Inside Value relationship occurs when the current day's value area is completely engulfed by the prior day's value area. This relationship usually indicates quiet trading behavior prior to the current session, which is also a sign of low volatility. Unlike the outside value day when market participants are happily trading within a range, the inside day suggests the market was in balance, but is now on the verge of a big breakout opportunity, as market participants will likely seek new value. On a day when an inside value relationship appears, you are more likely to see an out of range and value opening relationship, as the market will usually open the day with a bang. This type of behavior usually leads to initiative participation that pushes price in the direction of the break, creating the makings of a Trend Day scenario.

The Inside Value relationship can trigger some of the biggest breakouts the market can offer. It pays to know when this relationship has formed.

The Inside Value relationship is usually a precursor to the out of value and range opening relationship, which we know to be extremely powerful. However, unlike the opening relationship, which requires you to wait for the opening price the next day, you can be alerted to a potentially big day by simply observing that the following session will be an inside day relationship.

Let's take a look at Figure 4.12, which shows two Inside Value relationships in the five-minute chart of the YM futures contract. Remember, just the fact that the current value area is confined within the range of the prior day's value area indicates the potential for a breakout opportunity. The best-case scenario for a breakout opportunity occurs when price opens the session beyond the prior day's range. In this case, both sessions, February 2 and 4, offered this opening print scenario, which confirmed both Trend Day types. Of course, the inside day setup is not fool proof and does not work perfectly every time, but understanding the relationship and its implications will keep you prepared for every potential outcome.

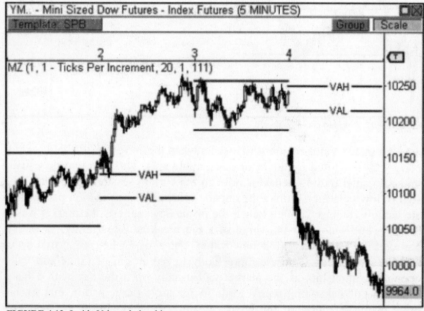

FIGURE 4.12: Inside Value relationship

BOSS IN ACTION

The Inside Value relationship can be a precursor to big moves in the market. As such, I like to be prepared and understand which days will have this setup *before* the market opens. The way I perform this function is by plotting the developing value area alongside the static value area. Keep in mind that the static value area plots the current day's levels, while the developing value area's ending values will become the static levels for the next session.

Let's take a look at Figure 4.13 to clarify this important point. Notice that this chart of Crude Oil has two sets of lines plotted, the static and developing Money Zone levels. The dynamically updating developing levels show that by session's end, both the upper and lower lines are *within* the day's static value area. This means the following session will have an inside value relationship and provide the potential for a big breakout opportunity.

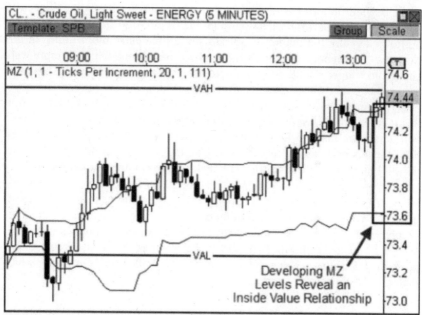

FIGURE 4.13: Deciphering the Inside Value relationship using the developing value area

Of course, knowing that the following day may result in a Trend Day scenario allows me to prepare accordingly, both mentally and strategically. The mental preparation involves switching from a short-term oriented trader to a "let it ride" type of persona. Remember, catching a ride on a Trend Day can make or break your month; therefore, it is important to switch your mentality from one that is "take what you got" to "take what you can." Strategically speaking, you will switch your focus from profit targets to wide trailing profit stops. If you are really confident in the day's action, you can use a Market on Close (MOC) exit, which will basically get you out of the trade when the session closes, since the biggest Trend Days will usually close at the day's extreme. In the software I use, OmniTrader and VisualTrader, there is a trade session boundary stop, which allows you to exit your trade a specified number of minutes before the close. This type of stop is essential for most styles of intraday trading.

Let's examine Figure 4.14, which is the actual breakout day in our Crude Oil chart. When I see that the following session will have an inside value relationship, it is my hope that the opening print will occur beyond the prior day's range. Remember, an open price that occurs beyond range and value indicates that sentiment has significantly shifted overnight and market participants are eagerly seeking new value, which embodies what a breakout day is all about. Our Crude Oil chart shows that the opening print did indeed occur beyond the prior day's range and value, which falls right in line with our best-case scenario. I will usually let the first five to fifteen minutes play out to make sure the market is able to sustain the early momentum. In this case, two consecutive higher closings in the five-minute bar timeframe were enough to trigger a long entry with stops below the day's lows. However, if the market opens out of range and value, but immediately retraces for a test back within the prior session's range, the market may be looking to affirm that it is ready to leave prior price levels and seek new value.

There are many different trade management methodologies that can be used for this particular setup, including partial exits and profit targets, but it is well known that during a true Trend Day scenario, the market will usually close at or near the day's extreme. Therefore, I will usually keep a relatively loose 2 ATR trailing stop with my sights set on exiting near the day's close, generally within the last fifteen minutes of the session. Remember, this type of breakout opportunity occurs only a few times per month, so the goal should be to make the most money possible when the ideal circumstances present themselves. Your trader personality will usually dictate which method you choose, however.

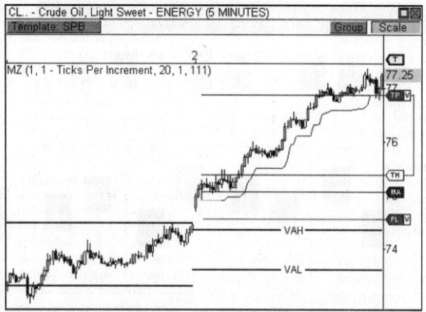

FIGURE 4.14: Inside Value relationship led to a big move in Crude Oil.

This particular setup is one of the most important and explosive that you will come across. Regardless of your trading style, the objective for all traders is to make money, and this setup delivers the biggest punch with the biggest profit potential. Remember, a day that opens out of value and out of range offers the most risk, but with high risk also comes big opportunity. Only a few days per month will generate a move of this magnitude, but participating on these days will allow you to make as much, or more, money than the other days of the month combined.

As a quick reference, Figure 4.15 illustrates each of the value area relationships. Remember, trading is about recognition. The best traders in the world are quickly and accurately able to recognize the pattern of the market and are able to deploy their capital in a confident and knowledgeable manner. Learning to recognize who is in control of the market, the types of market days, key setup opportunities, and value area relationships are all extremely vital to profitably engaging the market. Each new concept is a piece to a larger puzzle. Therefore, continue to learn and understand the interrelated concepts, as each new concept will be related to the last.

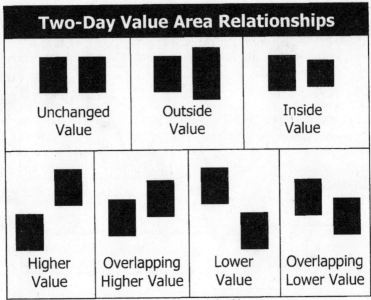

FIGURE 4.15: Diagram of the seven value area relationships

VALUE AREA WIDTH

The width of the value area can be an important part of the puzzle when planning for the current session's activity. If the width of the value area is of typical size, then not much information can be gained other than current market activity is proceeding like normal. However, if the width of the value area is extremely wide or narrow, these characteristics can be very telling of potential price movement in the upcoming session.

The width of the Money Zone value area can be a big determining factor on price movement if the range is abnormally wide or narrow.

A wide value area indicates that the prior session had a large range of price activity. This can be the result of several day types, including Trend, Double-Distribution Trend, and Expanded Typical Days. If today's value area is extremely wide due to yesterday's range of movement, this is an indication that today's market will be rather quiet, leading to either a Typical, Trading Range, or Sideways Day. The market will typically alternate between high range and low range days. That is, the market will consolidate after a big move, and will usually get a big move after a Sideways Day. If the width of the value area is wide, you will usually look to trade within the extremes of the initial balance, as these will likely hold throughout the session. Therefore, when the value area is wide, you will be preparing to trade a Typical, Expanded Typical, Trading Range, or Sideways Day. This will usually be the case during an Outside Value relationship day.

Conversely, if the width of the value area is extremely narrow, this is an indication that the prior day's range of price activity was small, which can be the result of a Trading range or Sideways Day. When this occurs, you will typically prepare for a Trend, Double-Distribution Trend, or Expanded Typical Day, as a breakout from the prior day's range will likely occur. In this instance, the outer boundaries of the initial balance may not hold throughout the session. Instead, market participants will likely overwhelm one or both sides of the initial balance, leading to range extension and one of the high-range day types.

Figure 4.16 shows a five-minute chart of Research in Motion, Ltd. that illustrates both narrow and wide value areas. Notice that the first day's value area is extremely narrow. When this occurs, you will be preparing for a potential breakout opportunity. The initial balance on this day is also narrow, which is indicative of a Double-Distribution Trend Day. Eventually, initiative buyers overwhelmed the top of the initial balance and proceeded to push price higher the rest of the session, causing a wide range for the day.

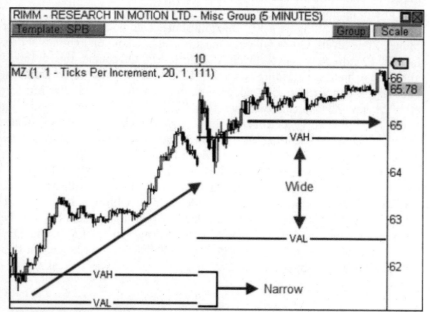

FIGURE 4.16: Value area width can help forecast trending or sideways market behavior.

As you recall, the market will typically alternate between high and low range sessions. The fact that the market rallied after the formation of a narrow value area caused the value area for the next session to be extremely wide. A wide value area will typically lead to Trading Range or Sideways Day behavior, which was the case the following day. When this occurs, the initial balance will usually be larger, as the market establishes the extremes for the day's trading activity, which usually results in a Typical, Trading Range, or Sideways Day.

BOSS IN ACTION

When the market has traded quietly sideways within the boundaries of an abnormally wide value area, I'm usually salivating at the idea of trading a major breakout from range in the upcoming session. During this type of session, a Sideways Day or Trading Range Day will usually occur. If the market remains true and trades sideways during a session with wide Money Zone levels, the conditions are ripe for a big breakout opportunity the following session by way of a very narrow Money Zone range. When this occurs, I will watch the opening print very closely for signs of a gap beyond the prior day's range to signify a true breakout scenario. If this occurs, I will trigger an entry in the direction of the gap with the hopes of riding a move to the close of the market.

Take a look at Figure 4.17, which illustrates both wide and narrow range Money Zone levels. Crude Oil got a magnificent breakout on February 4 due, in part, to extremely narrow Money Zone levels. Of course, this occurred after a day that saw trading range behavior with a wide value area. On February 3, Crude Oil traded sideways throughout the session after forming wide Money Zone levels, which set up perfectly for a breakout play on February 4. As we've discovered throughout the chapter, the big money paydays occur on trending days. Given that the market traded quietly sideways on February 3, the Money Zone levels for the following session were extremely narrow, setting the stage for a nice breakout opportunity.

I approach a narrow range breakout opportunity with the same confidence and enthusiasm as I would a day with an Inside Value relationship. Again, I will look for an opening print that occurs beyond the prior day's range and value, which sets the stage for a true Trend Day scenario. If this occurs, I will enter the market with a loose trailing profit stop with the hopes of riding the wave as long as I can, as was the case in this instance.

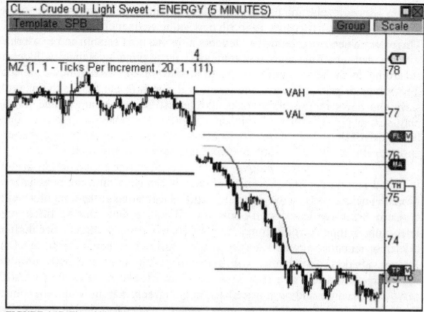

FIGURE 4.17: The width of the value areas helped forecast price behavior in Crude Oil.

There are countless setups that occur throughout the session. The key is to find the setups that fit your trader profile. As such, I usually look to trade scenarios that offer the best opportunity for success given my personal profile. Therefore, with a narrow range breakout opportunity, I like to see the opening print occur beyond the prior day's range, which usually sets up nicely for big movement (but not always). However, what happens if the market does not open beyond the prior day's range and value? What if the market opens within the day's narrow Money Zone range? In this case, the market's perception of value has not changed significantly enough to force initiative participants to enter the market in search of new value. Therefore, you are less likely to see fireworks in the market even if a breakout occurs at some point during the session, although a slim chance does still exist. Therefore, a breakout from the narrow range Money Zone levels may spark key price movement, but confirmation past the prior days range will need to be seen in order for a move with true market participation to occur.

VIRGIN MONEY ZONE LEVELS

Unlike other indicators, prior Money Zone levels can be extremely important and influential in the current trading session. Remember, the

Money Zone levels are based on *actual* trading that occurred in a prior session. Market participants establish new value areas with each passing day. Therefore, when price returns to a value area that was established in a prior session, market participants will remember these price levels and will react according to their perception of value at the present time. Of course, the importance of prior Money Zone levels will diminish the longer the market stays away from these price zones. While last week's Money Zone levels may still play an important role on current price behavior, Money Zone levels established three months ago may not be remembered by the market and, therefore, will have vastly reduced significance, if any at all.

A Money Zone level that was never touched during its session of origin is called a *virgin Money Zone level*, which can also be known as naked levels. These levels have special significance because the market will typically see these levels as it does an unfilled gap that must be filled at a later point in time. Virgin Money Zone levels will usually attract price during a later session, serving as a sort of magnet to price. When a virgin level is formed, market participants will remember this level and will usually approach it for a test in a later session. A test at a virgin level will usually serve as resistance and push price back in the direction from whence it came. Basically, market participants must see if any new business will be conducted beyond the virgin level before they can push price into a new direction. When initiative participants do not enter the market beyond the virgin level, responsive participants take control and push price back toward fair value.

A virgin Money Zone level can be an extremely important reference point, as market participants will usually drive price back toward this untouched level for a test at a future point in time.

Not all virgin Money Zone levels must be "filled," however. Actually, I find that only two of the three levels will have the most relevance after their formation. The first, and most obvious, virgin level to be concerned with is a *virgin point of control* (VPC). The point of control is the fairest price to both buyers and sellers in a given timeframe. Traders will watch this level closely and judge current price against it to trigger responsive or initiative actions. To say that this level is important is an understatement. Therefore, when price moves aggressively away from the point of control during its session of origin without testing it, traders will take notice and use this level as a key reference point at a later date.

Let's take a look at Figure 4.18, which is a five-minute chart of Heating Oil futures. On December 2, price moved aggressively away from the POC during its session of origin, thus creating a virgin point of control. Price stayed away from this level for two days, but eventually needed to return to this level for a test before new lows could be seen in this commodity. On December 4, price rallied aggressively to begin the session and tested the VPC almost to the penny before dropping sharply to new lows within the current downtrend. Your knowledge of the types of market days, the types of buyers and sellers, and the basic candlestick formations can easily give you the instant recognition required to enter this trade at the best price. If we break this trade down into these key components, you will find that entering this trade short at or above the $2.08 level offers a high probability outcome.

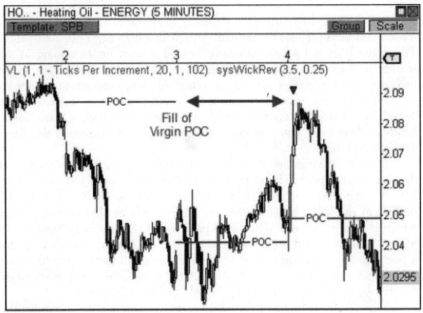

FIGURE 4.18: Heating Oil responds to a virgin point of control.

First, we know that when the market opens the day aggressively, there is a chance for either a Typical Day or Expanded Typical Day formation, which means the day's initial balance could contain the day's extremes throughout the day, or at least most of it. In our figure, when price rallied to the VPC and began to hold, you could assume with confidence that the boundaries of the initial balance had been set for the day, thereby creating the potential high for the session. Secondly, since price rallied away from the day's POC any indication of weakness at highs would likely trigger responsive selling activity, as price would be considered overvalued by these market participants. Third, since the fourth candlestick of the day was a bearish wick reversal setup, we had a trifecta of market activity that could have easily triggered a short entry into this market. Once in the trade, a stop loss could be set above the day's highs beyond the virgin Money Zone level, with our sights set to a target at the day's lows, which was easily reached. I like a target at the day's lows because, as you know, a Typical Day scenario would indicate that the extremes of the initial balance will hold, which indicates price will likely reach the day's lows, but may not surpass this price level. A partial exit methodology could work as well, wherein you exit part of the trade at the day's lows while letting the rest of the position "ride" with a trailing profit stop or additional profit targets. This scenario would allow you to capture a larger move if price were to break through the initial balance low.

I have successfully triggered this entry many times and it still impresses traders that I can pick such a difficult entry with a high degree of confidence. This setup does not require anything beyond a basic understanding of the market and its tendencies. Knowing there is a virgin POC above price indicates that the market may try to retest this level several days after its creation. Moreover, once the virgin level is tested, we know that responsive sellers may enter the market, which will push price back toward value. Lastly, having basic entry setups to trigger your entry completes this easy, yet powerful trade.

The second virgin level that I pay attention to is the Money Zone level that is closest to price. Therefore, if the market moves rapidly away from the Money Zone levels to create virgin lines, the level that I will watch closely, outside of the VPC, will be either the virgin VAH or VAL, depending on which is closest to price. That is, if price drops sharply away from virgin Money Zone levels, then the VAL and the POC will be the ones to watch for a potential "fill" in an upcoming session, as these will become the first lines of defense should a test occur. Conversely, if price rallies away from virgin MZ levels, then I will watch the VAH and POC for a test ahead.

Take a look at Figure 4.19, which is a five-minute chart of the E-Mini NASDAQ 100 futures contract and shows a virgin VAL at work. The market opened the day with a gap up and rallied to "fill" the virgin VAL that was created in the prior session. After price put in the initial low after the opening gap, I was fairly confident that the test at the virgin level would be the upper extreme of the initial balance, as a typical or expanded Typical Day would likely develop. Again, entering the market short based on this information allowed me to become a responsive selling participant, essentially pushing price back toward value. Entering the trade with a fixed loss stop above the virgin MZ level and a target back at the day's lows would have easily created a recipe for success on this day. Take note, however, that this type of trade usually works best at the beginning of the day. While these levels can be "filled" at any point during a session, a tradable reaction will usually occur during the first part of a session, generally within the first sixty minutes of the day. If price approaches a virgin level late in a session, it is best to use the level as a target, rather than trying to fade the reaction.

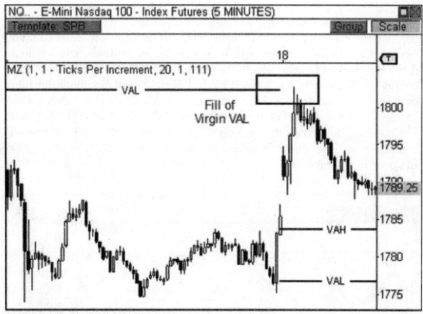

FIGURE 4.19: The E-Mini NASDAQ 100 responds to a virgin VAL

BOSS IN ACTION

Let's take a look at how I would normally play this setup. Figure 4.20 is a five-minute chart of Research in Motion, Ltd. that shows a test at the most recent virgin POC. There are two main factors that I look for when considering this setup for a fade opportunity: the trend and a morning test. First, I like to play a fade in the direction of the existing short-term trend, which can be as short as two days. As long as price is trading within a discernable short-term trend, a pull-back within the trend makes for an easy prospect for a fade opportunity. In Figure 4.20, you will notice that RIMM has been trending lower over the last several days of trading, making a pull-back on January 21 a prime prospect for a fade at the virgin POC. The second criterion that must be fulfilled is a morning test of the virgin level, preferably in the first thirty to sixty minutes of the session. I prefer this timing because it coincides within the natural reversal times in the chart. Moreover, this timing also runs parallel to the creation of the day's initial balance.

Looking at the chart, you see that RIMM rallied early in the session, but immediately halted the advance once the virgin POC was filled at $65.33. Instead of blindly submitting an order to sell the virgin POC, I usually look for signs of exhaustion at this level. I do this by studying the development of the candlesticks at this level to gauge the actions of responsive market participants. Have any of my key candlestick reversal patterns formed, like the extreme reversal or wick reversal setups? Have any candlesticks turned bearish after the early advance? If the answer to any of these questions is yes, then I will submit an order to sell the virgin POC with my stop loss set above the high of the session and a target back at the day's low. I choose this target because if the market does indeed reverse from the virgin POC, then chances are good that the market has established an early range for fair trade facilitation. Therefore, the market is likely to trade back within the boundaries of the initial balance, thereby testing the day's low, which occurred in this case.

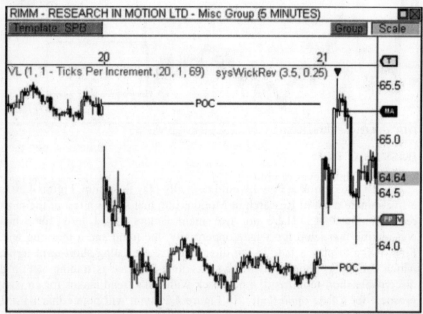

FIGURE 4.20: Fading a test of a virgin POC in RIMM

Virgin Money Zone levels are extremely valuable zones to monitor. A high percentage of virgin levels are usually filled within days of their creation. Actually, I've read research that indicates that upwards of 80 percent of virgin levels are "filled" within a week of their creation, so marking these levels for a potential test in the future is a good habit to keep.

These levels also become extremely useful when they are created within a trend, as a pull-back to a virgin level will usually offer a solid entry back in the direction of the current trend.

UNDERSTANDING VOLUME AT PRICE

The *volume at price* indicator is a visually powerful tool. This indicator is quite unlike the typical volume indicator that most traders use, which only plots volume at a bar. Instead, volume at price plots a horizontal histogram of volume at a price, and is overlaid directly on the price pane. This gives you visually significant market-generated information. Plotting this indicator allows you to see the market at work in a way that no other indicator offers, and it actually gives you the closest representation of the Market Profile structure.

Perhaps the most significant aspects of the volume at price indicator are the volume peaks, or *High Volume Areas* (HVA), that are formed day after day. These peaks visually highlight high traffic price levels where the most trade occurred between buyers and sellers. These peaks are extremely relevant in the charts because they signify price levels that offered fair facilitation of trade. As you know, the market solely operates to facilitate trade; therefore, these peaks visually display satisfied customers. Price will usually move freely between peaks, using prior peaks as both support and resistance, as market participants search for price zones that offer fair trade. More than one peak can be created in a single day, like on a Double-Distribution Trend Day, but the highest peak of the day will be crowned the *Volume Point of Control (VPOC)*, which indicates the fairest price of the day as seen through the eyes of volume. This level will usually be the same as the price-based POC, but can differ at times since it is based on volume.

Take a look at Figure 4.21, which is a five-minute chart of the Silver futures contract. Notice how price trades freely between volume peaks over the course of several days, as the market tests, and retests, high volume clusters. Basically, the market is operating in a matter that allows for easy facilitation of trade. Price is basically trading from one high volume cluster to the next in order to satisfy different market participants at different prices.

FIGURE 4.21: Price moves freely between high volume areas in Silver futures.

While the peaks offer extremely important market-generated information, the volume valleys, or *Low Volume Areas (LVA)*, can be quite important as well. A significant LVA that forms between two distinct volume peaks can usually indicate a price range that can be easily penetrated, similar to a single TPO price print in the Market Profile structure (see Figure 4.22). When this occurs, you may see price easily push through the LVA in order to get to the next volume peak, which is considered an area where fair trade is conducted. Think of an LVA as a hallway that separates two rooms, which are the HVAs. People will walk through the hallway freely and easily to get to the rooms at either end. While people can stand and congregate in the hallway, they are more inclined to do business in either of the two rooms, which offer more convenience and can accommodate more people. Knowing where the LVAs are located will allow you to prepare for a potential price probe to the next HVA.

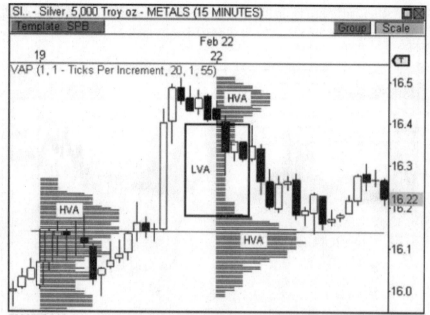

FIGURE 4.22: Price will move easily through an LVA between volume peaks.

The Unchanged VPOC Relationship

The *Unchanged VPOC relationship* can help forecast one of the most explosive breakout opportunities in the market. This relationship occurs when the volume point of control is virtually the same price for two or more days in a row. Basically, when this relationship develops, the market is currently in a virtual standstill, as market participants are trading quietly and happily within the boundaries of a clearly-defined range. Eventually, price will break free from the range, as market participants will look to seek new value, which usually sparks the beginning of a significant move. This unchanged relationship can deliver one of the biggest trending days of the month, especially when coupled with an open that occurs out of range and value.

Take a look at Figure 4.23, which is a five-minute chart of First Solar, Inc (ticker: FSLR). First Solar developed a clear two-day Unchanged VPOC relationship, which is our first indication that a breakout opportunity may be seen. Typically, I look to trade an emphatic breakout via an opening print that occurs beyond the prior day's range, but this criterion cannot always be satisfied. In this case, First Solar opened the day within the prior day's range, but immediately began to break two-day support, which essentially sparked heavy selling pressure in the stock. The first leg of the breakout generated a move of about $5, but the stock eventually reached the $110 level for a total range of $8 points on the day.

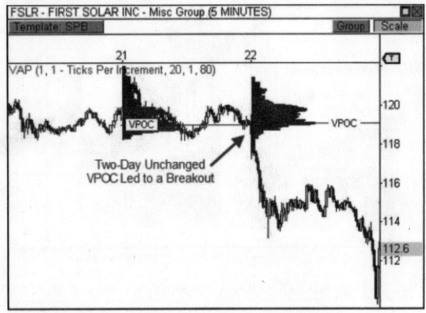

FIGURE 4.22: An Unchanged VPOC relationship leads to a breakout in FSLR.

THE VIRGIN VOLUME POINT OF CONTROL

A VPOC that is not touched during its session of origin is called a *Virgin Volume Point of Control*. Like a normal volume peak, a virgin VPOC, also called a naked VPOC, can attract price at a later date. However, virgin levels will usually have more gravitational pull, as the market will treat them like gaps that must be filled. On the whole, market participants do not like gaps to remain unfilled, as this usually leads to a feeling of unfinished business. As such, the market will usually return to a virgin VPOC and test it within a week of its creation. However, the farther price moves away from this level, or the longer price stays away from it, the less significance the level will carry in the future.

Let's take a look at Figure 4.24, which is a fifteen-minute chart of Research in Motion, Ltd. This chart clearly shows the formation of two virgin VPOCs in a three-day span. In the days that followed, price rallied and dropped to fill both of these important levels, as naked levels usually attract price like a magnet. Once a virgin level is filled, market participants are likely to reverse price back in the direction of the original trend, unless more virgin levels lie ahead.

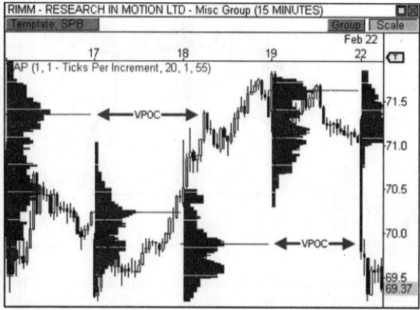

FIGURE 4.24: Two virgin VPOCs were filled within days of their formation in RIMM.

Let's turn our attention to Figure 4.25, which is a five-minute chart of Gold futures that illustrates the power of multiple virgin volume points of control. In this example, Gold futures created two virgin VPOC levels in a three-day span, which were both filled on the fourth day. The fact that virgin levels will usually be filled allows you to use these zones as potential targets for your trades. Gold futures began the day with heavy selling pressure via a breakaway gap against the current trend, indicating there was a good chance that the day would develop into a Trend Day scenario. As such, short positions taken in the first twenty minutes of the session could have used the virgin POCs as targets the rest of the day, incrementally scaling out of your position as the day progressed.

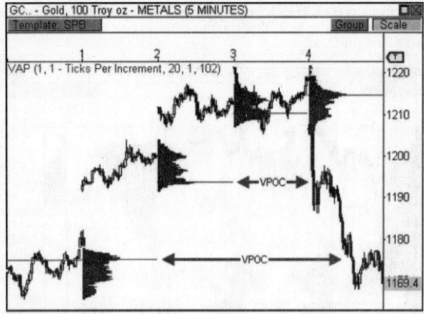

FIGURE 4.25: Gold fills two virgin VPOCs

Virgin POCs can also be used as major reversal points as well, as long as these levels are tested early in a session. For example, Figure 4.26 shows the Mini-Sized Dow futures contract responding to a virgin VPOC that was created four days earlier. The Dow broke out of a consolidation early in the session and raced to "fill" the naked level at around 10,235. Since the test happened early in the session, there was a chance that a reversal could be seen in the Dow, as responsive buyers entered the market en masse due to the short-term oversold conditions in the market. Responsive participants helped drive price quietly higher the remainder of the day, allowing the virgin VPOC to be used both as a target for morning short positions, and as a launching point for responsive long positions in the afternoon.

It is important to note that reversals at any virgin level usually occur early in a session, rather than late. First of all, a virgin level that sparks a reversal earlier in the day will likely coincide with the creation of the day's initial balance, which can usually set the extremes of the day's trading action. Therefore, a reversal at a virgin level that occurs within the first thirty to sixty minutes may have more help from responsive market participants looking to set the day's trading extremes. Conversely, if a test at a virgin level occurs late the session, this level should be viewed more as a target, rather than as a reversal point. This is due, in part, to initiative participants mainly ruling the afternoon's trading activity, especially if range extension is occurring late in the day.

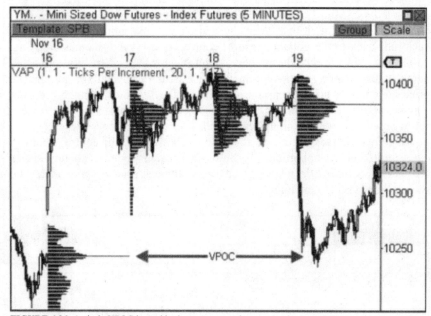

FIGURE 4.26: A virgin VPOC is used both as a target and reversal point in the YM.

USING VOLUME AT PRICE IN A TREND

While we have already covered several methods for using the volume at price indicator, probably the easiest method is using it in a clearly established trend. A trending market truly offers one of the best trading opportunities around. This type of market environment offers clear directional conviction, highlights when price is a bargain or overvalued, and packs enormous profit-making potential. It's no wonder so many trading strategies and approaches fixate on trend determination.

When the market is trading within a clearly established trend, the Volume at Price indicator becomes a great "bargain shopping" tool that allows you to buy the dips and sell the rips alongside the market's elite traders. That is, professional traders will usually wait for a pull-back before entering an established trend. Professionals wait to buy when price at or below value, and will sell when price is at or above value. Unlike many other indicators, volume at price illustrates real market activity at every price level during the course of a day. When these days are connected in a trend, price levels that are at, below, or above value jump right off the chart.

Let's use Figure 4.27 as an example. This chart shows a fifteen-minute chart of the E-Mini NASDAQ 100 futures contract during a trend in mid-February 2010. Notice that when the market is in the midst of an uptrend, each pull-back to the volume point of control, or a HVA, becomes a buying opportunity. In a trend, these areas depict clear zones where price is at or below value, therefore, illustrating the best areas to buy within the current price advance. If price opens the day above the session's volume point of control, any pull-back should be seen as a buying opportunity, with targets set to new highs within the uptrend. In each of the three days shown below, price opened the session above the day's volume point of control, making every pull-back an opportunity to buy at a cheaper price. I call this visual setup the *Escalator Effect*, since price uses volume at price as an escalator, or staircase, to push to new highs.

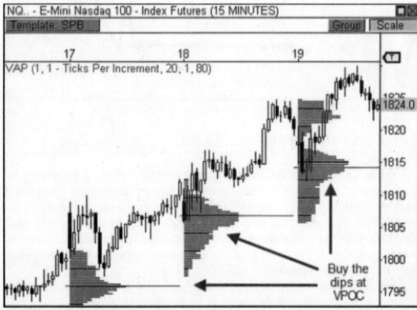

FIGURE 4.27: Buying the dips in an uptrend using VAP in the NQ

Let's take a look at an example where price is trending down. Figure 4.28 shows a three-day view of a fifteen-minute chart of Silver futures during mid-January of 2010. Notice that every pull-back to the volume point of control is a selling opportunity within the current down move, as this level clearly illustrates an area where price is at or above value. Professional traders will wait for a pull-back in price before entering into a trend, essentially profiting from the reverse Escalator Effect, as price bounces lower off the VAP indicator. By waiting to sell a pull-back in the commodity at or above value, you are improving your position by choosing a better trade location before price returns lower in search of lower valuation. This is one of the oldest, yet simplest lessons of the market.

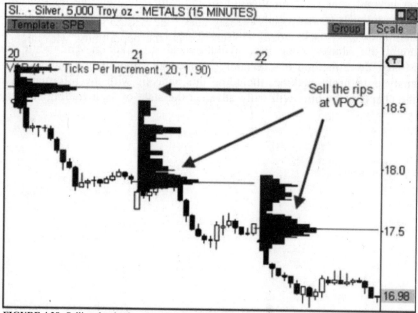

FIGURE 4.28: Selling the rips in a downtrend using VAP in Silver futures

Keep in mind there are several factors that contribute to the success rate of this setup. First, the market must be in an established trend. Second, the market must open in the direction of the existing trend: *above* the VPOC in an uptrend, and *below* the VPOC in a downtrend. Third, the day's closing price must be in the direction of the existing trend: *above* the VPOC in an uptrend, and *below* the VPOC in a downtrend. If these three factors are in agreement, the chances for successful bounces within the trend increase significantly. Otherwise, one simple stray can change the tide of the trend and the setup completely. An opening or closing price that occurs against the trend (beyond the VPOC) is usually enough to kill the validity of this setup.

THE MONEY ZONE REVOLUTION

The Money Zone offers an ultra powerful view of the market that allows you to analyze and trade the market in a much more informed manner. The Money Zone is much more than just a collection of lines on a chart. These levels offer important market-generated information that goes far beyond your typical collection of indicators. Judging the relationships of these levels reveals another realm of information about the market that is very hard to come by when using standard forms of analysis. There is no doubt the Money Zone has revolutionized my trading. And while the Money Zone method has certainly boosted all areas of my trading, from analysis to profit making, including this analysis with the information in the chapters to come will truly advance the state of your trading success.

CHAPTER 5

INTRODUCING
FLOOR PIVOTS

"I do not undertake the work unless I see my way clear to a profit."
- Jesse Livermore

The first significant awakening of my trading career occurred when I first discovered the power of Floor Pivots. Until then, I was trading solely off chart patterns and candlestick combinations and never knew there was an underlying road map to each chart I traded. Once the Floor Pivots were revealed me, however, a completely different gear was reached in my trading and market analysis. I felt as though I had finally joined the trading elite.

Floor Pivots have been around for a long time and many traders have used these pivots to master the market for decades. Larry Williams re-popularized the formula by including it in his book, *How I Made One Million Dollars Last Year Trading Commodities*, in 1979. He described the "Pivot Price Formula" that he used to arrive at the next day's probable high or low. Many great traders have adopted the pivots and have even incorporated them into many indicators that you may know today.

While these pivots can go by many names, including Pivot Points, Floors, or just pivots, I typically call them the Floor Pivots since they really became popular once traders on the floors of the exchanges began to use them. The pivots were a simple way for floor traders to forecast the day's potential support and resistance levels, since they didn't have sophisticated computers on the floors of the exchanges at the time. This name also helps to distinguish them from other types of pivot points, since there are other types that are unrelated to the ones we will discuss in this book.

Floor Pivots are extremely powerful price-based support and resistance levels that are calculated using a prior period's high, low, and close.

Floor Pivots offer an amazing way to view the market. They are like night-vision goggles, illuminating the moves of the market even in the most uncertain of times. As you begin to study the pivots on a deeper level, you will begin to see the correlated nature between the Floor Pivots and price behavior. The main reason these pivots can be so unbelievably accurate is the simple fact that market participants are watching and trading these key levels. Trader psychology, and human nature for that matter, has remained the same for centuries due to fear, greed, hope, and uncertainty. These are the reasons why traders continue to react to key levels in the charts the same way over and over again. This is also the reason why these pivots have stood the test of time and will continue to work into the future. We will delve deeper into Floor Pivots in this chapter and will unlock extremely powerful concepts that run deep in the market.

THE STANDARD FLOOR PIVOTS FORMULA

While Floor Pivots have been around for decades, they can still cause confusion due to the fact that several variations of the formula can be found. However, there is one formula that is widely considered to be the standard which I will divulge in a moment. Once you plug in the high, low, and close of the prior day (or week, month, and year), the formula will automatically calculate the central pivot, three resistance levels (R1 to R3), and three support levels (S1 to S3) that are to be used for the current day's trading activity. That is, seven pivot levels are plotted on your chart. The high, low, and close are used for the equation because they are the most important values for any given time period, whether it be a single bar or an entire day or month. The high and low represent the most bullish and bearish of expectations for the market for that period of time, thus making these values important reference points. Likewise, where the market closes can give insight into the collective minds of the market heading into the following period of time. Without further delay, the standard Floor Pivots formula is as follows:

Standard Floor Pivots Formula
R3 = R1 + (High - Low)
R2 = Pivot + (High - Low)
R1 = 2 × Pivot - Low
Pivot = (High + Low + Close)/3
S1 = 2 × Pivot - High
S2 = Pivot - (High - Low)
S3 = S1 - (High - Low)

TABLE 5.1: Standard Formula

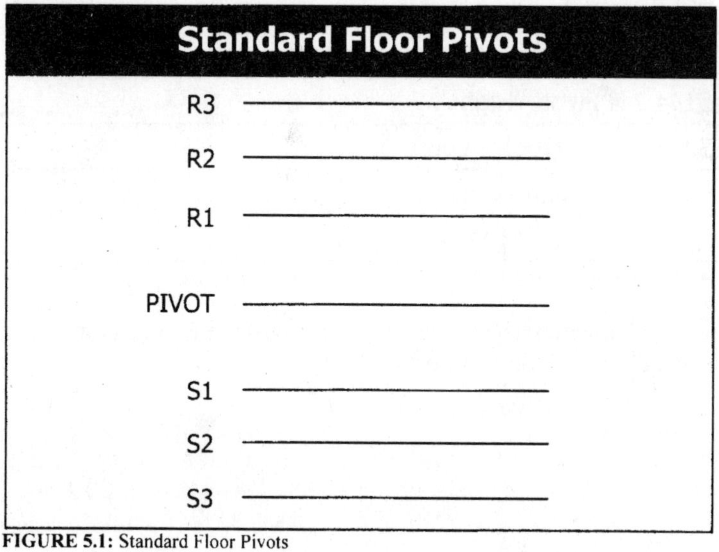

FIGURE 5.1: Standard Floor Pivots

THE EXPANDED FLOOR PIVOTS FORMULA

I did take liberty with the formula by adding four more levels to the charts that, in my opinion, make the indicator exponentially more dynamic. Given today's volatile markets, a third level of support and resistance can be quite shallow due to the explosive moves we see today. As a matter of fact, the volatility was even less of a factor in 1979, as the formula that Williams produced only offered two levels of support and resistance. However, I added a fourth level of support (S4) and resistance (R4) to the equation that falls in line with the general theme of the original levels. Moreover, taking a page out of Mark Fisher's book *The Logical Trader*, I added the pivot range (TC and BC) to the indicator, which in itself is extremely powerful. We will cover the pivot range in extensive detail in Chapter 6. The expanded formula is as follows:

Expanded Floor Pivots Formula
R4 = R3 + (R2 - R1)
R3 = R1 + (High - Low)
R2 = Pivot + (High - Low)
R1 = 2 × Pivot - Low
TC = (Pivot - BC) + Pivot
Pivot = (High + Low + Close)/3
BC = (High + Low)/2
S1 = 2 × Pivot - High
S2 = Pivot - (High - Low)
S3 = S1 - (High - Low)
S4 = S3 - (S1 - S2)

TABLE 5.2: Expanded Formula

Figure 5.2 illustrates the expanded version of the Floor Pivots, which we will use and discuss throughout of the book.

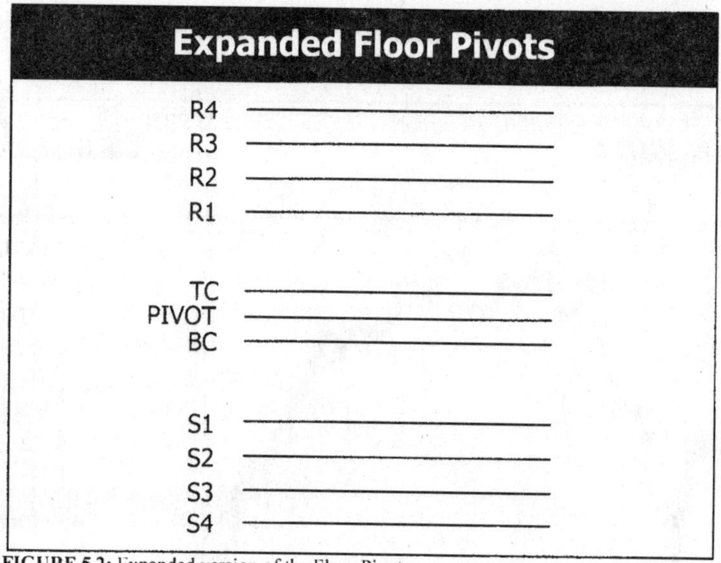

Expanded Floor Pivots

R4 ————————————
R3 ————————————
R2 ————————————
R1 ————————————

TC ————————————
PIVOT ————————————
BC ————————————

S1 ————————————
S2 ————————————
S3 ————————————
S4 ————————————

FIGURE 5.2: Expanded version of the Floor Pivots

APPLYING THE FORMULA

When I first discovered the pivots, I manually had to draw each pivot level with a line drawing tool onto my charts. I would input the high, low, and closing price into a spreadsheet I created and the next day's pivots would calculate automatically. I then carefully placed each pivot level onto my charts, which was very clumsy at times, and repeated this process day after day. The word tedious is a vast understatement.

However, many trading applications these days have the Floor Pivots as an indicator in their base indicator library, which means my rain dances appear to have worked. This level of automation actually unlocked many of the secrets that I will reveal to you in later chapters, including higher timeframe pivots, pivot trend analysis, and multiple timeframe pivot combinations, which are some of the most powerful techniques used in all of technical analysis.

First, however, let's learn more about these fabulous lines, and how they apply to a single session. Figure 5.3 shows a five-minute chart of the Mini-Sized Dow futures contract. This is just your Typical Day in the market, but this chart is sans the underlying road map to the market. On this day, the Dow futures contract rallied early in the day, but reversed off the 7,800 level and dropped three hundred points to 7,500. The contract then reversed sharply from the 7,500 low and rallied to 7,700 where it closed the session.

That's a lot of movement for one day, with lots of intraday swings and reversals to boot.

FIGURE 5.3: Mini-sizedDow Jones without the Floor Pivots

Figure 5.4, however, reveals the Floor Pivots for the same day and clearly illustrates how each turn in the market was orchestrated by reactions at these levels. The YM began the day right at the top central pivot and rallied through R1 resistance straight to R2. The contract then consolidated at highs beneath R2 and eventually dropped to S1 support for a brief moment before heading precisely to S2 at 7,500. The index then reversed sharply from S2 support and rallied back to R1 at 7,700, where it closed the day. Essentially, the high and low of the day was captured precisely by the pivots of this indicator, which is both fascinating and amazing.

FIGURE 5.4: Mini-sized Dow Jones with the Floor Pivots revealed

If this doesn't blow your mind, then you might not be impressed by the pyramids at Giza, the miracle of birth, or time travel. It's hard to argue against this type of incredible precision in the stock market, where price movement often seems unruly at best, and a complete enigma the rest of the time. As long as there is proper liquidity and volatility in the market, the pivots will work on any chart, market, and timeframe. Even in the most challenging of market environments, these pivots light up the charts for your trading pleasure—and profit! This is trader voodoo at its best.

Let's take a quick look at how to calculate the levels using the formula. On March 24, the YM had a high of 7,743, a low of 7,587, and a close of 7,618. To find the central pivot for March 25, you would take the high, low, and close from March 24 and then divide the sum by 3, thus, 7,743 + 7,587 + 7,618 = 22,948; 22,948 / 3 = 7649. To find S1, you would multiply the central pivot by 2 and then subtract the high from March 24. Thus, 7,649 × 2 − 7,743 = 7,555. To calculate R1, you would multiply the central pivot by 2 and then subtract the low, therefore, 7,649 × 2 − 7,587 = 7,711. You would continue in this manner until all the pivots have been calculated.

As I mentioned before, most trading platforms offer this indicator in their base indicator library, so actually plotting them by hand becomes an afterthought. Even if your platform doesn't offer this indicator, a basic knowledge around a spreadsheet can calculate these levels quickly and easily for you once you have provided the high, low, and close of the day. Moreover, many free pivot calculators can be found online at trading sites across the worldwide interwebs.

FOLLOW THE LEADER

Part of what makes the Floor Pivots so exceptional is the fact that they are based purely on price. It is this fact that gives pivot traders a huge advantage over other types of indicator-based traders. As you have already learned from the Money Zone, price-based indicators reveal true market-generated information. Traders that use price-based indicators are using the earliest price information available. Traditional indicators are lagging indicators, which means as soon as they confirm a move, most price-based traders have already identified a reversal and are already profiting in their trades, leaving the indicator-based bunch to scrounge for "seconds." The truth is the best leading indicators are always price-based, like Floor Pivots and the Money Zone. Anything less and you'll be trading from the back of the crowd instead of leading from the front.

Take a look at Figure 5.5. This chart typifies a lagging indicator being dominated by our price-based Floor Pivots. On this day, R1 resistance on the E-Mini NASDAQ 100 futures contract is 1,296.50 and the central pivot for the day is 1,281.50. Since R1 resistance is widely known prior to the day even starting, pivot players had already identified this pivot as a clear zone for potential short opportunities, since it is clear that responsive sellers are likely to enter the market once this level is tested. Therefore, when price rises cautiously into R1 resistance, pivot players pounce on price as responsive sellers and ride the move lower. However, a classic lagging indicator-based system like the Stochastic Crossover, for example, doesn't recognize the reversal until late in the move at 1,290.50. That means our price-based pivots signaled a reversal a full six points earlier than this traditional lagging indicator.

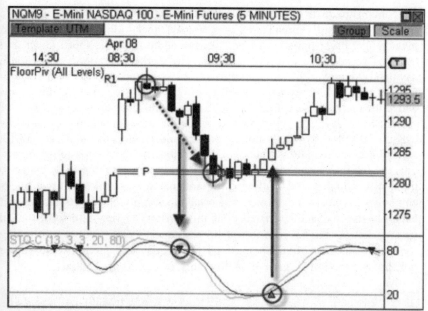

FIGURE 5.5: Price-based pivots versus a typical lagging indicator

Taking this example a bit further, pivot players will see a target at the day's central pivot point at 1,281.50 since it has a 63 percent chance of being reached at some point during the day, thus allowing this group of traders to take the entire fifteen-point move. However, traders using a lagging indicator didn't receive a crossover signal to exit the trade until 1,285.50 after the bounce had already occurred. Instead of picking up a full fifteen-point trade, the lagging indicator-based system only delivered a five-point trade. On the bright side, at least the trade didn't turn into a loss.

It is easy to see why insider's love to use these price-based pivots. They are unlike any other technical indicator on the shelf due to the fact that they are solely based on price.

Price is pure, unfiltered truth in the markets. Price is king.

THE FOURTH LAYER

Switching gears for moment, I mentioned earlier in the chapter that I added the fourth layer of support and resistance to the Floor Pivots indicator. I cannot take credit for discovering this formula, as it was already widely available to traders. However, I believe that I helped to make the fourth layer more mainstream to the trading public by including it in our company's software platforms (OmniTrader and VisualTrader), along with the central pivot range. Pivot purists may not like the addition of the fourth layer, but traders I've talked to love this addition. The market is more dynamic these days and the moves are more explosive. As such, the addition of the fourth layer of support and resistance helps to provide an extra target for those days where the market has exploded through the second layer of the pivots.

Just two days ago, a mechanical system of mine fired a buy signal in the Russell 2000 Index Mini Futures contract and entered the trade at 530.10, seen in Figure 5.6. The system's signal generation is unrelated to the pivots, thus the reason it fired long at R1 resistance. In any case, the trade began to trend nicely higher and I allowed the automated system to continue on its course, as I typically do. However, I became very interested in the trade as it began to rise above R3 resistance, as this territory is very rare for a typical trading day. As the TF rose to test R4 resistance, I called out to my trading room that this was officially the high for the day and promptly closed the position at 546.40 for a gain of 16.30 points, or $1,630 per contract.

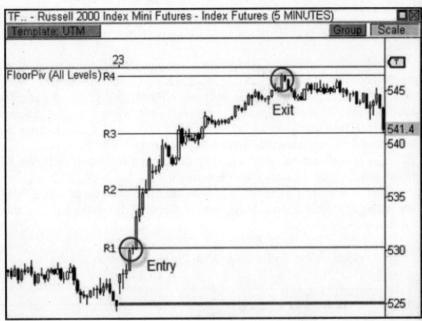

FIGURE 5.6: The Russell 2000 Mini Futures contract rallies to R4 resistance

As you can see, R4 resistance became the high for the day and the TF quietly proceeded to trend lower back toward R3, where it closed the session

The mechanical system would have closed the trade at 543.30 for a gain of 13.20 points ($1,320 per contract), but I was able to best that amount with my knowledge of the pivots. You see, the fourth layer of the pivots is only tested 5.5 percent of the time, with closures beyond this level occurring only 3.0 percent of the time. Therefore, there was a 97 percent chance that price would close below this pivot level, thus the reason for my exit. To learn more about how I arrived at these percentages, see Appendix A for an excerpt of my Floor Pivots research.

Let's take a look at Figure 5.7, which shows an extremely bullish day when the E-Mini S&P 500 opened the session above R1 resistance via a breakaway gap. As you may recall from previous chapters, gaps that occur beyond the prior day's range and value are likely to spark major trending moves in the direction of the break, as market sentiment has clearly changed overnight, which causes initiative participants to seek new value aggressively. Initiative parties have greater conviction behind their actions, which is clearly illustrated on these types of days.

FIGURE 5.7: The E-Mini S&P 500 closes the day at R4 resistance

In Figure 5.7, the ES rallied through R2 and eventually to R3 before resting at the highs of the morning. The ES then formed a higher low at R2 and rallied the rest of the session, reaching R4 in the process. For those purists that only use a second or third layer of support or resistance, the rest of the ride higher could feel like trading with your eyes closed. However, using the fourth layer of the indicator gave us another target to watch for a potential test ahead. In this case, the ES rallied to R4 and eventually closed the day *precisely* at this level.

Learning to read the cues of the market and the pivots prepares you to know when to switch from "reversal mode" to "trending mode." In this case, the market gapped *above* R1 resistance at 780 to begin the day. When the market gaps beyond the first layer of support or resistance, you may be on the verge of a nice, trending session toward the third or fourth layer of the pivots. The first thing to do is look to the pivot that was surpassed via the gap and watch for a test at this level on a pull-back. If the market reverses from the gap and successfully tests R1 from above, there's a 63.9 percent chance that it will test R2 and a 34.4 percent chance that it will test R3. Again, you can discover how I arrived at these percentages in Appendix A.

On this particular day, the ES was so strong at the outset that it never even pulled back to test R1, which is the first indication that continued strength lies ahead. In fact, on days when the central pivot is not reached at all during the session, you typically see the instances of touches at the first layer of the indicator drop significantly to 33.9 percent from 73.3 percent. This means that the market has gapped beyond R1 or S1 and is powering toward the next layers of pivots. Over 70 percent of the touches at the third and fourth layer of the pivots occur on Trend Days like the one in Figure 5.7, which is a day that offers the most explosive moves in the market. I will discuss how to capture this type of move using the Floor Pivots in Chapter 6.

THE DATA DEBATE

One important discussion that must not be overlooked is the extended-session data versus session-only data debate. Basically, pivot purists believe that the "true" pivots are only revealed when you plug in the high, low, and close of the prior day's full trading activity, including pre- and post-market trading. Therefore, you may be plugging in the high that occurred overnight, the low that occurred during pre-market trading, and the close that occurred at session's end. Moreover, the close should be the settlement price if you are trading futures, like E-Mini contracts or energy futures. This is important because the settlement price is the official closing price that the market "settles" at *after* the market has actually closed and all the orders have been sorted out, thus making it the official closing price. The process of reaching a settlement price can take anywhere from five to ten minutes after the actual close of the session. Typically, the settlement price is automatically reflected in your chart via your data provider, so this is not much of an issue.

The easiest way to get the extended-session data values (high, low, and settlement) is to flip to a daily chart of the instrument you are trading. Most data providers and charting software automatically include extended-session data when presenting the daily bars. Just take the high, low, and close from the daily bar, and you'll have the inputs for the next day's pivots.

While pivot purists believe that using the entire day's trading activity is the way to go, others believe the "real" pivots are revealed when using the day's regular trading hours, since this is when the vast majority of the day's volume is traded. Therefore, you are using the high, low, and close (or settlement) that occurred during normal trading hours from 9:30 A.M. to 4:00 P.M. ET for stocks (or 4:15 P.M. ET if you are trading E-Mini futures).

The good news for you is that I have researched, studied, and traded on both sets of pivots and find both to be extremely reliable. Figure 5.4, along with the rest of the examples thus far, shows pivots derived from session-only data. The moves during this day were so incredibly accurate that it is hard for pivot purists to discriminate against session-only data. In this book, I will include both session-only data and extended-session data in my examples. However, don't get bogged down on which set I'm using.

The concepts and setups that I will discuss throughout the book are equally effective regardless of which method you choose to use.

I have provided a handy table that shows my favorite markets to trade while also listing the times to watch for the two differing methods of calculating the pivots. Notice that the extended-session hours *do not* span from midnight to midnight. Rather, they begin at the end of one session and end at the close of the following session.

Standard Session	
Equities	9:30 A.M. to 4:00 P.M. ET
E-Mini's	9:30 A.M. to 4:15 P.M. ET
Energy	9:00 A.M. to 2:30 P.M. ET
Metals	8:20 A.M. to 1:30 P.M. ET
Extended Session	
E-Mini's	4:15 P.M. to 4:15 P.M. ET
Energy	2:30 P.M. to 2:30 P.M. ET
Metals	1:30 P.M. to 1:30 P.M. ET

TABLE 5.3: Using the right data for your pivot calculations

PIVOT TREND ANALYSIS

Once you begin to get a feel for the pivots, you will begin to develop your own ideas for how to incorporate them into your trading. Throughout the book, I am providing you with incredible insight that took me many years of study, research, and practice. But if there is just one concept you take away from this book, it is the one I am about to share with you at this moment:

Buy at support in an uptrend and sell at resistance in a downtrend.

This is a simple concept that can be easily overlooked, but it is one of the most powerful concepts that you can take away from using pivots, or any form of technical analysis, in your trading. Earlier in the chapter, I mentioned Larry Williams divulged his "Pivot Price Formula" in his book *How I Made One Million Dollars Last Year Trading Commodities*. In the text, he also provides this valuable insight:

"In all fairness, I should add that the projected high and low prices are best to use along this manner; if you expect tomorrow to be an up day, then run the formula for the high. That's the one most apt to be correct. By the same token, the low forecast will most likely be correct only if the commodity declines from the next day."

Essentially, Williams laid the foundation for what would become pivot trend analysis and pivot filtering. John Person took the concept a step further in 2007 with his book *Candlestick and Pivot Point Trading Triggers* by including his method for auto-filtering the pivots based on the current trend of the market. In essence, Person filters all pivots except S1, R2, and the central pivot point when the market is in an uptrend. In a downtrend, all pivots are filtered except R1, S2, and the central pivot point.

Basically, filtering the pivots in this manner forces you to become disciplined to the trend, which increases your chances for a profitable outcome. Filtered pivots decipher the trend for you, allowing you to focus on playing the pivots that are more prone to reversals within the corresponding trend. If you remove all the pivots below S1 support, you are forced to remain disciplined to a bullish trend by looking for long opportunities at S1 and the central pivot range. Likewise, removing all pivots above R1 forces you to prospect in the direction of a bearish trend.

This seems like a simple concept, but many traders can lose focus of the trend through all the noise that comes along with trading. This is especially the case for intraday traders. The fact is, when the market is moving within an established trend, certain pivots become "retired" for that particular trend. It is at this point that your focus should shift to the pivots that are active for key trading opportunities. For example, in a bullish trend, any pivot level below S1 support is usually just taking up real estate on your chart, since these levels are not tested during a true bullish advance. Likewise, any level above R1 resistance is just noise during a bearish trend, as these levels are rarely tested during a true decline. Therefore, if the market is trending higher, you will look to buy at support at either S1 or the central pivot range with your target set to a new high at either R1 or R2. Likewise, if the market is trending lower, you will look to sell at resistance at either R1 or the central pivot range with your target set to a new low at either S1 or S2. This pattern of trending behavior will usually last as long as price remains above S1 support while in an uptrend, or below R1 resistance while in a downtrend.

Let's take a look at Figure 5.8, which is a fifteen-minute chart of Google, Inc. (ticker: GOOG). In this example, Google trended lower beneath the R1 level for six straight days, allowing you to play the reversals within the downtrending market. Notice that the bearish trend remained firmly intact while trading below the R1 resistance level. However, on the seventh day, the stock jumped above R1 for the first time and closed beyond this level for the day. The adverse close beyond R1 caused a shift in the trend to bullish from bearish, which also caused a shift in the way the pivots would then be played. Notice that once the trend changed, the stock trended steadily higher above S1 support until price closed beneath this level for the day, which occurred six days later.

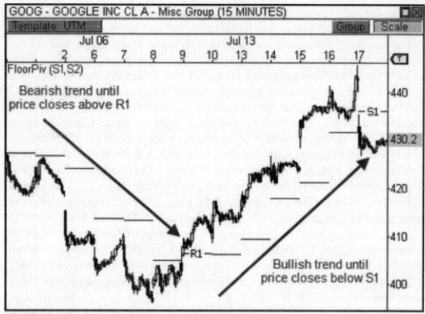

FIGURE 5.8: The first layer of the pivots directs the flow of the trend.

Let's take a look at Figure 5.9, which is a fifteen-minute chart of Google, Inc. The stock got a bullish breakout on April 12, 2010, which sparked a four-day rally. During the advance, GOOG remained above S1 support the entire time, and never even tested this pivot. When this occurs, you should obviously be in "bull mode" and look to buy pull-backs to S1 or the central pivot range, which act as support in an uptrend. Furthermore, being in "bull mode" also means setting your targets to a new high at or above R1 resistance. After all, being in an uptrend means higher lows *and* higher highs. Therefore, if you buy the pull-backs within an uptrend (higher lows), your goal then becomes to reach a new high within the uptrend (higher highs), which usually means playing the trade to R1 or R2 resistance. Every pull-back to the pivot range became a high probability buying opportunity during this four-day stretch, which was clearly identified by the pivots.

FIGURE 5.9: Every pull-back to the pivot range became a buying opportunity.

Let's take a look at an example of pivot trend analysis when the predominant trend is bearish. Figure 5.10 shows a fifteen-minute chart of Research In Motion during a four-day downtrend. During this decline, price remained firmly below the R1 pivot level, which means you should obviously be in "bear mode." During this type of market, you will look to sell every pull-back to R1 or the central pivot range. Furthermore, every trade taken should have a target of reaching a new low within the trend at either S1 or S2 support. While the market clearly trended lower during this stretch of time, notice how emphatic the reversals were at highs. Each test at the central pivot range or at R1 resistance led to a significant wave of selling pressure, as responsive sellers clearly went to work at these levels.

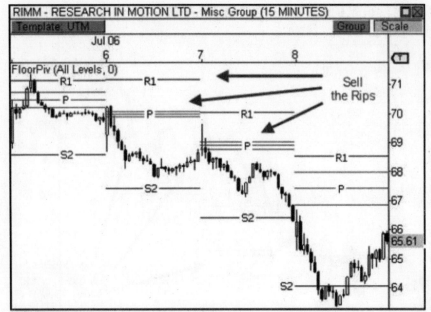

FIGURE 5.10: Selling at resistance in a bearish trend

BOSS IN ACTION

The pivots offer one of the best and easiest ways to profit from well-defined trending markets. However, the market doesn't always provide clearly established trends. In fact, it is estimated that the market only trends an average of 30 percent of the time, which means you must remain focused and demonstrate the proper discipline to wait for prime trending opportunities.

One of my favorite trending setups occurs when the market finally breaks a dominate trend and begins to move in the opposite direction. It takes a lot of conviction to break a trend and push prices in the other direction, which means if you are able to identify the change in trend early enough, you can profit from a very enthusiastic price move, which can last a day, or even weeks. For a case in point take a look at Figure 5.11, which shows a daily chart of Research In Motion, Ltd. This stock had been trending steadily lower for the better part of four weeks before a highly bullish day occurred on July 15, 2010. Price rallied over 6 percent during this session and pushed to new five-day highs, which indicated a potential change in trend. If price is to continue to push higher, a perfect "buy the dip" opportunity will likely be seen at S1 support or the central pivot range, which you can then ride throughout the day, or as long as the trend lasts. The key is to be ready to buy upon any pull-back to S1 or the pivot range, as these are the zones that will likely incite responsive buyers to enter the market.

FIGURE 5.11: RIMM begins to break a dominant trend with a big one-day rally

Let's take a look at how the following day turned out in Figure 5.12, which now shows a five-minute chart of RIMM. After a highly bullish rally in the prior session, price pulled back early the following morning. As long as price opens above S1 support, but below R1 resistance, you will look to buy any pull-back to S1 or the pivot range. In this case, price dropped right to the central pivot range and began to find initial signs of strength, as responsive buyers began to enter the market. After the first fifteen minutes passed, a bullish wick reversal candlestick pattern formed, which triggered my entry at $69.55. With my fixed loss stop set to a new low, I looked for price to rally to R1 resistance. While R2 can also be a target during this type of trade, the prior day's price range was extremely large, which caused the pivots to be wide-set on this particular day. When this occurs, you will usually look to trade to the closest pivot.

Price stalled for a bit, but eventually formed a higher low and a bullish extreme reversal setup, thereby confirming my trade entry. Eventually, price pushed higher and ultimately reached R1 resistance, where my fixed profit stop automatically liquidated my trade for a nice gain of 1.45 points—not bad for a lazy summer day. As it turns out, price proceeded to trend higher over the next two weeks and eventually reached the $80 price level.

FIGURE 5.12: Buying the dip in RIMM the next morning

Trending markets have an interesting dynamic with the pivots. As you have already seen, the market will remain strictly above S1 in a bullish trend and below R1 in a bearish trend. This will last as long as the market adheres to this paradigm. However, once a severe breach occurs through the first layer of the pivots, you typically see a shift of the trend toward the opposite extreme. That is, a bullish trend becomes a bearish trend, and a bearish trend becomes a bullish trend.

This type of analysis is extremely powerful for all types of traders, including intraday, swing, and position traders. It allows you to focus your attention on two key buying or selling zones, S1 and the central pivot range in an uptrend, and R1 and the central pivot range in a downtrend. By limiting your focus to these levels, you are eliminating the noise and expanding your attention to detail to the trend at hand. As a day trader, you know that when price reaches either the central pivot range or S1 whilst in an uptrend, you will be looking for signs to buy. Conversely, you will be looking for signs to sell at R1 or the central pivot range when the market is trending downward. This cannot be overstated, as most traders, even seasoned pivot traders, have not yet made this fascinating correlation. Instead, most traders will hesitate at S1 because they can't decide whether the market is going to break through this level or bounce off it. Buy at support, sell at resistance.

THE BREAKAWAY PLAY

In Chapter 4, I introduced how I play highly profitable breakaway days using Money Zone concepts like inside value and narrow value area relationships. While the Money Zone allows you to spot a potential Trend Day easily, the Floor Pivots make entering the trade far easier. First of all, when the market has formed a low-range day in the prior session, the pivots are likely to be tight, or narrow. As I discussed in Chapter 4, and will also cover in Chapter 6, narrow pivots foster breakout and trending sessions. Therefore, you have advanced notice that a potential trending day may be seen in the upcoming session if the pivots are abnormally narrow. Furthermore, if the market opens the session with a gap that is beyond the prior day's price range and beyond the first layer of the indicator, the chances of reaching pivots beyond the second layer of the indicator increase dramatically.

The breakout play is similar to a great hand in poker. When you have a full house or straight flush, you go "all in" and bet big. Sure, someone might have a better hand than you, but the odds of winning far outweigh the alternative. Similarly, the fact that you are able to anticipate a breakout day allows you to prepare for a potentially big payoff by betting big. Remember, on a true breakaway or trending day, initiative market participants are the driving force behind the market. Initiative buyers and sellers push price to new value by aggressively buying or selling, which invites additional market participation. This conviction leads to explosive moves in the market.

Let's take a look at an example. Figure 5.13 shows a fifteen-minute chart of NVIDIA Corporation (ticker: NVDA) on a day when price rallied to R4 resistance. Price opened the day with a gap that occurred beyond the prior day's price range and above R1 resistance. When this occurs, I study price behavior very closely in order to determine if the pivot that was surpassed via the gap will hold. If the pivot holds as support, you will look to enter the market long with your sights set on R3 or R4 as the target.

In this case, the first fifteen-minute bar of the day initially tested R1 from above and immediately saw buying pressure enter the market at this pivot level. The fact that this pivot held its ground as support gives you the confidence to pull the trigger in one of three ways: at the open of the next fifteen-minute bar, upon a new fifteen-minute high, or by using the *ambush entry* technique. I typically like to wait for the first fifteen-minute bar to complete before I enter the trade upon the open of the new fifteen-minute candle. However, traders that have nerves of steel can employ the ambush entry technique, which requires you to place a Limit order at the pivot level that was surpassed in anticipation of a test at that pivot level. When price retreats to test this pivot, your order to buy or sell is already waiting to be filled. After the trade has been entered, you are typically looking for price to reach the third or fourth layer of the indicator. Remember, since the pivots are extra narrow on this type of day, price has a greater chance of reaching pivots beyond the second layer of the indicator. Moreover, the third and fourth layers are 30 percent more likely to be tested when price gaps beyond the first layer of the indicator.

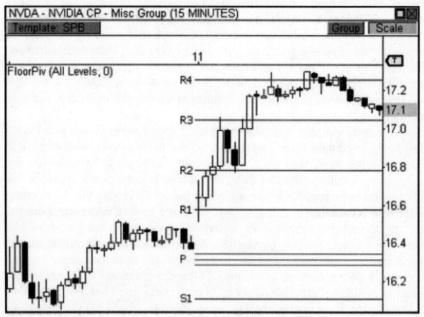

FIGURE 5.13: A bullish breakaway play usually leads to R3 or R4 resistance.

BOSS IN ACTION

When trading the Breakaway Play using the Floor Pivots, I typically like to see the gap occur beyond the prior day's range and value, preferably just beyond the first layer of the indicator. In addition, the gap should occur no farther than the second layer of the pivots. That is, I like my chances for a Trend Day scenario if the gap occurs beyond R1 for a bullish play, or S1 for a bearish play. If price gaps to the second layer, I will consider the play as long as price is not too far past this zone. If these criteria are satisfied, I will allow the first candle of the day to play out, as price tests any of the pivots that were surpassed via the gap. If a successful test occurs, I will enter the trade in the direction of the gap looking to capture as much of the move as possible.

Let's take a look at Figure 5.14, which you may remember from Chapter 1. This is a fifteen-minute chart of the E-Mini Russell 2000 futures contract on a day when a major breakout occurred. Notice that price opened the day beyond the two-day range and above R1 resistance. Immediately after opening above R1, price reversed to the pivot for a test, which was successful. What I like to see from a test is a touch at the pivot, with a sharp intra-bar reversal that causes the bar to close bar near the high of its range. When this occurs, you usually see a bullish wick reversal setup develop, which was the case in this instance. Since price confirmed the breakout opportunity, I entered the trade at the open of the following bar at 655.60 and set my fixed loss stop below the low of the day. I then allowed the 1.5 ATR cushion on my trailing profit stop to do the rest of the work, which kept me in the trade throughout the day. My trade session boundary stop automatically liquidated my position fifteen minutes before the close of the session at 664.90, giving me a very nice gain of 9.3 points, which amounts to $930 per contract traded.

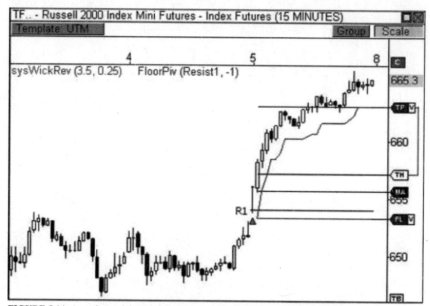

FIGURE 5.14: A gap beyond the prior day's range and value led to a breakaway rally.

You will notice that this particular day had a very narrow central pivot range, which might as well be a dinner bell since experienced pivot players come running out of the woodwork to trade this magnificent day. I will discuss this concept in great detail in the following chapter, as I will cover advanced Floor Pivots concepts using the central pivot range.

BUILDING YOUR KNOWLEDGE BASE

Without a doubt, the Floor Pivot indicator was the first price-based indicator to single-handedly kick my trading into a higher gear. The pivots opened my eyes to the underlying framework from which the market operates, which allowed me to align myself with a higher caliber of trader. Any time you're siding with knowledgeable market participants, you are giving yourself the best shot at a profitable outcome. The pivots have also allowed me to diversify my trading approach, giving me a wider variety of trading setups, entries, and targets. Individually, these concepts are quite powerful and valuable to your trading, but they are only the foundation to a greater structure of pivot knowledge. As we move forward, I will continue to expand your knowledge base with layers of new topics, further strengthening your bond with these amazing pivots. It is my sincere hope that the pivot combinations, trading setups, and overall market analysis contained herein will be nothing short of game-changing in your trading endeavors.

CHAPTER 6

THE CENTRAL PIVOT RANGE

"The way to make money is to make it. The way to make big money is to be right at exactly the right time."

- Jesse Livermore

The *Central Pivot Range (CPR)* is absolutely, without a doubt, the most powerful part of the Floor Pivots indicator. Some authors have called the range the meat of the market, while others refer to the central pivot point as the heartbeat of the indicator. In my opinion, the central pivot range is the Swiss Army knife of pivots. At any given time, the range can be support or resistance, it can forecast trending or sideways price behavior, dictate the day's direction, or serve as an integral part of a trend. This range can tell you so much about the potential movement of the upcoming day and even how the prior day transpired. Moreover, the placement of the CPR can give you a certain bias about the upcoming day. Knowing the location of the CPR at all times allows you to keep your finger on the pulse of the market and provides you with a significant trading edge. In trading, an edge is all you need to make money.

Like the Moon, the central pivot range controls the tides of the market.

Mark Fisher introduced the concept of the pivot range in his book *The Logical Trader*. He explains the pivot range concept in great detail and illustrates how he combines the range with his ACD Method to profit in the market. While he only uses the outermost boundaries of the range, I prefer to include the central pivot point to add another dimension to the range, which I affectionately call the *centrals*. To refresh your memory, I've included the formula for the centrals below; where TC is the top central pivot, BC is the bottom central pivot, and pivot is the central pivot point:

The Central Pivot Range Formula
TC = (Pivot - BC) + Pivot
Pivot = (High + Low + Close)/3
BC = (High + Low)/2

TABLE 6.1: Central Pivot Range Formula

It is important to note that I am referring to the level *above* the central pivot point as TC, while the level *below* the central pivot point is BC. However, depending on the market's activity the prior day, the formulas for TC and BC may lead to the creation of the opposing pivot level. That is, at times, the formula for TC may in fact create the level for the bottom central pivot, and the formula for BC would create the level for the top central pivot. This is just something to be aware of if you are calculating the pivots by hand. Using our company's software, however, the highest level of the two is automatically designated TC, while the lowest level is always assigned the label of BC. This is done seamlessly behind the scenes.

Figure 6.1 illustrates the central pivot range along with the first layer of support and resistance. As I mentioned in Chapter 5, the central pivot range is not part of the traditional Floor Pivots indicator. The standard Floor Pivots indicator includes only the central pivot point, along with three levels of support and three levels of resistance. When our company decided to include the Floor Pivots to our base indicator library for our customers many years ago, I decided to include the pivot range to the indicator to create a more dynamic and unique trading tool. By adding this range, the indicator becomes exponentially more valuable in helping traders keep an edge over their competition.

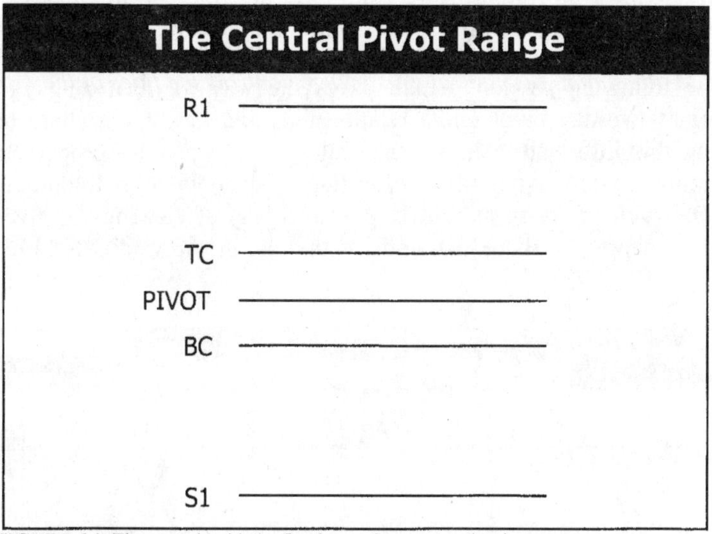

FIGURE 6.1: The centrals with the first layer of support and resistance

To my knowledge, we were the first company to release this version of the indicator to the trading public. Due to this fact, I have provided the code for the central pivot range indicator (file name: iCentralPivotRange) in Appendix B since this indicator may not be included in your platform's base indicator library. The CPR indicator solely plots the pivot range without the support and resistance levels, thereby reducing the clutter and allowing you to focus on important pivot range analysis, which will be a huge emphasis in this chapter.

THE DEVELOPING PIVOT RANGE

In keeping with the theme of the developing Money Zone indicators, I conceptualized the idea for creating a developing pivot range indicator that shows the central pivot range as it dynamically develops throughout the day. I typically code my own VBA indicators, systems, and stops because our scripting language is easy to learn and is quite efficient compared to other trading platforms. In this case, however, I asked one of our company's bright, young developers to code the indicator for me, as this particular script was a bit beyond my capabilities. Needless to say, I was ecstatic when I received the code that very same day!

The *Developing Pivot Range (DPR)* indicator dynamically calculates the central pivot range in real time as new data enters the market bar by bar. Essentially, this indicator allows you to see the "meat of the market" as the day's trading activity is taking place. More importantly, however, the closing values for the indicator tell you where the central pivot range will be located for the following session, which paves the way for analyzing extremely important two-day pivot range relationships and key width characteristics. Having this information in advance allows us to prepare properly for the upcoming session. After all, preparation is paramount to trading success. This indicator offers an extremely powerful way of viewing the pivot range and I'm happy to share the code with you in Appendix B (file name: iDevPivotRange).

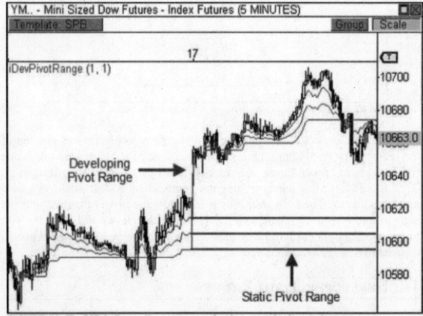

FIGURE 6.2: The DPR indicator allows you to see the pivot range for the next day.

Figure 6.2 shows the developing pivot range indicator plotted on a five-minute chart of the Mini-Sized Dow futures contract. Notice how the central pivot range dynamically updates throughout the session as new data enters the market. Pay special attention to where the indicator closes the session, however, as these ending values will become the levels for the static central pivot range for the following day. That is, the levels for tomorrow's central pivot range are derived from the ending values of the developing pivot range indicator. Therefore, looking at the chart shows the developing values closed February 16 from 10,595 to 10,614, which essentially became the levels for the static pivot range for the following day, February 17.

Throughout the rest of the chapter, I will explain how powerful and useful the central pivot range and the developing pivot range can be to your trading. From serving as support or resistance to forecasting price behavior and directing price trends, the pivot range is a multi-faceted tool that can certainly bring a huge boost to your bottom line.

TWO-DAY PIVOT RANGE RELATIONSHIPS

In Chapter 4, I introduced seven value area relationships that are very important when trading with the Money Zone. The same type of analysis can be used when trading within the central pivot range. While the value area and the central pivot range differ from one another on most days in terms of price location, this type of analysis still offers important market-generated information. Understanding how the current central pivot range relates to a prior day's CPR will go a long way toward understanding current market behavior and future price movement.

To refresh your memory, there are seven types of pivot range relationships that should be considered when analyzing the current strength and attempted direction of the market: *Higher Value, Overlapping Higher Value, Lower Value, Overlapping Lower Value, Unchanged Value, Outside Value,* and *Inside Value.* Each pivot range relationship brings with it a directional bias or expected outcome, which can prepare you for certain types of trading scenarios in the upcoming session (see Table 4.2).

Two-Day Pivot Relationships	
Higher Value	Bullish
Overlapping Higher Value	Moderately Bullish
Lower Value	Bearish
Overlapping Lower Value	Moderately Bearish
Unchanged Value	Sideways/Breakout
Outside Value	Sideways
Inside Value	Breakout

TABLE 6.2: Two-Day Relationships

Each of the seven pivot range relationships depend on two important prices: the prior day's closing price and the current day's opening price. Where the market closes in relation to the pivot range gives you an initial directional bias for the following session. The next day's opening price will either confirm or reject this bias, which then gives you a road map for which type of trade you should be prospecting. Understanding this dynamic will allow you to better diagnose the market's behavior, thus giving you the opportunity to enter trades on the right side of the market.

Let's take a look at the first two-day relationship: the Higher Value relationship. This relationship occurs when the current day's pivot range is completely higher than the prior day's pivot range. Therefore, today's bottom central pivot point is higher than the top of the prior day's pivot range. This is the most bullish relationship of the seven two-day combinations. Therefore, when this relationship develops, your initial directional bias will be bullish. If price closed above its pivot range in the prior session, the market is positioned to move higher in the upcoming session. However, how the market *opens* the day will either confirm or reject this initial bias. If the market opens the day anywhere above the bottom of the pivot range, you will look to buy a pull-back to the range ahead of a move to new highs. This is especially the case if price opens above the top of the range.

Let's take a look at an example. Figure 6.3 shows a fifteen-minute chart of the E-Mini Russell 2000 futures contract when a two-day Higher Value relationship developed. Notice that the TF closed the prior day above its pivot range and opened the current day above the central pivot point and pulled back early in the day. This pull-back was met with responsive buying participation at the bottom of the pivot range, which sparked another move to new highs within the current uptrend. This is a textbook "buy the dip" opportunity using the central pivot range to trigger your entry. Once in the trade, you are looking for price to reach a new high, usually at R1 or R2 resistance.

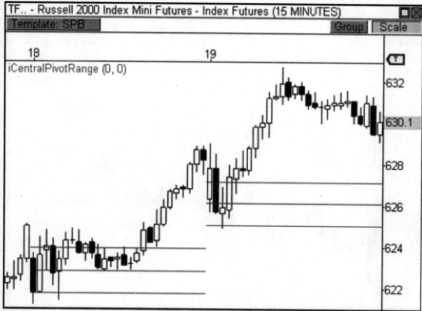

FIGURE 6.3: The Higher Value relationship

Let's take a look at how we anticipated this two-day relationship using the developing pivot range indicator. Figure 6.4 shows a fifteen-minute chart of the TF the day before the "buy the dip" opportunity. There are two sets of pivot ranges plotted on this chart: a static pivot range and a developing pivot range. Notice that the developing pivot range closed the day well above the values of the traditional pivot range, thereby indicating a bullish Higher Value two-day relationship for the next session. It is also important to note that the TF closed the day above both sets of indicators, thus confirming a bullish bias for the next session. As long as the market opens the following day above the bottom of the pivot range, but preferably above the top of the range, any pull-back to the range should be seen as a buying opportunity, which turned out to the case.

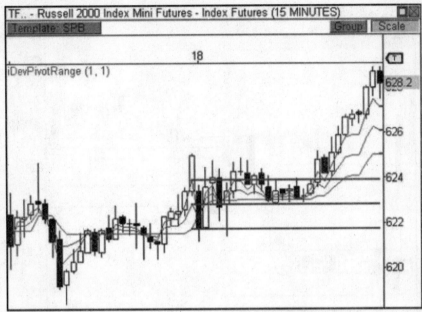

FIGURE 6.4: Identifying the Higher Value relationship using the DPR indicator

The most important factor that contributed to the positive outcome was the acceptance of directional bias by the day's opening print. The fact that price opened the day above the bottom of the range indicated that market sentiment remained bullish overnight. When this occurs, any pull-back to the range will likely be met with responsive buying activity. If the TF had opened the session below the bottom of the central pivot range, a completely different outcome would have been the result. That is, if the opening print had occurred at or below 624, price may have used the central pivot range as a fade opportunity in order to push price to lower value.

For example, Figure 6.5 shows a fifteen-minute chart of the E-Mini NASDAQ 100 futures contract on a day when a Higher Value relationship is present in the market. The fact that price closed above its pivot range in the prior session in addition to the Higher Value relationship indicated that continued strength should be seen the following day, as long as price opened above the bottom of the pivot range. However, the opening print rejected the bullish directional bias by opening well below the pivot range, adding a very bearish tilt to the morning. When this occurs, you must observe price to pivot behavior as a test occurs at the pivot range. A rejection at the pivot range should yield another round of selling pressure that pushes price to new lows, which was the case in this instance.

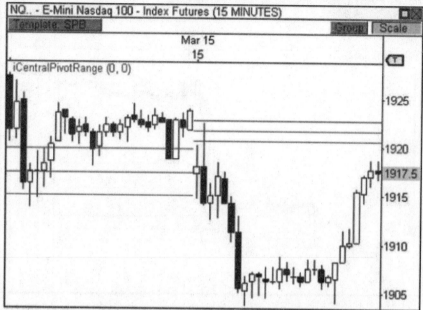

FIGURE 6.5: You must let the market prove each relationship through the day's opening price.

The next pivot range relationship is the Overlapping Higher Value relationship, which offers a moderately bullish outlook for the upcoming session. This relationship occurs when today's pivot range is higher than yesterday's range, but overlaps to some degree. Therefore, the top of the range is higher than the top of yesterday's range, but the bottom of the range is lower than the top of yesterday's range. The same closing and opening price dynamics are in effect for this relationship as well. If the market closes above its range in the prior session, a bullish bias should be assigned to the following day. However, where the market opens in the following session with either reject or accept this directional bias. In Figure 6.6, First Solar, Inc. clearly opened the day with a gap above the day's central pivot range, which was clearly bullish. Typically, you will look to buy a pull-back at the central pivot range ahead of a push to new highs. However, in this case, price opened beyond the prior day's range and value, which is clearly a breakout opportunity. When this occurs, you look for signs of bullish confirmation and enter the trade in the direction of the break in hopes of riding the trend as long as possible.

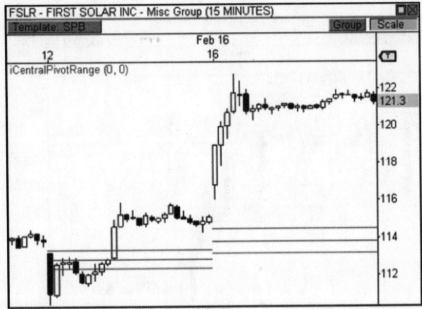

FIGURE 6.6: The Overlapping Higher Value relationship

The next type of pivot range relationship is the Lower Value relationship, which occurs when the current day's pivot range is completely lower than the prior session's range. This is the most bearish two-day relationship and typically leads to further weakness should the current day's opening price confirm the directional bias. If price opens the session below the central pivot range, you will look to sell any pull-back to the range ahead of a drop to new lows within the current trend.

Let's take at look at Figure 6.7 as an example, which is a fifteen-minute chart of Natural Gas futures. The two-day relationship is clearly a Lower Value situation, which points to continued weakness in the upcoming session. This bias is confirmed by the fact that price closed the day below its pivot range. Moreover, price opened the current session *below* the central pivot range, which offers the best opportunity to sell a pull-back should price test the pivot range. In this case, price pulled back modestly into the range, but was immediately met with selling pressure, which led to another wave of weakness in this contract. When this type of price to pivot behavior occurs, I look for confirmation that a potential sell-off may occur. In this case, an indecisive doji candlestick formed thirty minutes into the day, offering a great indication that price was likely to push lower, thus signaling a potential short entry play.

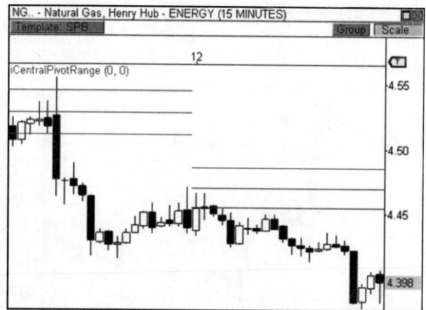

FIGURE 6.7: The Lower Value relationship

Let's take a look at how the developing pivot range indicator looks the day before this two-day Lower Value relationship develops. Figure 6.8 shows a five-minute chart of the same Natural Gas chart as above, but shows the day before the actual trade opportunity. Notice that the developing pivot range indicator closes the day well below the day's static pivot range, which means the following day will carry a bearish Lower Value relationship. Moreover, the commodity closed the session below both the static and developing pivot ranges, setting the stage for a "sell the rally" opportunity the next day. Therefore, if price opens the following session below the top of the pivot range, but preferably below the bottom of the range, any pull-back to the range should be a selling opportunity, which turned out to be the case.

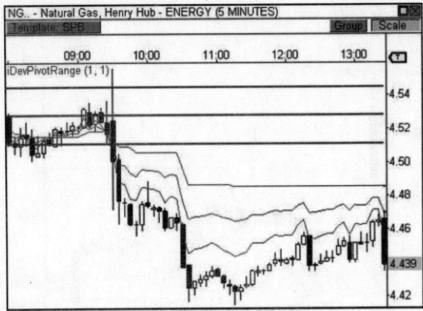

FIGURE 6.8: Identifying a Lower Value relationship using the DPR indicator

It must be reiterated, however, that just because a two-day relationship implies a certain behavior in price, this bias must be confirmed by the opening print. While a Lower Value relationship is the most bearish two-day relationship, perhaps the biggest rallies occur when the opening print rejects the original bias. Take a look at Figure 6.9, which is a fifteen-minute chart of Research In Motion, Ltd. It shows a two-day Lower Value relationship. Notice that the opening print did not confirm the bearish directional bias of the two-day relationship. Instead, price opened the day *above* the central pivot range and *beyond* the prior day's price range, which is emphatically bullish. This is a perfect example of a drastic shift in market sentiment occurring overnight. When this occurs, initiative participants are extremely eager to push price to new value, which sparks a major move in the direction of the break, which was up in this case.

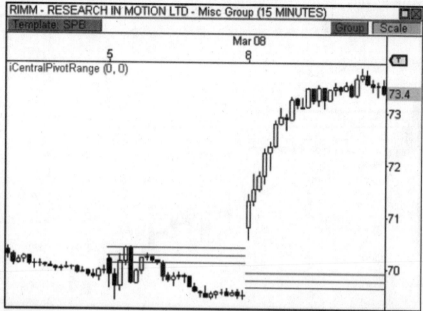

FIGURE 6.9: Price opens the day in stark contrast to the two-day relationship

The next two-day relationship is the Overlapping Lower Value relationship, which occurs when the current day's pivot range is lower than the prior day's range, but overlaps to a degree. That is, the current day's bottom central pivot is lower than the bottom of the prior day's range, but the top of the current day's range is higher than the bottom of the prior day's range. This relationship indicates a moderately bearish outlook for the forthcoming session. That is, if price opens within or below the pivot range, price should continue to auction lower. Any pull-back to the range should be seen as a selling opportunity.

Take a look at Figure 6.10, which is a fifteen-minute chart of Baidu, Inc. (ticker: BIDU) that shows a clear Overlapping Lower Value relationship. In this case, price opened the day below the pivot range, essentially accepting a bearish directional bias. If price were to rally into the pivot range, there is a good chance that the advance would be met with selling pressure, thus allowing you to sell a pull-back ahead of a potential push to new lows. In the chart below, BIDU opened the day with a highly bearish gap that occurred beyond the prior day's price range, essentially sparking a bearish breakaway opportunity, which confirmed the bearish nature of the two-day relationship.

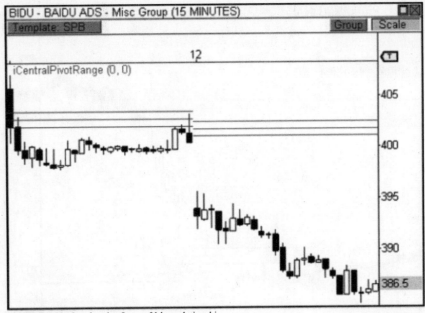

FIGURE 6.10: Overlapping Lower Value relationship

The two-day Unchanged Value relationship occurs when the current pivot range is virtually unchanged from the prior day's range. Of the seven two-day relationships, this is the only one that can project two very different outcomes, posing a bit of a dichotomy. On the one hand, a two-day neutral pivot range indicates that the market is satisfied with the facilitation of trade within the current range. When this occurs, the market will trade quietly within the boundaries of the existing two or three day trading range. On the other hand, however, a two-day unchanged pivot range relationship can indicate the market is on the verge of a major breakout opportunity, similar to when the market has formed two, or more, points of control that are unchanged. The outcome is typically driven by the opening print of the current session. If the market opens the day near the prior session's closing price and well within the prior day's range, the market will likely lack the conviction necessary for a breakout attempt. If the opening print occurs beyond the prior day's price range, or very close to an extreme, the chances are good that a breakout opportunity may lie ahead.

Take a look at Figure 6.11, which is a fifteen-minute chart of the Russell 2000 Index Mini Futures contract that shows a two-day Unchanged Value relationship. On this particular day, price opened the session with a noticeable move away from the prior day's closing price, indicating that market sentiment had changed overnight. Moreover, the opening print came very close to occurring beyond the prior day's price range, which means initiative sellers are beginning to enter the market with conviction. This type of opening sequence usually yields a very nice breakout opportunity, which was the case in this instance.

FIGURE 6.11: Unchanged Value relationship

The Outside Value relationship occurs when the current day's pivot range completely engulfs the prior day's range. This two-day relationship typically implies sideways or trading range activity, as the market is happy with the current facilitation of trade in the current price range. The width of the pivot range will usually lead us to this conclusion as well, since a wide range will usually indicate trading range behavior, which we will discuss shortly. Figure 6.12 shows a fifteen-minute chart of Silver futures on a day when the pivot range completely engulfs the prior day's range. Notice that price basically traded quietly sideways throughout the day, as opposed to the wide-ranging day in the prior session. When this two-day relationship develops, I will usually stand aside and look for a better opportunity in a different market, as the conviction necessary for intraday movement is clearly not present. The lone exception is when a clear trading range environment has formed, which can then offer nice intraday moves within the boundaries of an established range. One last thought, this relationship is much more telling if the current day's pivot range is significantly wider than the prior day's range. Otherwise, merely engulfing the prior day's range without the necessary width may lead to the same result, but with less accuracy.

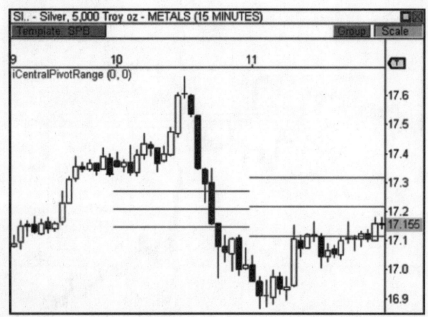

FIGURE 6.12: Outside Value relationship

The last two-day pivot range relationship is the Inside Value scenario, which occurs when the current day's pivot range is completely inside the prior day's range. This two-day relationship typically implies a breakout opportunity for the current session, as the market is likely winding up ahead of a breakout attempt. If the market opens the day beyond the prior day's price range, there is a very good chance that initiative participants will enter the market with conviction in order to push price to new value, since market sentiment has clearly changed overnight.

Take a look at Figure 6.13, which is a fifteen-minute chart of Copper futures. This commodity formed a two-day Inside Value relationship, which sparked a bearish breakout opportunity via an opening print that occurred beyond the prior day's price range. If the market had opened the day within the prior day's price range, a breakout opportunity could still be had, but with much less conviction. This two-day relationship doesn't occur frequently, but

I pay very close attention on the days when it develops, as these usually lead to major trending sessions.

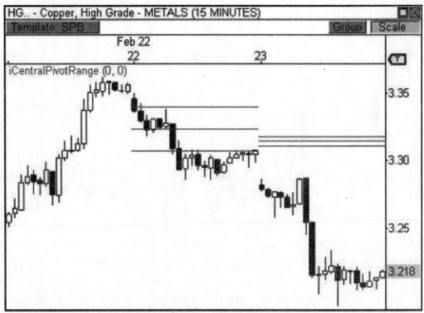

FIGURE 6.13: The Inside Value Relationship is the most explosive relationship.

Let's take a look at how the developing pivot range indicator looks the day before the actual breakout occurs in Copper futures, seen in Figure 6.14. Notice that the developing pivot range closed the session well within the boundaries of the day's static pivot range. Moreover, mere ticks separate the top of the developing range from the bottom, indicating that the next day's pivot range will be very narrow compared to the current session, which is another indication of a breakout opportunity. Arming ourselves with this knowledge in advance allows us to prepare for a major breakout opportunity in this commodity, which was indeed the case the next day.

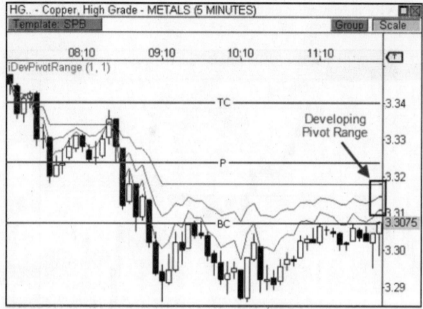

FIGURE 6.14: Identifying the Inside Value relationship using the DPR indicator

The one factor that I really like to see when this relationship develops is a noticeable difference in width between the two pivot ranges. If the prior day's pivot range is noticeably wider than the inside day pivot range, you are more likely to see a breakout opportunity, especially if the current day's pivot range is very narrow. This basically confirms that price has been winding up toward a virtual apex and is on the verge of a breakout attempt. If both pivot ranges are virtually the same width, but technically meet the inside requirement, the rate of success will noticeably drop.

As a quick reference, Figure 6.15 illustrates each of the two-day range relationships. Like the Money Zone, the two-day pivot range relationships offer guidelines for trading virtually any type of market: trending, breakout, and trading range. It is your job to properly diagnose the two-day relationship and apply proper confirmation before entering a trade. As always, the faster you can recognize the pattern of the market, the faster you will be able to deploy your capital in a confident and profitable manner. Anybody can plot the Floor Pivots on their screen, but the traders that have a keen understanding of the market's behavioral tendencies with regards to the pivots are the ones that will profit by using these amazing levels. Sometimes the tendencies have a penchant for the obvious, while other times are more subtle. However, with continued practice, every opportunity will become an obvious opportunity.

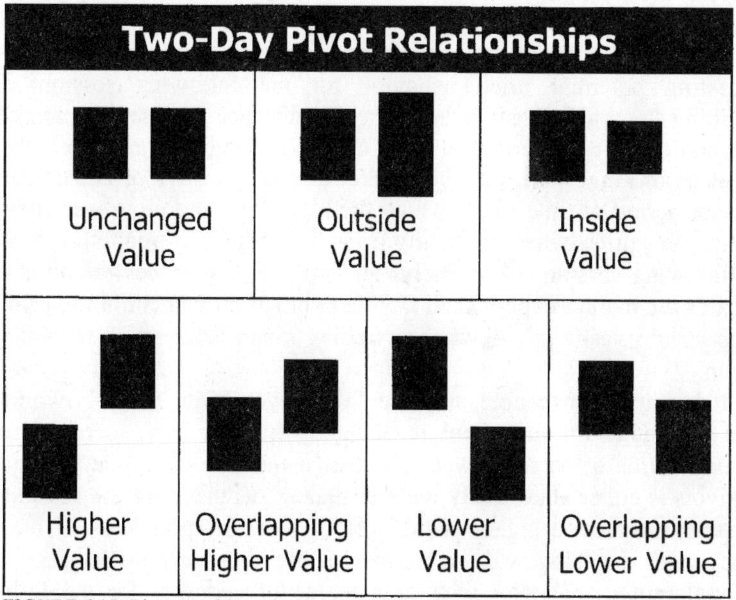

Two-Day Pivot Relationships

Unchanged Value	Outside Value	Inside Value
Higher Value	Overlapping Higher Value	Lower Value	Overlapping Lower Value

FIGURE 6.15: Diagram of the seven two-day relationships

PIVOT WIDTH FORECASTING

Pivot width forecasting is a consistent theme throughout the book, as each of the major forms of pivots, from the Money Zone to the Camarilla Equation, reveals major behavioral cues based on the day's pivot width. Since the prior day's trading activity leads to the creation of today's pivots, it is extremely important to understand how the market behaved in the prior day in order to forecast what may occur in the upcoming session. More specifically, if the market experienced a wide range of movement in the prior session, the pivots for the following day will likely be wider than normal, which usually leads to a Typical Day, Trading Range Day, or Sideways Day scenario. Conversely, if the market experiences a very quiet trading day in the prior session, the pivots for the following day are likely to be unusually tight, or narrow, which typically leads to a Trend Day, Double-Distribution Trend Day, or Extended Typical Day scenario. It is important to understand the pivot width concept, as this information allows you to prepare properly for specific day types in the upcoming session. If you are able to anticipate the market's likely behavior, you are giving yourself the best chance at success because you are able to deploy specific setups that are tailored for certain types of days. Any time you have an idea of how the market will behave in the following session, you are giving yourself a significant trading edge.

The width of the central pivot range is perhaps my favorite method for forecasting potential price behavior for the following session. When describing the width, I am referring to the distance between the top central pivot and the bottom central pivot (TC - BC). Typically, an extremely tight central pivot range indicates the market traded sideways or consolidated in the prior period of time (from which the high, low, and close were derived). As such, this price behavior usually leads to breakout or trending behavior in the following session. Conversely, an extremely wide central pivot range indicates the market experienced a wide range of movement in the prior day, which usually leads to sideways or trading range behavior in the following session.

It is important to note, however, that pivot width analysis works best when the range of movement is distinctly high or low, thereby creating unusually wide or narrow pivots. That is, it must be clear that the width of the pivots is either abnormally wide or narrow, as these are the sessions that lend themselves to a higher probability of forecasting success. If the pivot width is not distinctly wide or narrow, it becomes very difficult to predict potential trading behavior with any degree of certainty for the following session. You must also keep in mind that this analysis is not without fault. Measuring pivot width gives you a significant edge in determining the potential behavior for the upcoming session, but like any form of technical analysis, this method is not always correct; therefore, use it as a guideline.

Let's take a closer look at the pivot width relationship that can lead to one of the most explosive days in the market: the narrow pivot range relationship. An unusually narrow pivot range usually indicates the market is primed for an explosive breakout opportunity. Therefore, it becomes highly beneficial to know when this relationship has formed. If you have studied chart patterns, you know that consolidations and trading ranges lead to breakouts and range expansion. Essentially, a tight pivot range is telling you the prior day was consolidating, which usually leads to a breakout on the day with the narrow pivot range, given the right opening characteristics. Also, most trending days occur when the central pivot range is considerably tighter than the prior day's range, especially if the prior day's pivot range is unusually wide.

A tight central pivot range can be dynamite. You want to be aware when a day has the potential to start off with a bang.

Let's take a look at Figure 6.16, which is a fifteen-minute chart of Amazon.com. In this example, AMZN traded quietly sideways throughout the day on March 5, 2009, which led to an extremely tight central pivot range for the following session. Remember, today's central pivot range is derived by using the prior day's high, low, and close prices. If the market breaks free from the prior day's price range, a Trend Day could be seen. On this day, price opened the day within the prior day's price range, which means you must wait for a violation of the prior day's range before entering a trade. Eventually, initiative sellers overwhelmed the bottom of the prior day's range, ultimately pushing price to lower value. When this occurs, the conditions are ripe for a beautiful trending day, which was indeed the case on this day.

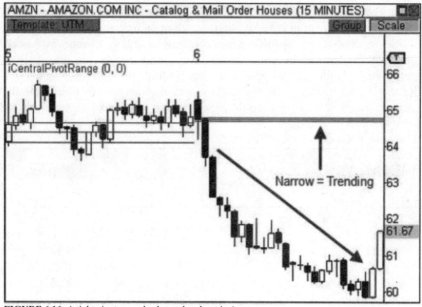

FIGURE 6.16: A tight pivot range leads to a breakout in Amazon.com

Look at it like this. If you were to remove all the pivots from the chart, you would see a consolidation and the breakout that followed. The pivot range confirmed this behavior, allowing you to anticipate a powerful breakout move. Why not look solely for consolidations then? The formula for the central pivot range is able to determine when price behavior is ripe for a breakout without an outright visual consolidation being present in the chart. This allows you to forecast when price is due for a breakout in markets where consolidations are blatantly visible and in markets when they are not so apparent.

The magic behind the CPR formula brings out the inherent details from price behavior when the chart sometimes does not.

For a case in point, let's examine Figure 6.17, which is a fifteen-minute chart of Amazon.com. In this example, AMZN traded in a fairly tight range on Friday, March 20. However, this quiet behavior was *not* in the form of a traditional consolidation. Despite this fact, the day's price activity led to the creation of an extremely tight central pivot range for the following session. As a matter of fact, the pivot range was so tight on this day that all three lines seemed to be at the exact same level, even though they were a few cents apart. When this occurs, the chart is telling you that the stock is about to explode in one direction or the other, depending on how the market opens the following day. If the opening print confirms a drastic change in market sentiment by opening beyond the prior day's price range, you are likely to see an explosive breakout opportunity. As it turns out, Amazon.com opened the day above the prior day's high and rallied nearly six points on the session, which is what you would expect to see when the pivot range is as tight as it was on this day.

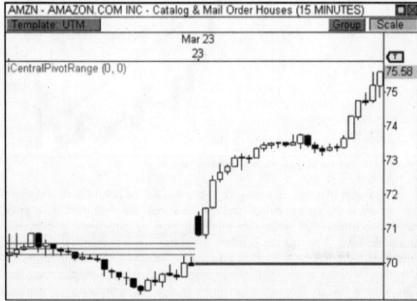

FIGURE 6.17: An extremely tight pivot range leads to a breakout in Amazon.com

BOSS IN ACTION

When the market develops an extremely tight central pivot range, I'm typically chomping at the bit to place a trade because I know that many of the biggest days of the month typically coincide with a narrow pivot range. My excitement grows further if the market opens with a bang via a breakaway gap since this usually indicates that market sentiment has shifted drastically overnight, which is fertile ground for trending behavior, as initiative participants are entering the market with conviction.

At the end of every session, I plot the developing pivot range indicator onto my charts and begin to record the two-day pivot range relationships and important pivot range width characteristics. When I come across a narrow pivot range for the upcoming session, I make a special note to watch that particular symbol closely for a potential breakout opportunity. On March 4, 2010, the indicator illuminated a great narrow range breakout opportunity in the E-Mini S&P 400 futures contract, seen in Figure 6.18.

FIGURE 6.18: Identifying a narrow pivot range using the DPR indicator

The top and bottom lines of the indicator closed the session within a half point of one another, which is an extremely narrow range for this particular futures contract. Remember, the closing values of the developing indicator tell you where the static levels for the central pivot range will be located for the next session. Therefore, I knew that a potential trending session could be seen the next day.

Looking at Figure 6.19 shows the market actually traded quietly sideways within an established two-day trading range prior to the formation of the narrow pivot range in anticipation of a potential breakout move. When price opened the day with a gap beyond the prior day's range and value, the groundwork for a major trending session was laid. I allowed the first fifteen-minute candle of the day to fully form in order to judge price behavior after the gap. After fifteen minutes passed, a bullish wick reversal signal formed, essentially triggering my entry near the open of the following bar at 762.80. I set my fixed loss stop below the session's low and allowed my 1.5 ATR trailing profit stop to manage the trade throughout the session. Price trended steadily higher throughout the session and eventually closed the day near the session's highs, which is very typical when a Trend Day has developed. Eventually, my trade session boundary stop automatically liquated my position fifteen minutes before the close of the session at 769.60, giving me a gain of 6.8 points, which amounts to $680 per contract traded.

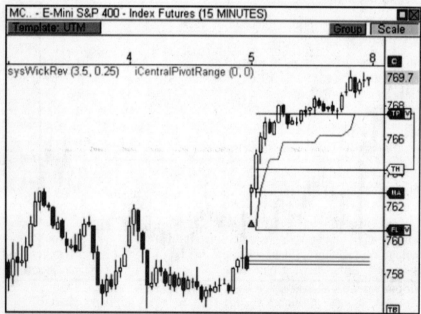

FIGURE 6.19: Identifying the narrow pivot range allowed me to hone in on this trade.

The key to this trade is the fact that I allowed a wider cushion than normal on my trailing profit stop. I use a 1.5 ATR cushion on days that I suspect will become Trend Days, as it is usually enough to capture an entire day's trending move in a fifteen-minute periodicity. Since a narrow pivot range indicated a greater range of movement for this day, I want to be able to hold on to the trade as long as possible, especially if the move is hot. My best-case scenario occurs when my trailing profit stop is never tested and keeps me in the trade throughout the day, allowing my mechanical trade session boundary stop to automatically exit my trade, which I set to fifteen minutes before the close of the market, as was the case in this trade.

Great poker players always know "when to hold them, and when to fold them." For traders, a tight central pivot range can help you to do just that. Entering a trade on a day when the centrals are tight should cause you to hold onto the position longer than you normally would, since the pivot range forecasts a wider range of movement on this day. As you may recall from Chapter 1, the market usually closes at the day's extreme on Trend Days, which means holding the position the entire day is usually the most profitable outcome.

Much to our dismay, the pivot range does not always offer a tight range that is ripe for beautiful trending behavior. Oftentimes, after explosive price movement, the calculation for the CPR yields a very wide pivot range, thus creating a role reversal. While quiet movement and a wide pivot range typically lead to a tight centrals range, the reverse happens after you see big movement in the market. That is, a day that has a wide range of movement, like a Trend Day, will lead to the creation of an abnormally wide pivot range for the following session. In this instance, you typically see a quieter atmosphere in the market, as dictated by the wide-set pivot range.

Why is this important to know? Wouldn't you want to know in advance that the market might not move much on certain days, thus allowing you to trade less or bet smaller positions? These types of days have much less volatility, which results in less conviction, smaller moves, and lots of whipsaw activity. Knowing when to spot these days in advance can save you a small fortune. When the pivot range is wider than normal, you either change your trading style to play smaller intraday swings or you avoid trading all together. Either way, the central pivot range gives you an advanced reading of what type of day the upcoming session may become, which allows you to adjust your trading plan accordingly.

Take a look at Figure 6.20, which is a sixty-minute chart of the GBP/USD forex pair that illustrates my point perfectly. On August 3, the pair rallied nicely on a day when the CPR was rather tight, which is what we would normally expect. However, this wide range of movement led to an abnormally wide pivot range for the following session, August 4. Since the centrals were unusually wide, we would expect quiet trading behavior, similar to a Sideways Day or Trading Range Day. Looking at price movement on this day, you see that the pair didn't really move at all, as it basically traded between the central pivot point and the top central pivot throughout most of the day. The wider-than-average CPR caused a lull in the market, which is your cue to either hang it up for the day, or trade smaller positions with tight stops and close targets. Actually, the activity on this day was enough to bore most traders to tears, and frustrate the heck out of those traders that didn't anticipate this behavior in advance.

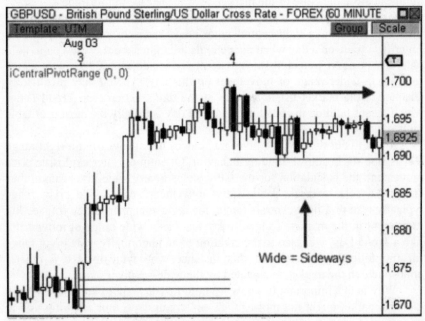

FIGURE 6.20: A wide pivot range usually leads to sideways trading.

Of course, the market isn't always so stagnant when the centrals are wide. Sometimes, a wide-set pivot range leads to nice trading range behavior that allows you to pick off quick intraday swings in the market, much like the Trading Range Day described in Chapter 1. Figure 6.21 shows a clear Trading Range Day in Natural Gas when the pivot range was unusually wide and the volatility low. The commodity bounced between S1 and the pivot range throughout the session, offering short-term intraday swings, which can be quite profitable for the traders that anticipated this behavior.

The key to trading a day when the centrals are wide is to identify the day's initial balance after the first hour of trading. If the initial balance has a wide enough width, you are likely to see trading range behavior within the high and low of the first sixty minutes of the day. Remember, the goal of the market is to identify price levels that easily facilitate trade. After the first sixty minutes have passed, the highest and lowest prices that the market will bear have been set (initial balance high and initial balance low), which then allows market participants to volley price back and forth within these extremes, which is especially the case during a Trading Range Day. If the initial balance coincides with key pivot levels, you have highly confirmed support and resistance levels that offer great opportunities for short-term bounces, as was the case in Figure 6.21.

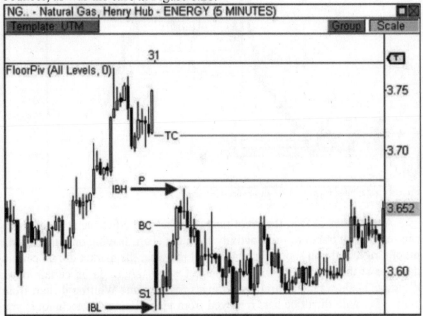

FIGURE 6.21: A wide pivot range leads to trading range activity in Natural Gas futures.

Oftentimes there can be a nice alternating pattern between days with unusually wide and narrow centrals. If the market consolidates, then tight centrals and a big move are likely to follow. After the big move occurs, wider centrals and lower volatility prevail, which again leads to tight centrals and a big move. And so the pattern continues. Figure 6.22 illustrates this recurring pattern perfectly. Whirlpool Corporation traded in a sideways pattern with wide centrals on March 17, which led to tighter centrals and a big rally on March 18. The rally then led to wide centrals and another dose of low volatility on March 19, which led to tight centrals and a breakout on

March 20. This pattern occurs time and again, which allows you to prepare in advance for big days with big profits, and quiet days with small ranges.

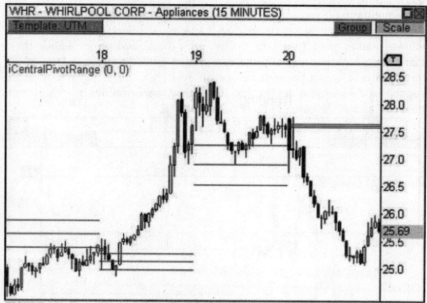

FIGURE 6.22: Pivot width can have an alternating behavior.

As a matter of fact, the pivot range can be so predictable at times that I can remove all traces of price activity from the chart, leaving only the central pivot range, and you should be able to tell me what the market did on certain days; or at the very least, what the market was *likely* to do on certain days. Figure 6.23 shows the central pivot ranges for the same Whirlpool chart from above, but with the price bars removed from view. Using this technique, you can clearly see the differences in width for all four sessions. Clearly, the market was going to have a greater propensity to trade sideways on the first and third days, while having an increased likelihood of trending on the second and fourth sessions. Understanding this dynamic allows you to anticipate potential price behavior well in advance, allowing you to deploy the right setups that are geared for specific day types.

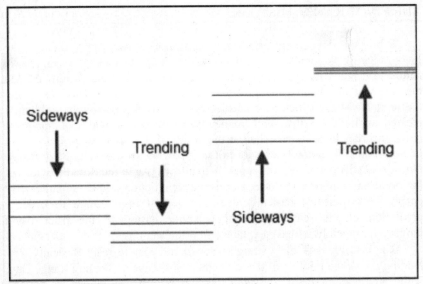

FIGURE 6.23: The pivot range allows you to guess market behavior.

Pivot width analysis also helps with trade target expectations. Oftentimes, a trader may enter the market at an excellent entry point, but mishandles the trade management aspect of the position due to an overly aggressive target, or one that is not aggressive enough. For example, the market has a much better chance to reach pivots beyond the second layer of the Floor Pivots indicator if the central pivot range is unusually narrow due to a low-range trading day in the prior session. Therefore, if a trader has entered a long position off the central pivot point, but takes his profits at R1, he is potentially leaving a ton of money on the table, as the market is likely to push to R2, or beyond, on this type of day. Conversely, a market is less likely to reach pivots beyond the second layer of the indicator if the central pivot range is unusually wide due to a high-range trading day in the prior session. Therefore, if a trader enters a long position off the central pivot point and looks to take profits at R4 resistance, he is doing himself a disservice, as price is not very likely to reach this target on this particular day due to the wide-set pivots. Instead, he should moderate his expectations and shoot for R1 as the target.

Being a trader means being prepared and anticipating what the market is *likely* to do. Any edge that you can capture that helps you toward this end is one that you should consider. By knowing in advance that the market may not move on a given day, or may move tremendously, you are allowing yourself to allocate your capital appropriately and judiciously.

THE PIVOT RANGE HISTOGRAM

While the developing pivot range indicator allows you to analyze the pivot range for the upcoming session visually, it still has a slightly subjective nature to it when judging the width of the pivot range. That is, how do you measure whether the pivot range is wide enough, or narrow enough to predict the next day's price behavior accurately? To solve this minor problem, I created an indicator that mathematically measures the width of the pivot range in order to decipher whether the width of the pivot range is likely to incite predictable market behavior in the following session. The *Pivot Range Histogram* (file name: iPivotRangeHIST) allows you to measure the width of the pivot range in order to forecast when a trending or sideways market may occur. This indicator basically uses the central pivot range to make a prediction on the day's potential behavior based on the prior day's movement, much like I have explained in prior sections.

The histogram is fairly straightforward and easy to read. Basically, any reading *above* the midline of 0.5 indicates a Sideways or Trading Range Day, while any reading *below* 0.5 indicates a trending type of day. A reading above 0.75 increases the likelihood of sideways trading behavior, while a reading below 0.25 increases the likelihood of a trending market.

Let's take a look at an example. Figure 6.24 shows the histogram plotted on a fifteen-minute chart of the Russell 2000 Index Mini Futures contract. In this three-day view, notice that the first and third sessions had a histogram reading that fell at or below the 0.25 level, which gave strong indications for trending markets. Conversely, the second day had a histogram reading above the 0.75 level, thus indicating the potential for a Sideways Day was high, which was indeed the case. In all cases, you would have been able to anticipate the day's market behavior, thus allowing you to plan your trading day accordingly.

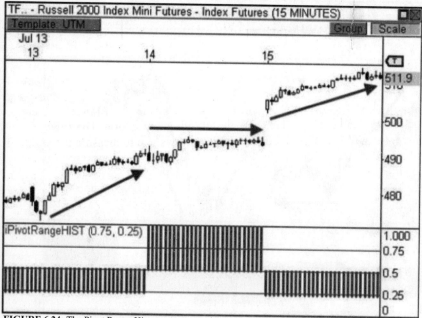

FIGURE 6.24: The Pivot Range Histogram accurately predicts trading behavior in this chart.

Being conscious of the width of the centrals gives you a huge advantage in knowing what type of market movement to expect for that particular session. I have included the code for this indicator in Appendix B to help you toward this end. Of course, since the histogram is *just an indicator*, it isn't always right. However, the frequency with which this indicator nails the market can be fascinating at times. Let's take a look at another example. Figure 6.25 shows a fifteen-minute chart of the Mini-Sized Dow futures contract for an entire week of trading. The Pivot Range Histogram accurately predicted the market behavior for every single day during this week of trading, calling out two days of sideways behavior and three trending days. Amazing!

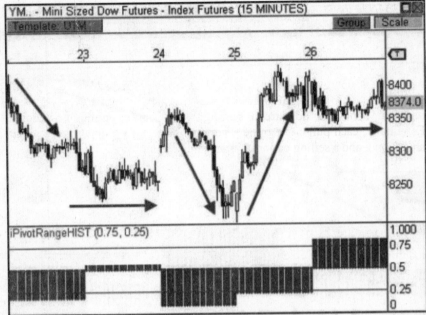

FIGURE 6.25: The Pivot Range Histogram accurately predicted the entire week of trading.

PIVOT RANGE TREND ANALYSIS

At some point in your trading endeavors, you have probably heard someone throw out the sage, but vague, advice "Buy the dips, and sell the rips." Many times, it's the first bit of strong advice offered by professionals, but remains vague enough to perplex amateur traders. Buying the dips means buying the pull-backs within an uptrend, while selling the rips means selling (or shorting) the rallies within a downtrend. While this sounds like great advice, how do I use this great knowledge? How does a trader know when a dip or rip is ripe for action?

In trading, there are many ways to capture a move. As such, there are many ways of capitalizing on buying and selling the waves of a trend. In my opinion, one of the best ways to buy and sell pull-backs in a trend is to play the bounces off the central pivot range, which is the method many professionals use. As you now know, the centrals can be one of the best sources of support and resistance in the market. Due to this fact, they can control the tide of a trend as good as any tool on the market since each day's pivot range serves as support or resistance whilst in a trend.

*Playing the bounces off the central pivot range in the direction of a
prevailing trend is a prudent course of action.*

Take a look at Figure 6.26, which is a sixty-minute chart of Energizer
Holdings, Inc. (ticker: ENR). This stock had three trends over the course of a
two-week span: two minor trends and one major trend. Notice how the
centrals remain beneath an uptrend to serve as support on the way up, while
remaining above a downtrend serving as resistance on the way down.
Essentially, each pull-back to the pivot range is a buying opportunity within
an uptrend, and a selling opportunity in a downtrend.

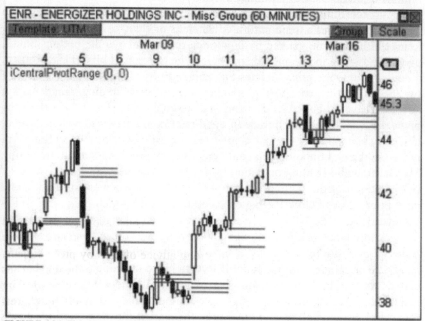

FIGURE 6.26: The pivot range dictates the trend in this stock.

Remember the two-day pivot range relationships we discussed earlier in
the chapter, like the Higher and Lower Value relationships? When these two-
day relationships develop, the goal is to play the bounces in the direction of
the trend. With longer-term pivot range trend analysis, the goal remains the
same, except many more days are strung together. Moreover, I discussed the
importance of understanding where the market closes in relation to the day's
pivot range. If the prior day's close was above its pivot range, the market will
likely carry a bullish bias. On the flip side, a market will likely carry a
bearish bias if the prior day's close was below its pivot range. The behavior

is exactly the same when discussing trends, only we're stringing together many days of pivots instead of just looking at two sessions.

Referring back to Figure 6.27, when ENR broke above the pivot range on March 10 and closed above this level, it essentially broke the existing downtrend and created a new bullish trend. When this occurs, you will look for price to hold above the central pivot range for two consecutive days. If price successfully uses the centrals as support during these first two days, any pull-back to the CPR during the uptrend should become a buying opportunity, otherwise known as "buying the dip." Notice how the stock bounced off the CPR the following three days, offering successful bounces into the direction of the prevailing trend!

Another thing to notice is how price remains above (or below) the centrals throughout a trend until it either stalls or changes direction. A strong trend can usually be gauged by how price remains above the bottom central pivot (BC) while in an uptrend, and below the top central pivot (TC) while in a downtrend. Once price violates this paradigm by closing beyond the range for the day, you see either a change in trend or a trading range market develop. Given this behavior, swing traders could enter the market once the pivot range is violated and trade in the direction of a newly-developed trend, holding their stops at, or just below, the opposite side of the central pivot range. In the chart above, you could enter the market long some time during March 10, while holding onto a multi-day position with your trailing stop set to a violation of the bottom central pivot. You would remain in the uptrend until price closes below the bottom central pivot, at which point you would liquidate your trade.

I know what you're thinking: *"What if we had an automated stop that uses the centrals as a trailing stop to capture long trending moves in the market?"* Great idea! In Appendix B I've included the code for a stop I wrote called the trailing centrals stop (file name: stoTrailingCentralsStop). This stop is ideal for capturing trending moves in the market using any timeframe. Basically, this stop allows you to stay in the market for those glorious trends by trailing your profit at the centrals and dynamically updating once a new pivot range appears the next day, month, or year (depending on the timeframe). Instead of keeping an arbitrary trailing stop, using the centrals allows you to keep your stop levels at key psychological points in the chart. For long positions, the stop will trail price using the bottom central pivot, while short positions use the top central pivot, and will exit once price *closes beyond* the pivot range. Figure 6.27 illustrates the trailing centrals stop in the same ENR chart that we've been analyzing. Notice how the stop automatically updates when new pivots are revealed with each passing day.

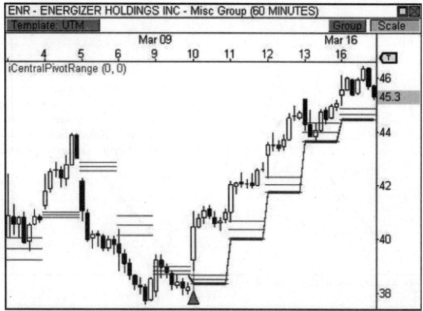

FIGURE 6.27: The pivot range can be used as a powerful form of trailing stop.

Using the central pivot range to gauge a market's trend is both extremely powerful and visually stimulating. As a matter of fact, I can remove price from the chart, leaving only the central pivot range, and you should be able to tell me what the market is doing—and still make money! Take a look at Figure 6.28, which is the same ENR chart that we have studied. I have removed all the candlesticks from the chart, leaving only the centrals in plain view. Even with price removed from view, you can easily see the trends of the market and could make money by only trading in the direction of the prevailing trend. While I don't suggest you trade this way, you can see that keeping your finger on the pulse of the centrals can help to remove the clutter from the chart, both literally and figuratively.

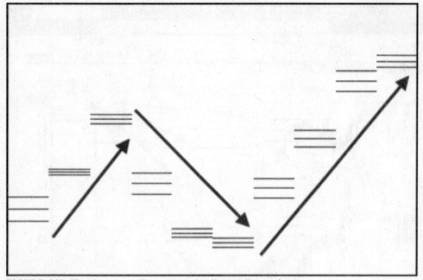

FIGURE 6.28: The pivot range allows you to visualize trending markets.

Take a look at Figure 6.29, which is a fifteen-minute chart of the Natural Gas futures contract. This chart illustrates the typical behavior at the central pivot range when a market is in an established trend. First, notice the market closed below the day's pivot range in every session in this sequence, thus painting the following day with a bearish bias. Second, notice how every pull-back to the CPR was met with selling pressure, thereby following the typical path of "selling the rallies." Moreover, every time price tested the pivot range it never closed beyond the top central pivot, instead leaving only wicks in its wake. Every test at the pivot range occurred early in the day and led to new lows by the afternoon, setting the stage for another round of anticipated behavior the following session. This is pivot range trend analysis at its best. Price movement becomes like clockwork: calculated and expected outcomes in an orderly trend.

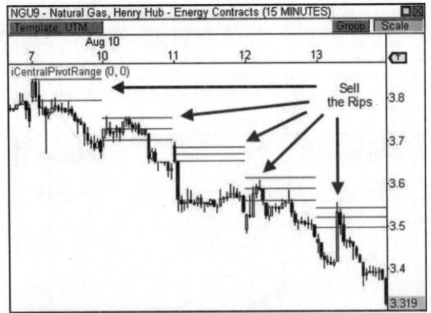

FIGURE 6.29: The pivot range acts as resistance in a bearish trend.

BOSS IN ACTION

I study price behavior closely at the central pivot range early in the day for signs of a bounce in the direction of the prevailing trend when the market has formed a Higher or Lower Value two-day relationship or a series of these relationships in a trend. I find that pull-back opportunities usually occur early in the session, with follow-through occurring the rest of the day. As such, any pull-back to the range early in the morning is a buying or selling opportunity depending on the direction of the trend. Once in the trade, the goal is to either ride the trade to a prior area of support or resistance, or to a new high or low within the trend.

Take a look at Figure 6.30, which shows a trade I took in the Mini-Sized Dow futures contract on July 8, 2009. The YM was in the midst of a four-day downtrend and formed a clear two-day Lower Value relationship. The fact that the YM closed well below the pivot range in the prior session gave me a very good indication that any pull-back to the pivot range could lead to nice short opportunity the following morning.

The YM opened the day with mild strength the next morning and pushed precisely to the central pivot range before forming a bearish wick reversal candlestick. Since I was fairly confident about the potential for a decline, I entered the trade during the formation of the bearish candlestick at 8,153, instead of waiting for additional confirmation. I set my stop loss above the top of the pivot range and looked to take profits upon price reaching a new low within the trend. Therefore, I set my profit target to 8,082 and let price do the rest. An hour later, my profit target was reached, giving me an easy 71 point gain in the trade, which amounts to $355 per contract traded. Not bad for an hour's work!

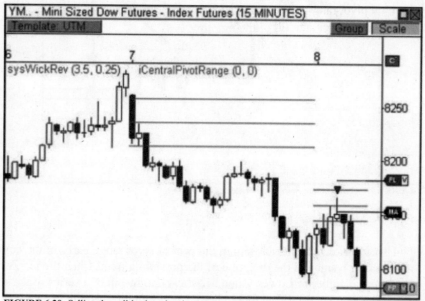

FIGURE 6.30: Selling the pull-back to the pivot range

It's easy to overlook how powerful this information can be. Many traders haven't a clue about pivots. They wake up every morning and wonder what the market will bring in the upcoming session, completely oblivious to the fact that the pivots may have already written the script for the day. Of course, not every day offers perfect trading opportunities. But understanding key pivot behavior allows you to wait patiently in the tall grass for a prime opportunity to pounce. Doing your homework prior to each market day allows you to study these important relationships and prepare for the upcoming session.

THE MAGNET TRADE

One of my favorite trading days occurs when the market gaps at the open of the session. When this occurs, I'm able to use the pivots to either trade a potential breakaway move, or fade the market for a fill of the gap. In either case, a gap at the open indicates that market sentiment has changed overnight and the market is poised to move in the current session. I've discussed my methods for snuffing out and trading the highly profitable breakaway days using the pivots. In this section, however, I will discuss how the central pivot range can have an amazing magnetic affect on price that can lead to a high percentage fill of the morning gap.

The central pivot range is the equilibrium of the market. As such, it can have an amazing gravitational pull on price, which becomes much more apparent on days when the market gaps at the open of the session. If price opens the day with a gap and the centrals are back near the prior day's close, you typically see a fill of the gap a high percentage of the time, given the right circumstances. I call this the *Magnet Trade*, since the centrals attract price, causing a fill of the gap. It is one of my favorite days in the market because I get to play a trade with a history of high percentage wins while making quick money, usually within the first thirty to sixty minutes of the day.

Let's take a look at an example. Figure 6.31 illustrates a perfect magnet trade in a fifteen-minute chart of Crude Oil futures. Crude opened the day with a gap up and formed a bearish doji reversal pattern in the first fifteen-minute bar of the day. Since the centrals were back near the prior day's close, there was a high probability that they would have a magnetic effect on price, which was indeed the case. The bearish doji reversal setup easily triggered an entry on this day, as price dropped steadily to the central pivot range before finding support. With the Magnet Trade, the pivot range becomes the play's target, as any of the three lines can be used as your exit. This particular trade netted a nice move of about one point in Crude Oil, which translates to $1000 per contract traded—not bad for forty-five minutes of work!

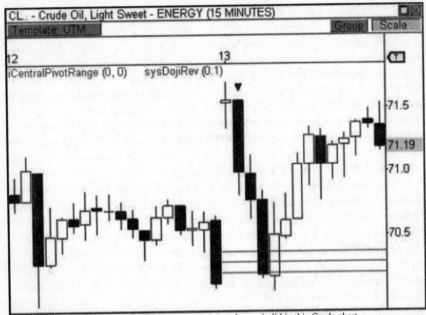

FIGURE 6.31: The pivot range can act as a magnet to price, as it did in this Crude chart.

This is one of my favorite setups due to its simplicity and the fact that it is a recurring pattern in the markets. Remember, the central pivot point is reached 63 percent of the time at some point during the day. When the market gaps at the open, the trade inherently has a 63 percent chance of being a winner.

While this trade is best served simple, there are a few additional tips that can help make this trade even more powerful and profitable. For instance, trading the right size gap greatly increases the success rate of this setup. Gaps that are too large don't tend to fill as easily as those that are moderate in size. Stick to the gaps that have a fighting chance to fill and the pivot range will help do the rest. Secondly, pivot range placement should be at, or very near, the prior day's closing price. When this is the case, the pivot range helps attract price to fill the gap. If the range is too close to price, however, it could hinder the market's ability to fill the gap. Also, you must remember that the goal of the trade is to play for a fade of the gap back toward the central pivot range, which means the trade will usually be short and sweet. If you can get a little more out of the trade then go for it. But don't wait all day for a gap to fill, because the longer the trade takes, the more unlikely it is to fill. Remember, pigs get fat and hogs get slaughtered.

Some trades are meant to go for the gold, while others are meant to go for golden nuggets. The more nuggets you collect, the bigger your pot of gold.

One interesting tidbit is the fact that this set up, and gap fills in general, seem to work best during earnings season, which are the months following the end of each quarter: January, April, July, and October. Trading this setup alone during these periods of time is enough to sustain a healthy lifestyle. You can literally trade just one setup four months a year and live off a generous income. That's how powerful this setup can be during earnings season.

The trend can also play an important factor in the successful outcome of a magnet trade. As you recall from earlier in the chapter, when a market has formed an established trend price will usually pull back to the pivot range before resuming in the direction of the trend. Therefore, if the market has formed an uptrend and price gaps in the direction of the trend (up), there is a very good chance that price will drop to the pivot range before another round of buying pressure is seen, thereby causing a fill of the gap. This market behavior aligns perfectly with the essence of the magnet trade

Let's take a look at an example. Figure 6.32 shows a five-minute chart of Entergy Corporation (ticker: ETR), which was in the midst of a three-day uptrend and had formed a two-day Higher Value relationship. The stock opened the day with a gap up, but showed signs of weakness after the first ten minutes of the session and began to auction lower. Price eventually filled the morning gap and reached the center of the pivot range at around $68.40, where responsive buyers entered the market and pushed price to new highs for the day, illustrating the CPR's ability to both attract and repel price in a single session. Notice that after price reached the pivot range to complete the magnet trade, an outside reversal setup fired a long signal to confirm a "buy the dip" opportunity, which preceded the rally to new highs within the established uptrend.

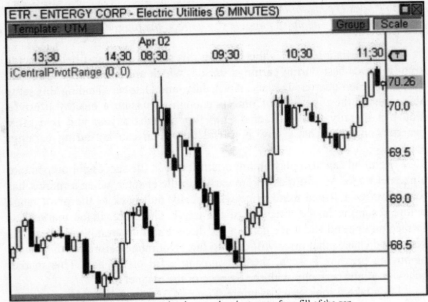

FIGURE 6.32: After a morning gap, price drops to the pivot range for a fill of the gap.

Another important factor to consider when trading this setup is looking for additional pivot confirmation that can add to the success of your trade. If price gaps up to R1 resistance, or down to S1 support, these pivots can serve as a barrier to a breakaway trade, which leads to a higher percentage of filled gaps. Knowing where these support and resistance levels are can help give you confidence in entering a trade, especially if the market gaps down at the open. I am much more open to trading this setup when the market gaps up at the open, rather than down. A gap down requires much more confirmation, conviction, and volume in order to fill the gap on most occasions. However, having clear pivot support at S1 can help price reach its objective in many cases.

Take a look at Figure 6.33, which shows pivot confirmation in a five-minute chart of the E-Mini S&P 500 futures contract. Price opened the day with a gap down and initially pushed quietly lower before reaching S1 support at about 842.75, essentially laying the foundation for a potential bounce and fill of the gap. The market tested the S1 pivot level several times, forming multiple wick reversal candlesticks at this level, which is usually indicative of a reversal. In this case, the market held nicely at pivot support and traded quietly to the prior day's close, filling the gap precisely at the central pivot range.

FIGURE 6.33: S1 support helps you identify a reversal in this magnet trade.

Sometimes, however, pivots can provide a roadblock to a perfectly good magnet trade opportunity, as is the case in Figure 6.34, which shows a fifteen-minute chart of Natural Gas futures. The commodity gapped *below* two key pivot levels, which would typically help to push price higher, but instead became resistance in this instance. That is, the very levels that are intended to be support served as resistance and stifled price throughout its upward attempt. Eventually Natural Gas succumbed to R1 resistance and failed to fill the very modest gap.

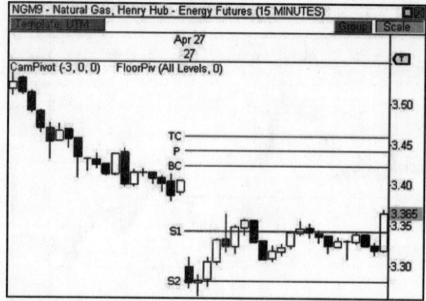

FIGURE 6.34: Too much resistance can be a pitfall when playing the magnet trade.

BOSS IN ACTION

A gap at the open of the day indicates the market is primed and ready for an active morning. While breakaway gaps offer some of the best money-making opportunities in the market, the magnet trade offers a level of accuracy and comfort that is highly unusual in trading, especially if the setup occurs in January, April, July, or October. I've actually created mechanical strategies that solely focus on this setup and have accuracy ratings well over 80 percent during earnings season.

My favorite magnet trades occur when the market takes a moderate gap up at the outset of the day, as was the case in the E-Mini S&P 400 futures contract in Figure 6.35. The fact that the setup formed in July during a two-week uptrend gave me extreme confidence that a fill would occur. Therefore, I scouted the three-minute chart to potentially capture an earlier entry point. Normally, I would enter the market directly after the first bar of the day forms a bearish wick reversal candlestick, as it did on this particular day. However, the fact that price gapped above R1 resistance provided a potential impediment, as this level can usually serve as support under these circumstances. When this occurs, I watch price behavior very closely at the pivot for signs a potential entry.

Since price held at R1 resistance through the first twelve minutes of the day, I submitted a stop market order just below the pivot at 599.20 in order to capture a potential decline back to the pivot range. Price eventually triggered my entry at this level and proceeded to drop quickly to the top of the pivot range, where my fixed profit target took me out of the trade just beneath the 596 level for a gain of 3.5 points, which translates to $350 per contract traded. The trade took all of six minutes from entry to target.

FIGURE 6.35: A break of R1 helped confirm the entry in this magnet trade.

The magnet trade is one of my favorite setups due to its simplicity. Oftentimes, the simplest trades are the most beautiful and profitable. Its ability to recur in the market while delivering a consistently profitable outcome makes this setup a mainstay in my trading arsenal.

The Central Pivot Range Revolution

The centrals are an extremely dynamic trio of lines that should find their way onto the charts of every trader. Knowing where these lines are in relation to your next potential trade can mean cash or crash. Two-day pivot range relationships, pivot width analysis, and pivot trend analysis offer extremely poweful methods for using the central pivot range. The pivot range offers a significant trading edge. Anytime you have an edge in trading, you are putting yourself in a position to profit.

CHAPTER 7

INTRODUCING THE CAMARILLA EQUATION

"When I couldn't play according to my system, which was based on study and experience, I went in and gambled."

- Jesse Livermore

I clearly recall one particular day when a group of traders were huddled around my computer at a trader boot camp as I taught the class. One trader asked me what the lines were on my chart and I told him they were the Camarilla pivots.

"Camarilla? That sounds more like the name of an enchilada dinner!" Trader Joe quipped.

To borrow a line from the famous Schlotzsky's slogan: *"Funny Name. Serious Trading Strategy."* The Camarilla Equation was first discovered by successful bond trader Nick Stott in 1989. He penned an equation that led to the brilliant, and oftentimes unbelievable, levels that so many of us have used to profit in the market. As we saw with the Floor Pivots formula, there are different versions of the Camarilla Equation as well. Adding further secrecy to the equation, the creator of the formula has not disclosed the official equation to the public, although many have reverse engineered the formula for our trading pleasure. As if the equation needed more mystery, the word "camarilla" literally translates to a group of secret, private advisors in Spanish.

You may also hear from certain Web sites that their Camarilla Equation is the only reliable equation, although they will only provide you with the levels for various tradable markets for a fee. I have not seen this equation and, therefore, cannot vouch for its accuracy in the market. In my opinion, what makes these pivot levels work so unbelievably well is the fact that traders are watching and trading by them, creating a self-fulfilling prophecy. The more traders that trade by the same equation, the more prominence these levels will carry. It is this sort of trading behavior that allows these levels to flourish. If a formula is kept secret, there are fewer traders honoring the levels, thus diminishing the formula's effectiveness.

THE STANDARD CAMARILLA EQUATION

The equation that I will discuss is the most commonly used Camarilla Equation. This equation is widely available to all traders and I have found it to be quite powerful for all timeframes in my trading. I have followed this equation for many years and have spent every market day studying and trading by these levels. I can certainly vouch for the value of this formula as it pertains to the market.

The basic premise behind the equation is very similar to that of the Floor Pivots: all time series typically revert back to the mean. This equation takes the prior day's high, low, and close to determine eight key levels on your charts; four support levels (L1 to L4) and four resistance levels (H1 to H4). The equation is as follows (keep in mind that RANGE is the high minus the low of the prior session):

Standard Camarilla Pivot Formula
H4 = Close + RANGE × 1.1/2
H3 = Close + RANGE × 1.1/4
H2 = Close + RANGE × 1.1/6
H1 = Close + RANGE × 1.1/12
L1 = Close - RANGE × 1.1/12
L2 = Close - RANGE × 1.1/6
L3 = Close - RANGE × 1.1/4
L4 = Close - RANGE × 1.1/2

TABLE 7.1: Standard Formula

The Camarilla Equation offers a series of price-based support and resistance levels, with each level carrying a specific call to action.

The Camarilla Equation offers a powerful method of trading the market because the call to action is always the same. The equation forces you to recruit your inner discipline to trade on the right side of probability. Traders take similar positions at each level, thus creating a powerful form of self-fulfilling prophecy. Moreover, the pivot levels in the indicator are usually color-coded to remind you which actions to take when certain pivot levels are tested. For example, the H3 and L4 pivot levels are typically colored red because these are the zones where you should be looking to sell the market. Likewise, H4 and L3 are typically colored green to indicate long action levels. Figure 7.1 shows each Camarilla level, including the first and second layers of the formula.

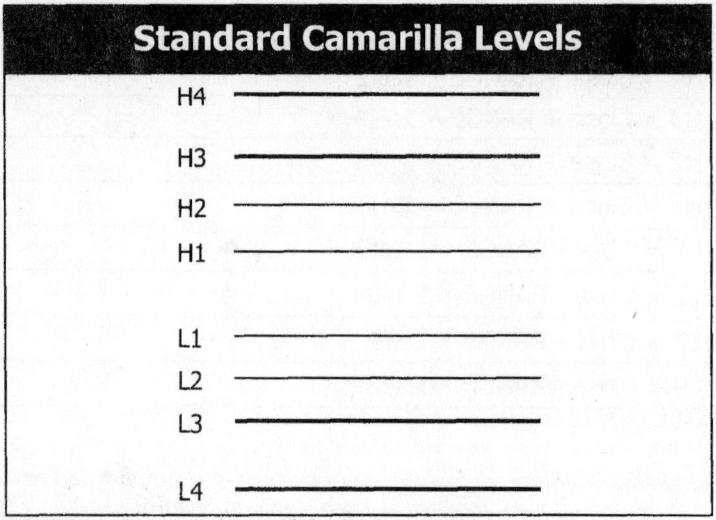

FIGURE 7.1: The Standard Camarilla levels

Traditionally, the most important levels are the third layer of support and resistance (L3 and H3). Once the market reaches these levels, you typically see a reversal back toward the mean. Therefore, you are typically looking to sell the market at H3 resistance, and buy the market when price tests L3 support. Once price pushes too far in one direction, responsive market participants enter the market in order to push price back toward perceived value. In essence, the third layer of the Camarilla Equation is visually displaying price levels on the chart where responsive market participants are likely to enter the market in order to push price back toward an area of prior value. This is the reason the third layer of the indicator can have such an impact on price on any given day, especially when the market displays certain market tendencies.

The first and second layers of the indicator (L1, L2, H1, and H2) are typically ignored and generally not even plotted. However, I will discuss how and when to use these levels in Chapter 9. On the other hand, the fourth layer of support and resistance (L4 and H4) is very important. This layer is seen as the last line of support or resistance and is watched very closely for a breakout or reversal. Traditionally, traders of this system will watch the fourth layer of the indicator for a breakout. Therefore, H4 resistance is usually colored green to denote a bullish breakout, while L4 is colored red to represent a bearish breakout. While the third layer of the indicator visually represents where responsive market participants are likely to enter the market, the fourth layer illustrates price levels where initiative market participants are likely to act. Since the fourth layer of the indicator is typically seen as the last line of support or resistance, it makes sense that a break would likely lead to range extension via initiative buying or selling pressure. Therefore, breaks through these levels usually lead to trending moves in the direction of the break. In addition to watching the fourth layer as a breakout zone, I have also found this layer to be as prone to reversals as the third layer, thus allowing me to play it as I would L3 and H3. Therefore, it could be said that the fourth layer of the indicator offers the most versatility.

THE EXPANDED CAMARILLA EQUATION

As with the Floor Pivots, I also like to include an extra layer to the Camarilla Equation. The fifth layer (L5 and H5) of the equation generally serves as a target should a breakout through L4 or H4 occur. Many traders I've talked to love this aspect of the indicator, but I cannot take credit for discovering the formula, as it was already widely available. In keeping with the color-coded theme of the indicator, I typically keep H5 and L5 as blue or black lines so they are not easily confused with any other Cam level. The formula for the expanded Camarilla Equation is as follows:

Expanded Camarilla Pivot Formula
H5 = (High/Low) × Close
H4 = Close + RANGE × 1.1/2
H3 = Close + RANGE × 1.1/4
H2 = Close + RANGE × 1.1/6
H1 = Close + RANGE × 1.1/12
L1 = Close - RANGE × 1.1/12
L2 = Close - RANGE × 1.1/6
L3 = Close - RANGE × 1.1/4
L4 = Close - RANGE × 1.1/2
L5 = Close - (H5 - Close)

TABLE 7.2: Expanded Formula

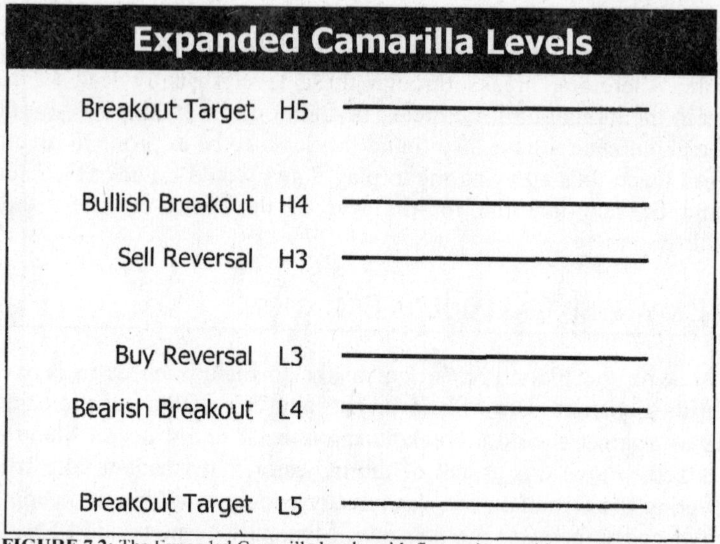

FIGURE 7.2: The Expanded Camarilla levels, with first and second layers ignored

Figure 7.2 illustrates the expanded Camarilla levels, which I will use the remainder of the book. This graphic shows each key Camarilla level and also includes the actions to be taken at each pivot. Remember, the third layer of the indicator is where the market is likely to reverse due to responsive parties, the fourth layer is where breakouts are likely to occur due to initiative parties, and the fifth layer serves as a target should a break occur through the fourth layer.

Let's take a brief look at the pivots in Figure 7.3, which is a five-minute chart of Heating Oil futures. Only the third layer of the pivots is visible in this chart. However, this layer is typically the most watched and most important layer of the equation. Notice how Heating Oil reacted cleanly off L3 and H3 throughout the day, making three great passes between the levels. Traders were clearly honed in to the reversal zones highlighted by this equation, which proved highly profitable on this day. As with the Floor Pivots in our prior chapters, the reactions at these key pivot levels can be simply amazing. In a time when the market can be all over the map in terms of volatility, these levels can provide a sense of calm while navigating the high seas of the market.

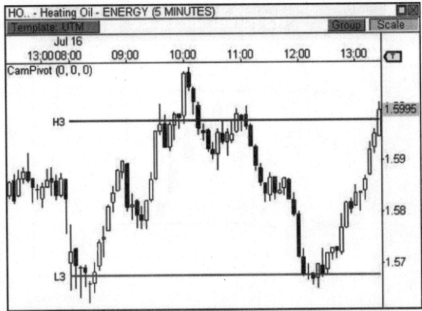

FIGURE 7.3: Heating Oil reacts to Camarilla pivot levels

THE STANDARD THIRD LAYER REVERSAL

The Camarilla Equation is like a built-in trading system, complete with entries, stops, and targets all built into one indicator. In this section, I will break down the conventional methods of using the Camarilla Equation in your trading. In Chapter 9, I will discuss more advanced trading techniques using this indicator. First, however, we need a Camarilla primer.

There are two basic setups that the Camarilla Equation offers: two reversal plays, and two breakout plays. The first setup I will discuss is the *H3 Reversal* trade, illustrated in Figure 7.4. This trade occurs when the market advances to the red H3 pivot level and begins to lose momentum. At this point, responsive sellers are likely to enter the market and push price back toward perceived value, essentially forcing price to revert back toward the mean. As such, any signs of weakness at H3 should be viewed as a selling opportunity, as this is the first major level of resistance identified by the indicator. According to traditional Camarilla strategy, any short position taken at the H3 pivot level should carry a stop loss at, or just above, the H4 pivot level. Along the same lines, your target should be set to the green L3 pivot level, which is the first major level of support identified by the indicator.

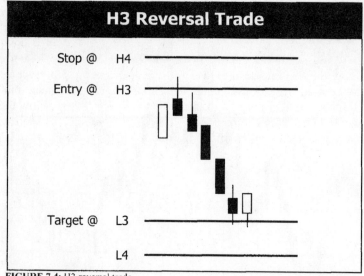

FIGURE 7.4: H3 reversal trade

While this is a simplified example of entering and exiting a trade, actual entries can be much more complicated at times. Specific entry methodologies can vary from trader to trader. In the illustration, you see the first candle that reaches and extends beyond H3 is a bearish candle, as evidenced by the wick at the top of the candlestick. This candle opened and closed below H3, but the wick extended beyond the pivot level, leaving a bearish shadow. As we learned in Chapter 2, this type of bearish reversal wick is the first indication of weakness at this level. Some traders may want to enter this trade based on this criterion alone.

However, some traders want to see a bit more confirmation at this pivot level. For example, does H3 coincide with visual price resistance in the chart? Has price been in a downtrend the last few days? Have any key candlestick setups formed at this pivot level? These are all prudent questions to ask when trading any set of pivots. A basic, yet powerful, form of confirmation is to see how the following bar reacts after the initial test at H3 occurs. If the following bar's high falls below H3 and its close is below the prior bar's close, you have all the confirmation needed to fire off a short trade. Your entry would occur at the close of the confirmation bar, or at the open of the following bar. You would then look to offset the trade once your target is reached at L3 support, as illustrated in Figure 7.4. I typically allow any of the major candlestick setups discussed in Chapter 2 to trigger my entries at a key Camarilla pivot level.

Let's take a look at an example. Figure 7.5 is a fifteen-minute chart of Natural Gas futures. Natural Gas opened the day with modest strength, but sheepishly rose to test H3 resistance in the first forty-five minutes of the day. The third candlestick of the day was our first indication that a downside reversal would occur off the H3 pivot level, as a clear doji had formed. Notice how the doji candlestick rose above H3 resistance, but reversed and eventually closed beneath this pivot. The following candle's open and high both fell below H3 resistance, with the close of the bar falling below the low of the doji candle, thus confirming the H3 reversal trade. This sequence of events triggered a short entry off H3 resistance, with our target set to L3 and stops set at the H4 pivot level. As you can tell, the trade worked out in textbook fashion, as Natural Gas reached the L3 target a few hours later.

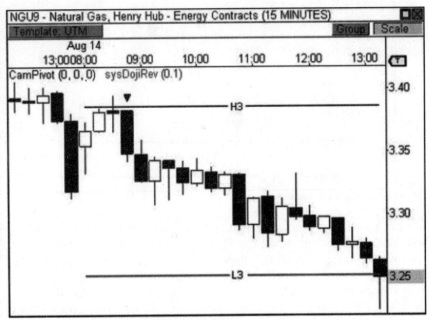

FIGURE 7.5: The H3 reversal trade in Natural Gas futures

The second version of the third layer reversal play is the *L3 Reversal* trade, which is basically an inverted version of the H3 reversal trade. The goal of this trade is to buy at L3 support with targets set to H3 resistance. Traditionally, stops would be held at, or just below, the L4 support level, as illustrated in Figure 7.6. Remember, if price drops to the L3 pivot level and begins to see initial signs of strength, responsive buyers are likely beginning to enter the market with the intent of pushing price back toward higher value.

That is, responsive buyers are seeing value at lower prices and are looking to capitalize on this bargain opportunity. As with the H3 reversal trade, a method for confirming the reversal would be to look to the bar that follows the initial test at L3 support. If this bar closes above the prior bar's close and its low is above the L3 pivot level, there's enough confirmation to fire off a long signal. Again, any of the major candlestick setups discussed in Chapter 2 are great triggers for the L3 reversal trade as well.

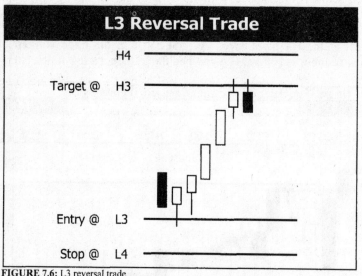

FIGURE 7.6: L3 reversal trade

Let's look at an example. Figure 7.7 is a fifteen-minute chart of Applied Materials, Inc. (ticker: AMAT). The stock opened the day with early weakness and quietly tested L3 support within the first thirty minutes of the day. After testing L3 support, AMAT formed a moderately bullish reversal wick at this level. The following bar's low was above the L3 pivot and its close was above the prior bar's high, completing the necessary requirements for a long signal. You would then enter a long position at the close of the second bar, or at the open of the following bar, with targets set to H3 resistance and stops at L4 support. In this case, AMAT trended nicely higher and eventually reached H3 resistance to complete a successful trade.

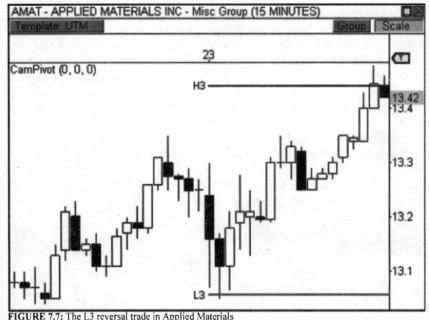

FIGURE 7.7: The L3 reversal trade in Applied Materials

BOSS IN ACTION

There are several factors that I look for when I have my sights set on a third layer reversal trade: the current trend, the prior day's price behavior, visual support or resistance in the vicinity, and price to pivot behavior. As you may recall from our study of both the Money Zone and Floor Pivots, the prior day's trading activity can have a huge influence on the next day's trading behavior. Therefore, if the prior session was a Trend Day, you are more likely to see trading range behavior in the next day's market, which means reversals at H3 and L3 are more likely to occur. Along the same lines, if the market has been trending higher for a period of time, any pull-back to L3 should be seen as a buying opportunity. Likewise, if the market is in an existing downtrend, any pull-back to H3 should be viewed as an opportunity to sell the rip. The ability to quickly recognize the market's context clues will allow you to get a feel for how price may respond to certain Camarilla pivots.

Let's take a look at Figure 7.8, which shows a five-minute chart of the Copper futures contract. Copper basically traded in a clear range the prior session, establishing clear areas of support and resistance. The fact that price opened the day firmly within the prior day's range was indicative that continued trading range behavior was likely to occur—at least until a breakout from the range proves otherwise. Copper reacted to both H3 and L3 pivot levels early in the day, but the wick reversal signals did not allow for proper trade location, as the candlesticks were quick large. Later in the day, Copper formed two bearish wick reversal candlesticks at H3 resistance, which was a level that had already proven to appeal to responsive sellers. I entered the trade short during the development of the second candlestick and set my target to L3 support, which was quickly reached for a handsome profit.

While this trade worked out perfectly for me, you'll notice that I did not rush an entry at either pivot level earlier in the day, as I was not completely comfortable with the size of the candlesticks, which seemed rather erratic. I did miss a perfect bullish outside reversal setup at L3 support just before my short entry, but such is the life of a trader.

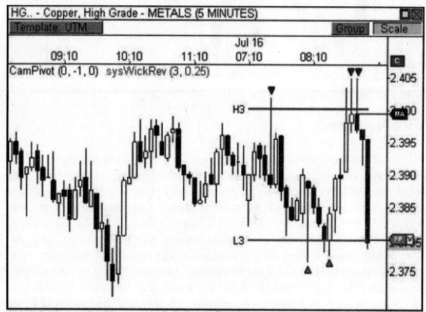

FIGURE 7.8: A perfect H3 reversal trade in Copper futures

THE STANDARD FOURTH LAYER BREAKOUT

The second type of Camarilla setup that I will discuss is the fourth layer breakout trade. Let's begin with the first version of this trade, which is the *H4 Breakout* trade (illustrated in Figure 7.9). The basic premise of this setup is to trade a breakout through H4 resistance with a target set to the H5 pivot level. Stops are traditionally held at, or just below, the H3 level. As I mentioned earlier, H4 represents the last line of pivot resistance, as seen through the eyes of the indicator. The market has to decide whether it will break through, or bounce off, this last line of defense. If a break occurs through this level, you typically see a rush of buying pressure that catapults price vastly higher, as initiative buyers begin to step into the market to advance price to higher value. When H4 is crossed with plenty of energy, the market can break away from the prior range at an advanced rate of speed, reaching the H5 target in a matter of minutes.

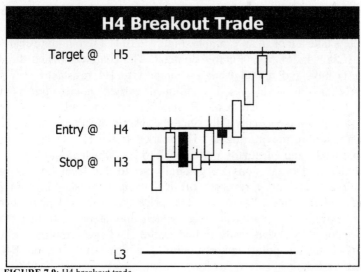

FIGURE 7.9: H4 breakout trade

While the H4 breakout play looks easy to trade, it can actually be quite difficult for traders that are new to trading with the Camarilla Equation. The reason is that H4 is typically considered a breakout level, but it is actually more of a last line of resistance. What happens when the market tests the last line of resistance? The market fights this level tooth and nail on most occasions, as bulls and bears battle for control. This struggle causes price to wick resistance many times before direction is ultimately decided. These wicks are what cause headaches and frustration for new traders of the equation. You see, when newbies to the Camarilla Equation learn that H4 is to be bought for a breakout opportunity, they generally buy the first touch at this level, which typically results in a losing trade. On most occasions, the market has to test this last line of resistance before making a decision to head higher. Therefore, the best course of action is to watch behavior at H4 and allow it to form a natural price resistance until a solid breakout occurs via a bullish candle. A close above this resistance level is typically the confirmation required for a bullish trade.

Referring back to Figure 7.9, notice the first five candles at H4 were basically testing this pivot level for either a breakout or reversal, with each candle closing below the pivot, but leaving wicks above it. Eventually, the sixth candle of the sequence led to a breakout through H4 and closed above the highs of the prior candlesticks. This is the candle that should be bought for a ride to the H5 target, as initiative buyers have clearly begun to step into the market. Obviously, not all H4 plays are the same (and we will review more advanced plays at this level in Chapter 5), but having this bit of knowledge will save you some frustration and will surely advance your learning curve.

Let's take a look at an example. Figure 7.10 is a five-minute chart of the Russell 2000 Index Mini Futures contract. The contract opened the day in strong fashion and rallied from L4 support to H4 resistance, but stalled precisely at this level. As I mentioned earlier, novice traders would automatically buy a touch at the H4 pivot level (after all, it is a breakout level), but this trade usually fails since the market must test the last level of resistance before moving higher. The market tested H4 several times with multiple wicks and eventually pulled back to H3, which would have stopped out novice traders, as stops are generally set to this level for this type of trade. Eventually, price reversed off H3, using it as support, and rallied through H4 resistance. The key is that price tested the H4 pivot level and *closed* above this line of resistance, which ultimately confirmed the long trade opportunity. Price easily rallied to the H5 target, resulting in a solid gain of about four points in forty minutes, which is worth about $400 per contract traded.

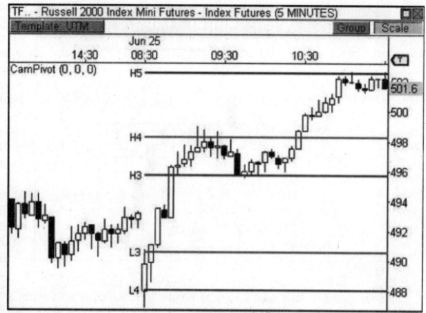

FIGURE 7.10: H4 breakout trade in the Russell 2000 Index Mini Futures

The second version of the fourth layer breakout is the *L4 Breakout* trade, which is basically the bearish version of the H4 breakout trade. For this trade, you would enter short trades upon a close *below* the L4 support level, while setting your stops at, or just above, L3 and your targets at L5 (illustrated in Figure 7.11). Again, since L4 represents the last level of pivot support for the market, you may see a struggle at this level before a breakout or reversal occurs, as bulls and bears battle for territory. Eventually, you want to see initiative sellers enter the market in order to extend the day's range downward. Watch price behavior closely at this pivot and look to play a close below the pivot through prior lows.

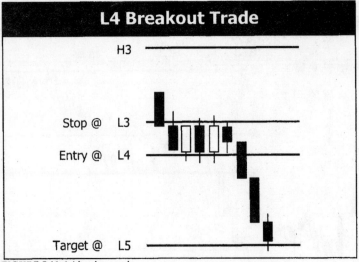

FIGURE 7.11: L4 breakout trade

As an example, let's take a look at Figure 7.12, which is a five-minute chart of Crude Oil futures. The commodity opened the day with clear weakness and dropped from H3 resistance to L4 support about twenty-five minutes into the market. As expected, L4 put up a fight at this level, as it was the last line of support, as seen through the eyes of the indicator. Price briefly reversed back to L3 and tested this level from underneath, using it as resistance. The fact that price used L3 as resistance is our first clue that Crude may take another shot at L4 support. Eventually, Crude dropped back to L4 for another test. This time, however, price broke through L4 support and closed beneath this pivot level, which triggered our short entry. After the successful break, price dropped quickly to the L5 target to complete the trade.

FIGURE 7.12: L4 breakout trade in Crude Oil

BOSS IN ACTION

As with the H3 reversal trade, there are several factors that can be judged to help you determine if a successful H4 breakout trade is likely to occur. The current trend, the prior day's trading behavior, and where price opened the current session in relation to the pivots all are key factors that can result in a high probability H4 breakout play, which we will discuss in Chapter 9. For example, if the market has been trending higher in the days leading up to the current session, you are likely to see responsive buyers enter the market upon a pull-back to the L3 support level. As you know, all too well, bullish trending markets form higher lows and higher highs. Therefore, if responsive buyers enter the market on a pull-back to L3 support, you are likely to see price reach a new high within the uptrend, which generally means a move to H4 or H5, once initiative participants take over the move. Likewise, if the prior session was a Trading Range or Sideways Day, price is likely to trend in the current session, meaning that a push to, and through, the fifth layer of the pivots is very likely. On the flip side, if the prior session had a wide range of movement, like on a Trend Day or Double-Distribution Trend Day, the market is likely to trade in a range in the current session, which doesn't bode well for a Camarilla breakout opportunity. This behavior actually sets up much better for the third layer reversal plays.

Figure 7.13 shows a recent L4 breakout trade I placed in the Mini-Sized Dow futures contract. Notice that price opened the day below L3 support, but within the prior day's range. Think of the area between L3 and H3 as the Camarilla Equation's version of the value area. When price opens beyond this zone, the market is likely looking to push price to new value. In this case, price opened between L3 and L4 support and traded above L4 through the first ninety minutes of the day, creating a natural price support at this level. Eventually, price pushed below L4 and closed below this level in a five-minute bar, which was enough to trigger my short entry at 10,538. I set my stop loss to L3 at 10,558 and my fixed profit stop to L5 support at 10,519, which was easily reached for a quick gain of nineteen points. By no means was this trade a home run, but it offered a high probability setup that delivered exactly what it was supposed to.

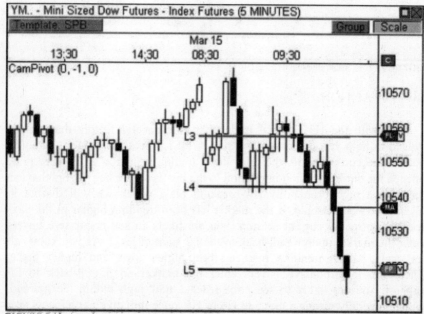

FIGURE 7.13: A perfect L4 breakout trade in the YM

ENGAGING CAMARILLA

The Camarilla Equation offers a powerful view of the market. The pivots highlight important levels in the charts and reveal inherent details about the market that are usually tough to uncover. Not many indicators or formulas can reveal such precise levels on the chart where both responsive and initiative market participants are likely to enter the market. What's fascinating about the indicator is that it can be used as a self-contained trading strategy, with all the entries, stops, and targets built right into the pivot levels. I am a strong believer in knowing the sequence of events that trigger any given entry. By trading this way, you are introducing discipline into your craft, while reducing the emotional aspect of trading. The Camarilla Equation definitely falls along these guidelines and provides even more powerful setups than the classic ones demonstrated in this chapter. Chapter 8 will further unlock the strength behind the equation and reveal some of my favorite setups using this indicator.

CHAPTER 8

ADVANCED CAMARILLA CONCEPTS

"A man may know what to do and still lose money—if he doesn't do it quickly enough."

- Jesse Livermore

Now that you have learned the basics of the Camarilla Equation and have a solid understanding of its self-contained trading strategy, we can move forward to more advanced concepts using the indicator. This chapter will be geared toward the intricacies of using the indicator and will also include many of the important relationships that we have already covered, like two-day pivot relationships, pivot width analysis, and pivot trend analysis. Since I've thoroughly covered these subjects with respect to the

Money Zone and Floor Pivots, I will spare you formal introductions and will jump straight into the material.

After trading with this indicator for many years, my brain has become programmed to sniff out winning and losing trades depending on market movement and price behavior at key pivot levels. The following material will be immensely powerful if you're serious about becoming a pivot player.

THE DEVELOPING CAMARILLA THREE INDICATOR

In addition to conceptualizing the idea for the Developing Pivot Range indicator, I also wrote the code for the *Developing Camarilla Three (DC3)* indicator, thereby completing the developing suite of indicators for the Money Zone, Floor Pivots, and the Camarilla Equation. The DC3 indicator plots the third layer of the Camarilla Equation in real time as it dynamically updates throughout the day. As is the case with the developing Money Zone and Pivot Range indicators, the day's ending values for the DC3 indicator will tell you the location of the third layer of the static Camarilla indicator for the upcoming session, thereby allowing you to analyze important two-day Camarilla relationships and pivot width characteristics. Remember, the advantage of the developing suite of indicators is to get a read on the market before anyone else. Having this information the day before important relationships develop allows you to engage highly profitable setups and predictable market behavior in a more informed and educated manner. As always, I have included the code for the DC3 indicator (file name: iDevCamarilla3) in Appendix B.

Let's take a look at the indicator in Figure 8.1, which shows a five-minute chart of the E-Mini NASDAQ 100 futures contract. Notice how the third layer of the equation dynamically updates throughout the session as new data enters the market. While the indicator will dynamically ebb and flow throughout the day, pay close attention to where the indicator closes the session, as these ending values will become the levels for the third layer of the static Camarilla indicator for the following day. That is, tomorrow's levels for the third layer of the Camarilla Equation are derived from the ending values of the DC3 indicator. Therefore, looking at the chart shows the developing values closed at 1,757.50 and 1,782.50 on January 28, 2010, which essentially became the levels for the third layer of the static Camarilla indicator the following day, January 29.

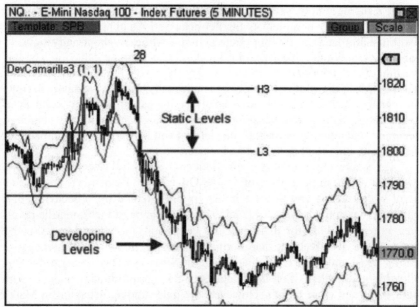

FIGURE 8.1: The DC3 indicator helps you see the third layer of the Cams for the next day.

I will use the DC3 indicator the rest of the chapter as I explain the most useful Camarilla pivot relationships. This indicator has been tremendous in helping me visualize and anticipate important, money-making Camarilla relationships ahead of other traders. It cannot be overstated how important preparation is to trading. Preparation allows you to analyze the market with a clear mind before real money is on the line and live bullets are in the air.

Preparation is what separates the Pros from the Joes.

PIVOT WIDTH ANALYSIS

By now, you already know how important pivot width analysis can be to anticipating potential market behavior. There is no doubt that pivot width analysis has been instrumental in my development as a trader and analyst. This analysis allows you to prepare for certain types of trading scenarios and utilize specific exit methodologies depending on the width of the pivots. As you recall, I judge the width of the value area when using this analysis with the Money Zone. For Floor Pivots, I use the width of the central pivot range. When using the Camarilla Equation for pivot width analysis, I use the width of the third layer of indicator, from L3 to H3.

It's such a simple, yet powerful concept. Pivot width plays an important role in your ability to anticipate market behavior. An abnormally wide pivot width usually leads to trading range activity, while an abnormally tight, or narrow, pivot width typically yields breakout and trending behavior. The key word here is "abnormally," which is to say the pivots are unusually wide, or narrow. When the width of the pivots is unusually wide or unusually narrow, the chances for forecasting price behavior increases. If pivot width is of average size, then no real behavioral cues can be gleaned with any degree of accuracy. Therefore, you must be disciplined and honest in your approach for deciphering important pivot width characteristics.

Let's take a brief look at pivot width analysis in full effect in Figure 8.2, which is a five-minute chart of Crude Oil futures. Remember, an unusual pivot width allows you to get a better fix on potential price behavior for a particular session. On March 11, 2010, the third layer of the Camarilla pivots was extremely wide for this particular commodity, as the prior day had a wider range of movement than normal. Naturally, this wide-set pivot range allows us to anticipate a Trading Range or Sideways Day scenario, thereby allowing us to either sit on the sidelines or trade brief intraday bounces with tight stops and close targets. However, the quiet trading behavior on March 11 led to the creation of an unusually narrow pivot width for the following session, which allowed us to anticipate a potential trending session, which was indeed the case.

It is important not to overlook the opening price in relation to range and value conversation from Chapter 4. Remember, how the market opens the session with regards to the prior day's range and value allows you to judge the market's conviction. There is acceptance or rejection for every analytical forecast given. If the pivot width is abnormally wide for the following day, it is safe to anticipate a Sideways or Trading Range Day. However, acceptance of this view will take place if the market opens within the prior day's range and within the third layer of the indicator for the current day, as was the case on March 11. If the market had opened the day outside the prior day's range, or outside the third layer of the indicator, market conviction would have led to a different outcome. Likewise, acceptance of a narrow pivot range forecast occurs if price opens the day beyond the prior day's price range and, preferably, outside the third layer of the Camarilla indicator. This indicates the market is ready to seek new value, thus confirming the breakout or trending behavior that narrow pivots typically forecast, which occurred on March 12.

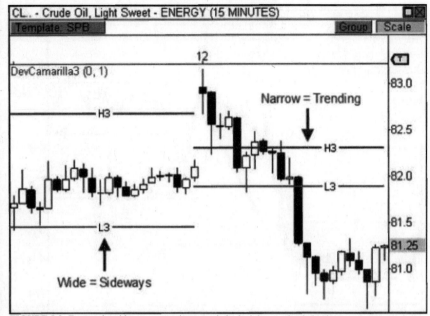

FIGURE 8.2: Extremely wide or narrow pivots can help decipher market behavior

Let's take another look at how the unusual width of the third layer of the pivots can influence price behavior. Figure 8.3 shows a three-day view of a fifteen-minute chart of Apple, Inc. (ticker: AAPL). Notice the first and third days have unusually wide pivots, which lead to quiet, sideways trading. Moreover, the quiet trading behavior of the first day led to the extremely narrow pivot width for the second day, which essentially led to an explosive breakout move. Of course, the breakout move of the second day led to the unusually wide pivots for the third day, which sparked sideways movement. Obviously, this isn't rocket science. However, pivot width analysis allows you to forecast potential price behavior with uncanny accuracy, which is why it remains a key staple in my trading arsenal.

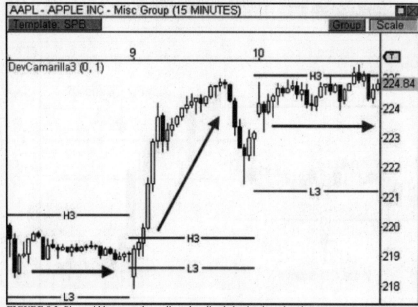

FIGURE 8.3: Pivot width accurately predicated trading behavior three days in a row.

TWO-DAY CAMARILLA RELATIONSHIPS

Two-day relationships are extremely important when using pivots in your trading. These relationships give you directional bias and allow you to anticipate potential market behavior for the upcoming session. I have extensively covered the seven two-day relationships in Chapters 4 and 7 using both the Money Zone and Central Pivot Range. These relationships are the same when using the Camarilla Equation, but the two-day analysis uses the third layer of the indicator, instead of the value area or the pivot range. Since I have already covered these topics in prior chapters, I will stick to real world application as it pertains to the Camarilla Equation. As a reminder, the seven types of two-day relationships are as follows: *Higher Value, Overlapping Higher Value, Lower Value, Overlapping Lower Value, Unchanged Value, Outside Value,* and *Inside Value* (see Table 8.1 and Figure 8.4).

Two-Day Pivot Relationships	
Higher Value	Bullish
Overlapping Higher Value	Moderately Bullish
Lower Value	Bearish
Overlapping Lower Value	Moderately Bearish
Unchanged Value	Sideways/Breakout
Outside Value	Sideways
Inside Value	Breakout

TABLE 8.1: Two-day relationships

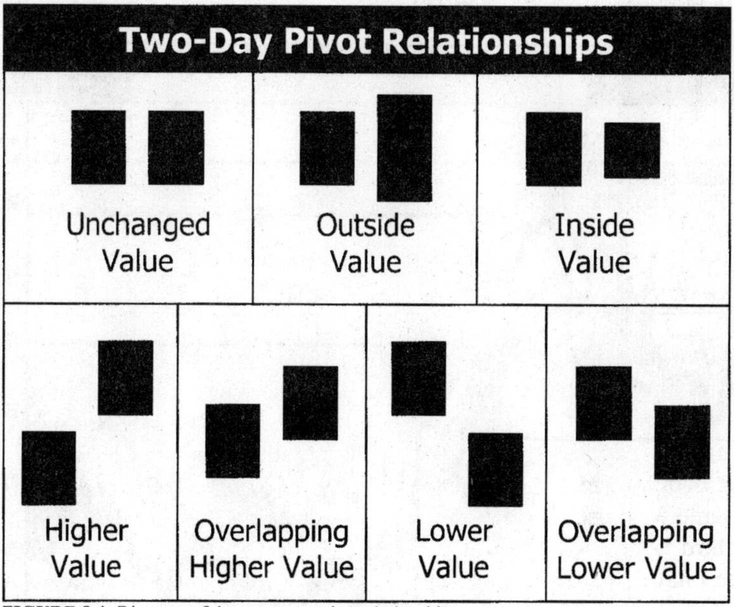

FIGURE 8.4: Diagram of the seven two-day relationships

When using two-day pivot analysis, a developing pivot indicator becomes a huge asset, as it allows you to see the next day's pivots on your charts before a tick is even recorded, unlike a spreadsheet or pivot calculator. This allows you to properly prepare for the upcoming day and visualize the market's anticipated behavior. Of course, the market will not always behave as expected, but preparing for a course of action allows you to know when the market is following the script, or tossing the script out the window.

Let's take a look at Figure 8.5, which shows the initial example used to explain the DC3 indicator earlier in the chapter. In this five-minute chart of the E-Mini NASDAQ 100 futures contract, price dropped steadily throughout the morning on January 28, 2010, and eventually settled within a range from 1,760 to 1,780 to end the day. As you can see, the day's third layer of the static Camarilla indicator ranged from 1,800 to 1,819 on this day, but the ending values for the DC3 indicator showed that the third layer of the Cams would be vastly lower in the following session, thereby creating a two-day Lower Value relationship. This relationship has the most bearish connotation and should be used to sell any pull-back to the H3 pivot level in the upcoming day, especially if the relationship forms in the midst of a bearish trend. Therefore, any pull-back to the 1,780 to 1,785 zone should be seen as a selling opportunity in the following day.

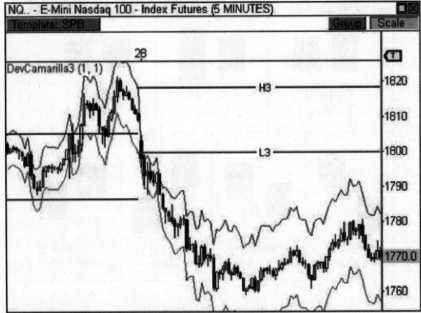

FIGURE 8.5: Identifying a Lower Value relationship using the DC3 indicator

The Lower Value relationship in the chart above gives us a course of action for the following session. If the market opens at or below the H3 pivot level, we will look to sell any pull-back up to this point, as this opening price would indicate acceptance of the current two-day relationship. Selling any pull-back will also carry with it an expected outcome of reaching a new low within the current bearish trend. However, rejection of the two-day relationship will occur if price opens above the H3 pivot level, as this opening behavior would indicate a vast change in sentiment from the prior day, thereby leading to a potential advance.

Let's take a look at Figure 8.6 to see how the following day transpired. Price opened the day *precisely* at the H3 pivot level, which poses an interesting dilemma: do we sell this "pull-back" or buy the "rejection"? Since price opened right at the H3 pivot level, neither acceptance nor rejection has been confirmed, but I would err on the side of acceptance, since price hasn't opened beyond the H3 pivot level. I would then look for any signs of weakness in order to confirm a potential drop to new lows. In this case, price was not able to confidently rise above H3 and instead formed a lower high before dropping to L3 support, and lower. In essence, our initial two-day pivot analysis helped us reveal 1,780 to 1,785 as the sell zone in this chart, which turned out to be spot on.

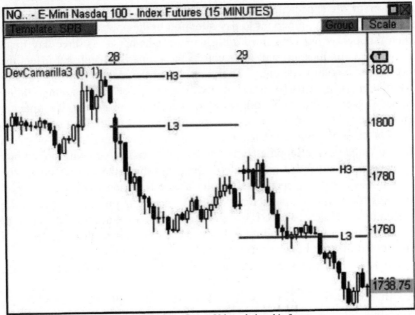

FIGURE 8.6: Sell the pull-back to H3 when a Lower Value relation ship forms.

Keep in mind there were several factors that led to the successful outcome of our initial analysis. First, the market had been in an existing downtrend over the prior two weeks, which means responsive sellers will be looking to sell any pull-backs in price. Therefore, you are aligning yourself with the right side of the market. Secondly, the two-day Lower Value relationship is the most bearish Camarilla relationship. This relationship indicates weakness for the upcoming session, which is complemented by the two-week downtrend. And last, while the opening price did not show full acceptance of our initial analysis, it also didn't reject our directional bias, thereby allowing us to scout H3 for a potential sell entry, which turned out to be the right pivot to watch for action.

This is the type of pre-trade analysis that allows you to prepare properly for the next day's price activity. If price trades according to the script, then you have already identified the action levels for the upcoming market. Likewise, you will not be caught flat-footed if price completely disregards the day's script, as you will be able to identify price behavior that is not consistent with your analysis. As a matter of fact, many of the biggest days occur when the market completely disregards the day's script and behaves in a manner that is unexpected.

One of the main components of two-day pivot analysis is acceptance or rejection of an expected outcome by way of the day's opening print. It becomes especially important to pay attention to the opening print of the day when the market has developed a clear trend, whether it's a three-day trend or longer, as its location will alert you to the Camarilla level that offers the best shot at a solid trade entry. Therefore, when the market develops a two-day trending Camarilla relationship, like Higher Value, Overlapping Higher Value, Lower Value, or Overlapping Lower Value, watching the opening print of the day will give you clues as to which pivot to play for a reversal.

For example, when the market is trending higher and has developed a Higher Value or Overlapping Higher Value relationship, you will look to buy a pull-back at either H3 or L3, depending on where the market opens the session. If the market opens the session above H3, then the H3 pivot level becomes the pivot to watch for a bullish bounce. If the market opens the session below H3, but above L3, then the L3 pivot level becomes the pivot to watch for a buying opportunity. Of course, if price opens the session in an unexpected manner beyond the L3 pivot level, and especially below L4, you will look to sell the market, as the tide has likely changed and a decline could be ahead.

In a bearish trend, you will look to sell any pull-back to L3 or H3, depending on where the market opens the session. Therefore, you will be looking to "sell the rips" if a Lower Value or Overlapping Lower Value relationship has formed, but the day's opening price will tell you which Camarilla pivot level to play. If price opens the day below L3, then you will look to sell a pull-back at the L3 pivot level. If the market opens the session above L3, but below H3, then you will look to sell any pull-back to the H3 pivot level. Again, a major gap against the trend above the H3 or H4 pivot levels indicates a likely change in trend. Therefore, you will look to buy any pull-back at H4, or maybe even H3, as the market is likely headed higher. The concepts for both the bullish and bearish entry options have been illustrated in Figures 8.7 and 8.8.

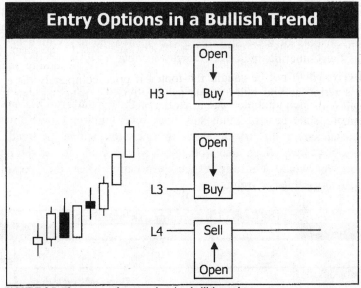

FIGURE 8.7: Three types of entry options in a bullish trend

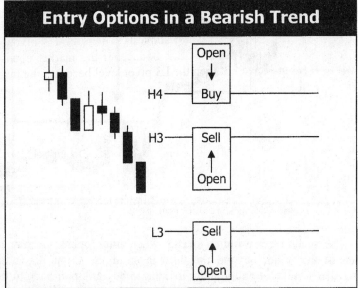

FIGURE 8.8: Three types of entry options in a bearish trend

The next three examples will illustrate each of the three options for entering bullish and bearish trends. The first example, Figure 8.9, shows a fifteen-minute chart of Research In Motion, Ltd. that has formed both Overlapping Lower Value and Lower Value relationships in consecutive sessions. Each of these relationships indicates continued weakness in the following session if the opening print accepts, or confirms, this expected behavior. In both of these sessions, price opened the day within the third layer of the Camarilla indicator, thereby leading us to watch H3 for any selling opportunities.

In both cases, price pushed higher in the morning and found responsive sellers at H3, which ultimately led to weakness the remainder of the sessions. Furthermore, since bearish trends have both lower highs and lower lows, the expected outcome is to play the move to a new low within the trend, or at least to a prior low, which also worked out as expected. This is the type of behavior you would typically expect, especially when the market has developed an established trend.

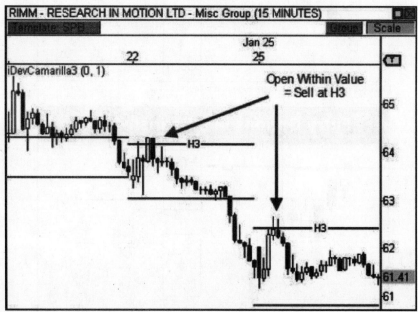

FIGURE 8.9: If price opens within value in a bearish trend, look to sell at H3.

The second entry option occurs when price opens the day in the direction of the trend, beyond the third layer of the Camarilla indicator. Therefore, in a bullish trend you are looking to buy any pull-back to the H3 pivot level if price opens the day above this pivot. Figure 8.10 shows a five-minute chart of the E-Mini Russell 2000 futures contract on a day when price opened the session beyond the H3 pivot level during a bullish trend when a two-day Higher Value relationship was present. The fact that price gapped above H3 is quite bullish and indicates continued bullish price movement. However, the task becomes to enter the market at a favorable entry near the H3 pivot level. Any signs of strength near the H3 pivot level should present a nice entry opportunity, with the intent of reaching H5, or beyond.

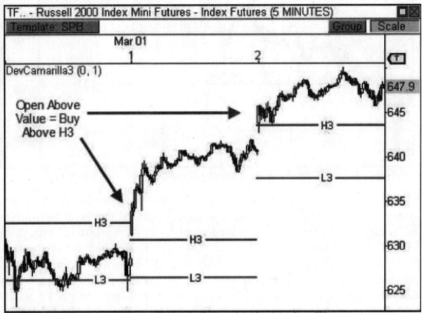

FIGURE 8.10: If price opens above value in a bullish trend, look to buy above H3.

Let's take a look at the third, and final, entry option during a trending market. Figure 8.11 shows a five-minute chart of the E-Mini NASDAQ 100 futures contract on a day when the DC3 indicator forecasts a Higher Value relationship for the following session, which would make two days in a row of this bullish relationship. Therefore, our initial directional bias is to buy any pull-back to the 1,778 to 1,780 area if price opens the day above the L3 pivot level. A rejection of this bias would occur if price opens below the L3 pivot level, thereby introducing a potential selling opportunity.

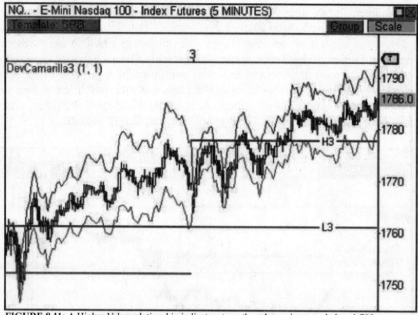

FIGURE 8.11: A Higher Value relationship indicates strength, unless price open below 1,780.

Let's take a look at Figure 8.12 to see how the day's events transpired. As it turns out, the NQ completely rejected the day's bullish bias by opening the session below the L3 pivot level. As a matter of fact, price opened the session below the 1,773.50 L4 pivot level, which is very bearish. This opening print completely rejected our initial bias, which means market sentiment changed drastically overnight, as market participants are now actively seeking lower valuation. While an opening print below L3 would technically confirm a rejection, the fact that price opened below L4 solidifies this fact, which steers your focus to the short side.

When price rejects expected market behavior outright, you are likely to witness an aggressive push to new value, as initiative market participations are likely controlling the market, thereby introducing more conviction. When this occurs, you will look for signs of a continuation to L5 and beyond. Looking at the chart shows price initially attempting to fill the gap, but was stifled at the L4 pivot level. Price then formed a bearish outside reversal signal, which confirmed weakness and provided your short entry. The market trended steadily lower on this day in an unexpected manner. However, the fact that we identified areas for acceptance and rejection using our two-day pivot analysis allowed us to go with the flow and profit from the move. Moreover, part of what led to this day's rejection of our analysis was the fact that the market had been trending lower over the prior two weeks, thereby reinforcing the importance of longer term pivot trend analysis.

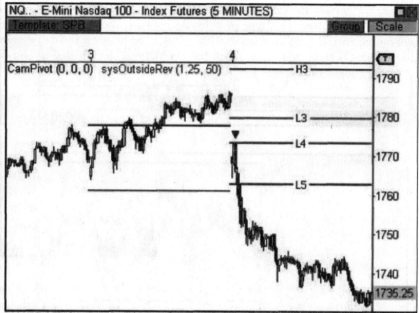

FIGURE 8.12: Opening print did not confirm strength, thus sellers entered upon a test of L4.

The opening print also plays a big role in the Inside Value relationship, which is a very powerful breakout setup. As you know, I am extremely fond of the Inside Value relationship because this formation typically leads to explosive breakout opportunities in the market. Identifying this formation in advance allows you to prepare for some of the biggest trending days in the market. The Inside Value relationship occurs when the third layer of the Camarilla indicator for the current session lies within the third layer of the indicator of the prior session. This two-day relationship is usually a precursor to a major breakout opportunity in the market, which is amplified if the current day's pivot width is unusually narrow.

Let's take a look at how I would scout this particular day in the market. Figure 8.13 shows a five-minute chart of the Crude Oil futures contract on February 3, 2010. Crude Oil traded quietly and formed a Trading Range Day, as the pivot width was wider than normal due to the prior day's trending behavior. Since Crude traded within a clear range throughout the session, this behavior led to the creation of a very narrow third layer of the indicator for the following session, as seen by the ending values of the DC3 indicator.

Moreover, the third layer of the Cams for the following day created an Inside Value relationship, which forecasted a potential breakout opportunity. Remember, in order for price to accept this forecast, I like to see the opening print occur outside the prior day's range, and preferable beyond the fourth layer of the indicator. This type of behavior indicates the market is actively seeking new value with conviction. Otherwise, if price opens the day within the prior day's range and value, much less conviction is anticipated, although a breakout could still occur.

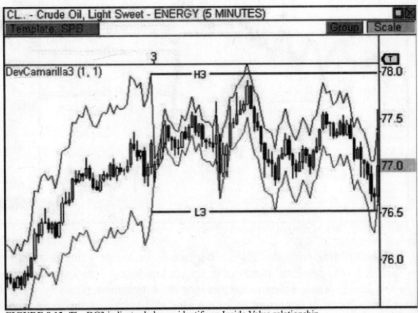

FIGURE 8.13: The DC3 indicator helps us identify an Inside Value relationship.

Let's take a look at Figure 8.14 to see how the Inside Value relationship fared the following day. As expected, price saw a powerful breakout right at the open of the market, which sparked steady trending behavior throughout the session. The opening print for the day confirmed our initial analysis by occurring beyond the prior day's range and value. Moreover, the gap occurred beyond the fourth layer of the indicator, which sweetens the pot for a breakout opportunity. Remember, this type of behavior is fueled by initiative market participants, which carry much more conviction than their responsive counterparts. If the market cannot rise to fill the gap within the first fifteen minutes a downside continuation usually occurs, which was the case in this instance. A bearish wick reversal setup formed after the first thirty minutes of trading, which helped to confirm the short opportunity.

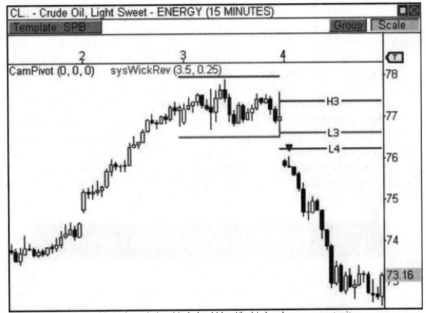

FIGURE 8.14: The Inside Value relationship helped identify this breakaway opportunity.

THE HIDDEN LAYERS

In Chapter 7, I mentioned most traders ignore the first and second layers of the Camarilla Equation, which I call the *Hidden Layers*. However, given the right circumstances, these levels can be extremely useful to your trading. Since the prior session's high, low, and close are used to calculate the pivots for the current day, the prior day's range will dictate when it is useful to trade from the hidden layers of the indicator. In other words, when the prior day's range is excessively larger than normal, the pivots for the following session become abnormally wide, thus allowing you to profit using these hidden layers. When this occurs, you can basically ignore all pivots outside of L3 and H3, as the market will likely become trading range bound. Therefore, unlike the Money Zone and Floor Pivot indicators, the Camarilla Equation provides a better way to play Trading Range and Sideways Days when the pivots are unusually wide.

For example, if the Mini-sized Dow futures contract were to have a range of over three hundred points, the next day's pivots will be vastly wider than normal. If you are looking to trade a reversal off H3 to the traditional target of L3, you are less likely to reach your target since these pivots are spaced wider apart than normal. Actually, you may not even have a chance to trade an L3 or H3 reversal because the pivots may be so wide that price may never venture out from the inner two layers of the indicator.

The first and second layers of the Camarilla indicator are like a swimming pool, you don't always use it, but when the day is nice you enjoy a swim.

Keep in mind that unlike the trading dynamic of H3 and H4 (or L3 and L4) where one pivot is played for a reversal and the other a breakout, the Hidden Layers (H1, H2, L1, L2) are always played for reversals just like the third layer of the indicator, see Figure 8.15. That is, H1 and H2 are to be played for bearish reversals like H3, and L1 and L2 should be played for bullish reversals like L3. This type of relationship falls perfectly in line with how a Trading Range Day should be played.

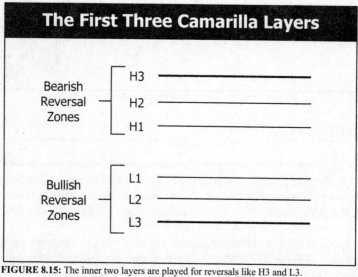

The First Three Camarilla Layers

Bearish Reversal Zones — H3 / H2 / H1

Bullish Reversal Zones — L1 / L2 / L3

FIGURE 8.15: The inner two layers are played for reversals like H3 and L3.

As a rule of thumb, anytime the market experiences a trending session or a session with a wide range of movement, you will want to consider turning on the hidden layers of the indicator the following day. In our software, the indicator has an option to hide or reveal the inner two layers of the indicator, which I usually hide unless the prior session has an abnormally wide range. I have actually created mechanical trading strategies that automatically determine which set of pivots to use depending on pivot width.

If the prior day's range is excessively wide, thereby creating wide pivots, the strategies will automatically trade off the hidden layers of the indicator. If not, these levels are ignored. Isn't it amazing what can be accomplished in our era of trading with the advents of sophisticated platforms and trading automation? Imagine what Jesse Livermore could have accomplished in our era of trading technology!

Let's take a look at an example. Figure 8.16 shows a five-minute chart of the Mini-Sized Dow futures contract. The prior session had a range of 194 points, which created a 107 point spread between L3 and H3. Since the YM saw a wide range of movement in the prior session, the hidden layers of the Cams should be revealed for the following day, as trading range behavior is likely to occur. Remember, the next day's opening price should confirm trading range behavior, however. That is, the YM should open the session within the range of the third layer of the indicator in order for price to accept the day's potential forecast. By price opening within this range, the market is showing a lack of conviction to seek new value. Therefore, the market seems content with current value and the facilitation of trade that it offers. As you can see, the hidden layers of the indicator played a key role in the day's trading, as responsive buyers and responsive sellers basically volleyed price back and forth throughout the day off these inner levels.

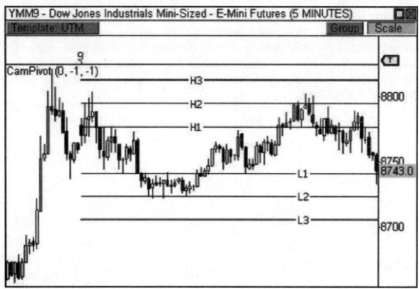

FIGURE 8.16: The hidden layers provided a method for trading sideways activity on June 9.

Professional traders are quite content taking smaller moves within a clearly defined trading range. They will continuously scalp twenty points on the YM throughout a session, hitting the ball out of the park by virtue of base hits. Not every trade becomes a one hundred-point winner, but every one hundred-point winner was first a twenty-point trade. Remember, traders do not like obstacles standing between their trades and potential profits. Trying to ride a trade to a one hundred-plus point intraday target (from L3 to H3 in this case) can be an obstacle on many days. Instead, the inner layers of the indicator provided the same reliable pivot behavior, but reduced the inherent risk typically associated with wide price ranges.

Great traders do not require profits to be large; only that profits are quick and painless.

Let's take a look at another example of how the hidden layers can be extremely useful on a day when the pivots are unusually wide. Figure 8.17 shows a two-day view of a five-minute chart of Apple, Inc. On July 13, AAPL had a wide range of price movement after the stock rallied five points from the low of the day, which caused the pivots for the following day to become extremely wide. As a matter of fact, the pivots were so wide, and price movement so stale, that price never tested the third layer of the indicator. This may seem rare, but this pattern occurs more often than you would normally expect, especially after the market experiences a wide-ranging day in the prior session. After a big rally (or sell-off), the market will usually use the following session to catch its collective "breath," as it digests the prior day's move. These make for great sessions to reveal the hidden layers of the indicator.

FIGURE 8.17: The previous day's wide price range led to wide pivots on July 14.

Now, let's take a look at AAPL on July 14, when the trading range behavior was clearly dictated by the inner two layers of the Camarilla indicator (Figure 8.18). Notice that every reversal on this day was quick and decisive, which is typical of a Trading Range Day. On this type of session, you must be decisive at the point of entry and steadfast to your target. Any of the key reversal patterns covered in this book can be very useful on this type of day, and the ambush entry technique becomes especially important as well. Remember, on these particular trading days, volatility is typically very low, therefore, you are looking to take quick profits, while limiting your risk. Needless to say, the inner layers of the Camarilla indicator could be your "ace in the hole" that gets you through this type of session profitably, while other traders are frustratingly getting whipsawed.

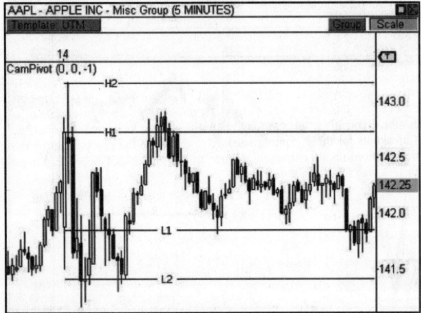

FIGURE 8.18: Reveling the hidden layers of the pivots in Apple, Inc.for July 14

THE CAMARILLA BREAKAWAY PLAY

The Trend Day can be one of the most explosive days the market has to offer. For this reason, it is very important to develop your ability to prospect and anticipate this type of session before it occurs. Your ability to properly diagnose and trade the Trend Day using the pivots can easily take your trading to the next level. While I wrote about trading this type of day using both the Money Zone and Floor Pivots, I will now reveal how I like to scout and trade this setup using the Camarilla Equation.

True Trend Days typically begin the day with a bang, usually with a price gap that occurs beyond the prior day's range and value. However, you do not want this to be your first indication that a Trend Day is in full swing. Instead, a fully prepared trader will use this information as confirmation that a Trend Day has started, since pivot characteristics would have already alerted the trader to the possibility of a Trend Day outcome. Therefore, pivot analysis like narrow pivot width or the Inside Value relationship would have tipped you off that the next day could offer a Trend Day scenario. While this analysis is not always perfect (what is?), it does give you a fantastic advantage in anticipating the next day's potential behavior.

One of my favorite methods for prospecting for a potential Trend Day involves using the two-day Inside Value relationship. The DC3 indicator makes scouting for this pattern effortless, as the indicator automatically calculates and visually displays the third layer of the Cams for the next day's trading. Take a look at Figure 8.19, which shows a fifteen-minute chart of Energizer Holdings on March 26, 2010. Notice that the DC3 indicator clearly alerts you to an Inside Value relationship for the next session, as both lines of the developing indicator lay within the third layer the static Camarilla indicator. Remember, this two-day relationship has a keen sense of snuffing out breakouts for the upcoming session, especially if the pivots creating the inside relationship are extremely narrow, as they are in this example. Armed with this insight, we can now wait for a gap at the open of the following session to *confirm* a potential Trend Day scenario, as a gap in either direction will likely spark a beautifully trending day. If a gap does not occur at the open of the following day, then you must watch the prior day's price range for signs of a violation in order to confirm range extension.

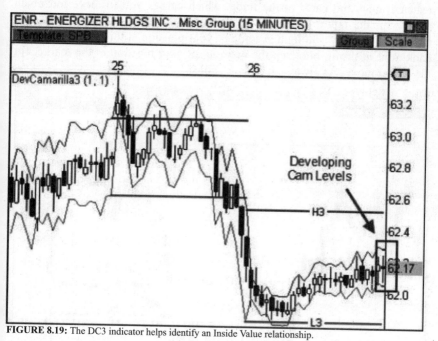

FIGURE 8.19: The DC3 indicator helps identify an Inside Value relationship.

Let's take a look at Figure 8.20 to see how the following day transpired. The stock opened the day with a bullish gap that occurred above the prior day's price range and above the current day's value, which is seen as the third layer of the Camarilla indictor. You usually want the gap to occur beyond the third layer of the indicator, but not beyond the fifth layer, as this gap may be too big for the market to digest. After the opening print confirms a breakout, I usually watch the first five to fifteen minutes of action for further confirmation that a continuation will occur. In this case, ENR raced out of the gates in the first fifteen-minute bar, which is enough confirmation to place a long entry at the open of the following candlestick, with the intent of riding the trend as long as possible using a 1.5 ATR trailing profit stop. Remember, true Trend Days usually close at, or very near, the day's extreme. This means that you will usually use a stop management approach that allows you to capture as much of the move as possible, which means you could sacrifice smaller gains in order to acquire a bigger winner. I am comfortable with this trade off for this particular setup.

Keep in mind, since the pivots are usually narrow on days when the market breaks out, you will not usually look to take profits at the fifth layer of the indictor, as this will not do your trade justice. This target is typically reached much too early in the trade, which causes you to leave too much money on the table. However, this target could be used in a partial exit approach, whereby you lighten some of your position at this level in order to bank a bit of profit, but keep the majority of your position in the market for the bigger move. As always, it is your choice.

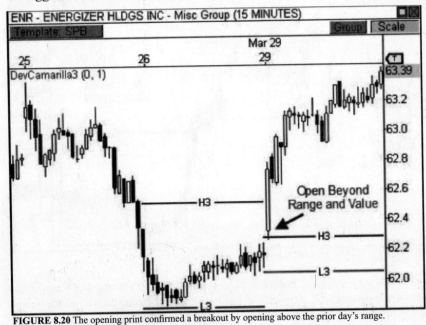

FIGURE 8.20 The opening print confirmed a breakout by opening above the prior day's range.

While narrow pivots and the Inside Value relationship allow you to spot a potential Trend Day easily for the upcoming session, sometimes it's the unexpected breakouts that can offer huge results. Earlier in the chapter, I covered the various entry options for trading in a trend while using the Camarilla pivots. In a bullish trend, you will look to buy any pull-back to L3 or H3, and in a bearish trend, you will look to sell any pull-back to L3 or H3, depending on where the market opens the day. However, if price opens the session with a gap that is completely against the grain, this is a big indication that market sentiment has changed and participants are likely seeking new value. Spotting these days can be easy, but only if you did your homework.

Let's take a look at an example. Figure 8.21 shows a fifteen-minute chart of Google, Inc. over the course of three days. During this three-day stretch, GOOG formed two Overlapping Lower Value relationships in a row, thereby illustrating a moderately bearish trend. If you had done your homework the prior day, you would have identified H3 and L3 as "sell zones" if price opened the session anywhere below H3, in anticipation of continued downtrending behavior. However, you would have also identified any gap above H3, and especially H4, as one that completely bucks the current bearish trend, thereby igniting a potentially bullish Trend Day.

As it turns out, Google opened the day with a gap above the H3 pivot level, and nearly beyond the prior day's range. Price pulled back to H3 for a brief test in the first fifteen-minute bar and then closed at the top of its candlestick, thereby confirming strength in this stock. Any long entry that followed would have easily allowed you to participate in the bullish outcome, as GOOG trended higher throughout the session.

This type of unexpected Trend Day usually occurs against grain of an existing trend, as seen through the eyes of two-day pivot relationships. In this case, the market formed a series of Overlapping Lower Value relationships, which implied continued weakness. When the opening print rejected this forecast, a major trend occurred in the opposite direction. It is important to note that these types of counter-trend breakout days usually occur when the market has formed overlapping two-day relationships, as opposed to Higher or Lower relationships. Remember, a two-day relationship that is completely higher or lower offers the most bullish or bearish expectations. On the other hand, overlapping two-day relationships offer a directional bias, but are not as strong as higher or lower relationships. Therefore, this particular relationship is subject to becoming overwhelmed by contrarian market participants that are ready to seek new value.

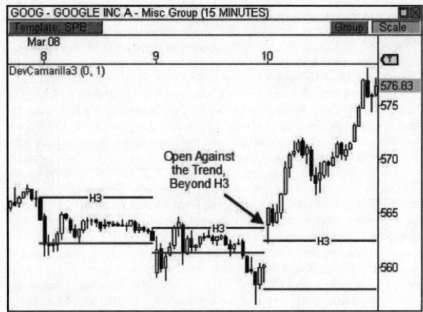

FIGURE 8.21: Price opens across the grain of the trend, sparking a breakaway move

BOSS IN ACTION

When I trade the Camarilla breakaway play, I typically like the gap to be beyond the fourth layer of the indicator on a day when price opens beyond the prior day's range and value. When this occurs, I study price behavior at the closest Camarilla pivot and enter the trade if a successful test occurs. Take a look at Figure 8.22, which is a fifteen-minute chart of the E-Mini NASDAQ 100 futures contract. Price opened the day above the prior day's range and above the H4 Camarilla level, which set the stage for a bullish Trend Day. I allowed the first fifteen-minute bar of the day to play out before entering the trade, as I want to see a bullish reversal from this pivot before I commit to the play. In this case, the NQ formed a bullish wick reversal setup, which allowed me to enter the trade near the open of the following bar at 1872.50. After the entry, I set my fixed loss stop below the day's low and used a 1.5 ATR cushion on my trailing profit stop, which kept me in the trade throughout the session. My trade session boundary stop automatically closed me out of the trade fifteen minutes before the end of the session at 1887, netting me a gain of 14.5 points, which amounts to $290 per contract.

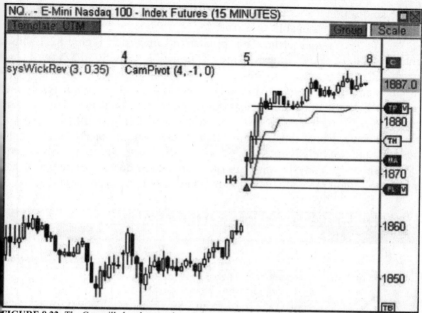

FIGURE 8.22: The Camarilla breakaway play work to perfection on the NQ.

PIVOT TREND ANALYSIS

Two days ago, potential investors visited our company's offices. When he CEO of our company brought the investors into the trading room, one nvestor asked me what the Dow was going to do the following session. At his point, the Dow had been trending higher for four straight weeks, but was n the midst of a two-day pull-back from highs, which was the largest retracement during this advance. Despite the longer-term uptrend, I had a feeling that we would see more short-term selling pressure. As such, I told him that the following day we would likely see an early rally in the first hour of the session, but that this advance would be met with another round of selling pressure that would push the Dow back to new lows within the current short-term retracement. Needless to say, the investor gave me an incredulous look as if to ask, *"Are you a time traveler? How could you possibly see the future?"*

No, I'm not a time traveler, much to the dismay of my wife, who is uper intrigued by time travel. But once you understand pivots and how narkets react at these key zones, you too will be able to anticipate future rice movement with the best of them. Of course, if your prediction does not come to fruition you can always save face by diagnosing the market as irrational and unreasonable!

Let's take a look at how my prediction turned out. Figure 8.23 shows the Mini-Sized Dow futures contract traded in exactly the way I had predicted! On August 25, 2009, the YM opened the session with early strength and traded *precisely* to the H3 pivot level, and was immediately met with selling pressure from responsive market participants. This selling pressure occurred within the first hour of the day, highlighted by the extreme reversal setup, which sparked immediate weakness that lasted throughout the session and essentially pushed price to new lows within the short-term downtrend. My analysis was spot on, showcasing how accurately you can predict potential price movement with pivots when price is trending.

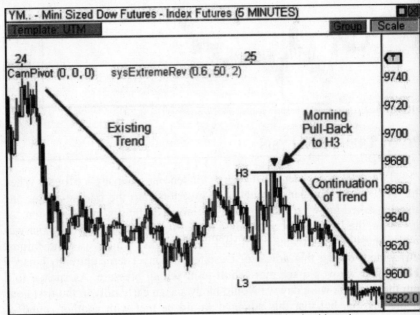

FIGURE 8.23: The YM opens within value and finds resistance at H3 in a bearish trend.

I do not claim to know what the market will do at all times, but when the market falls into a familiar routine, it is my responsibility as a trader to quickly and accurately identify and diagnose the situation so that I may deploy my capital in the most responsible manner. Trading is about finding those familiar patterns in the market and capitalizing on the highest probability opportunities. Even in the shortest of trends, you will begin to see how every pull-back to L3 or H3 will be an opportunity to either buy the dip or sell the rip. The smart money enters positions at the most favorable spots in the chart, and pivot trend analysis allows you to spot these opportunities with the best of them.

Pivot trend analysis is one of the most powerful and successful ways to analyze and trade a trending market.

Throughout the book, I have discussed the importance of recognizing the trend of the market while playing the pivots. To fully appreciate and profit from the pivots, you must buy at support while in an uptrend, and sell at resistance during a downtrend. Every pull-back becomes a buying opportunity in an uptrend, while every rally becomes an opportunity to sell in a downtrend. Understanding this axiom will allow you to hone in on the high probability buy and sell zones of the market. Obviously, the Camarilla indicator makes this process as elementary as possible due to the color-coded pivots that direct you to buy or sell at certain levels.

Up to this point in the chapter, we have looked at two-day pivot relationships to give us a feel for potential behavior in the upcoming session. Pivot trend analysis is basically the same, but strings together multiple days during trending markets. The concept remains the same; buy at support in an uptrend, and sell at resistance in a downtrend. Every pull-back to H3 should be a selling opportunity during a bearish trend, while every retracement to L3 should be a buying opportunity during bullish trend.

Let's take a look at an example. Figure 8.24 shows a fifteen-minute chart of Natural Gas futures during a five-day bearish trend. The contract pushed lower within a clearly defined downtrend throughout the beginning of August and followed the basic framework that you would expect from a trend. That is, every rally within the downtrend was met with selling pressure, which created new lows within the trend. Looking closely, you notice that every pull-back to H3 resistance led to another round of selling back to new lows within the bearish trend at either L3 or L4, which is exactly what you would expect within a clearly defined trend. This process repeats day after day until the trend is broken. In this example, I have manually "filtered" the pivots to show only the most pertinent pivots when price is in a bearish trend (H3, L3, and L4). Manually, or automatically, filtering the pivots in this fashion forces you to become disciplined to the trend. This method forces you to focus on the right actions at the most important levels, which inherently improves your potential for success. So what do we do with this information? If the market closes the day lower within the bearish trend, the next morning you will be ready to sell any advance to H3 resistance, should you have proper confirmation. Once in the trade, you will look to cover the position at either L3 or L4 support. Likewise, if the market has developed a bullish trend, you will be looking to buy the dip at L3 the next morning, with your target at either H3 or H4 resistance.

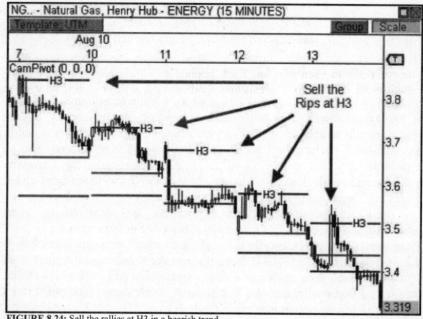

FIGURE 8.24: Sell the rallies at H3 in a bearish trend

Pivot trend analysis may seem like common sense after it has been illustrated and explained, but trust me, many inconsistent traders have not yet made the correlation between this type of market behavior and how pivots factor into a trend. The use of pivots in a trend, whether Camarilla-based, Money Zone, or otherwise, offers you the most accurate method of forecasting turning points in a trend. Your ability to accurately diagnose the trend and identify the right actionable pivots can definitely put you ahead of the herd.

Of course, your definition of what constitutes a trend does not have to be rigid. Not all trends are long, glorious moves in the market. A two-day move in the same direction may be classified as a short-term trend, which can still allow you to take advantage of market moves using the appropriate pivots. Identifying the most pertinent trend will allow you to utilize the right Camarilla levels for the best results.

Let's take a look at a bullish example. Figure 8.25 offers an excellent example of the type of pivot behavior you can expect when a market has established a bullish trend. I have also manually "filtered" the pivots for this example, leaving only the pivots that are the most pertinent in a bullish trend (L3, H3, and H4). When the market has developed a well-behaved uptrend, you should see a clear pattern of buying pressure at L3, with targets at H3 and H4. In this chart, the E-Mini Russell 2000 futures contract began a new uptrend when price closed beyond H4 resistance on September 3, 2009. The price behavior that followed was a clear pattern of "buying the dips," as three of the next four sessions saw buying pressure enter the market when L3 was tested early in each session. Each bounce at L3 support led to new highs within the uptrend to H3 resistance and beyond, which is exactly what you would expect when the market falls into this type of predictable behavior.

In other words, during a bullish trend, price typically pulls back from highs at some point the next morning, which offers a buying opportunity for savvy traders. This buying opportunity is usually seen at L3 support, as this level offers traders a high value entry point versus buying a new high, a method that is usually reserved for amateurs. This is the same type of consumer mentality that you would see in any marketplace around the globe. Why buy a product for a higher price at one store, when you can shop around for the best price at other stores or on the Internet? Trading is always about getting the best price you can find, whether it's buying as low as possible, or selling for as much as you can get.

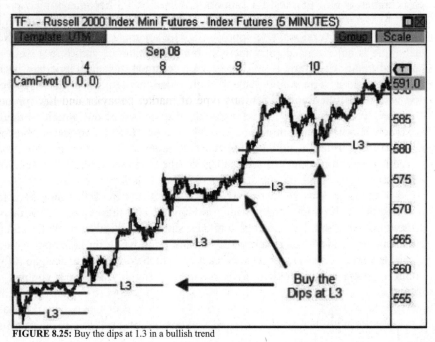

FIGURE 8.25: Buy the dips at 1.3 in a bullish trend

BOSS IN ACTION

Let's take a closer look at this phenomenon, and how I would approach it for executing a trade. Figure 8.26 shows the last two days of the bullish trend from the previous example. I remember September 10 clearly because I had a strong belief that we would see early selling pressure that would offer a bargain buying opportunity, since the market had developed such a strong trend over the prior week of trading. As you are now familiar, having an educated guess about what the market is likely to do in the upcoming session is only the first part of the puzzle before you can pull the trigger on a trade. You must also get acceptance from the market in other forms, like the opening print in relation to value, pivot confirmation, and even candlestick setup confirmation.

Now that I am armed with an idea of how the market may behave in the upcoming session, I set out to confirm the trade. Before the market opens the session, I take a look at the pre-market futures data to get a feel for where the market is about to open the day. Remember, since this particular contract has been rising in a bullish trend, I want price to open the day anywhere above L3 support, but not beyond H4 or H5. The fact that price eventually opens the session above L3, but below H3, lets me know that if price is going to push higher, it will first test L3 support. Essentially, L3 becomes my action level. Any signs of strength at this level should become a buying opportunity.

There are several ways to approach L3 for an entry. The ambush entry technique is an advanced entry method, but this technique shines in a well-behaved trend. Therefore, if you are going to dust off this entry type, now is the time to do it. You would place a Limit order entry to buy at L3 support and wait to be filled upon a test at this level. If you pass on this entry type, however, you can opt to wait for candlestick confirmation, which is the approach I took on this morning. The TF dropped into L3 in an expected manner and formed a bullish wick reversal setup at this level, essentially triggering my long entry at the open of the following bar. This entry confirmation also gave me my stop loss placement, as I was able to place my fixed loss stop below the low of the wick reversal candlestick. I now focus my efforts on the trade target, which is H3, H4, or a new high within the current bullish trend. I chose to go with H3, since the spread between L3 and H3 is a little wider than usual, which means price has a bit of distance to cover. Eventually, the H3 target was reached, which completed a nice gain of about 7 points on this trade, which amounts to roughly $700 per contract traded.

FIGURE 8.26: Buying the dip at 1.3 in a bullish trend.

It cannot be overstated how important pivot trend analysis can be to your trading. From time to time, the market can move in highly predictable waves. The pivots allow you to capitalize on this predictable behavior by offering you calculated value areas of support and resistance in your charts. The ability to program your brain to sniff out these opportunities will allow you to be a highly consistent trader for many years to come. Be aware, however, that the market only trends an average of 30 percent of the time, which means you must have the patience to wait for a confirmed trend in order play this type predictability in the market. The rest of the time is perfect for two-day pivot analysis, pivot width analysis, and golf.

THE CAMARILLA REVOLUTION

I have to admit, I was quite skeptical of the Camarilla pivots when they were first introduced to me. I had already been firmly entrenched into my own world of Floor Pivots and I wasn't going to let go of them easily. As a matter of fact, I had written off the Cams as a viable trading method after hastily reviewing them on a handful of charts. However, like many traders that are new to a concept, I did not have the proper understanding of these powerful levels. Fortunately, I gave the Cams another shot, and this time, the opportunities for profit became exceedingly clear. Concepts like two-day pivot relationships, pivot width analysis, and pivot trend analysis are the cornerstone to making big money with this indicator, and any pivot-related indicator. However, these concepts took me many years to discover and develop. As an old timer would say, *"I wish I knew then what I know now."*

Thankfully, I didn't have to dispense of my beloved Floor Pivots either. Instead, the combination of the two sets of pivots led to some of the most powerful discoveries that I've come across in trading. The inclusion of the Money Zone further amplifies these combinations, creating incredible multi-pivot discoveries, which I will share in Chapter 11. But first, let delve into Higher Timeframe Pivot Analysis.

CHAPTER 9

HIGHER TIMEFRAME PIVOT ANALYSIS

"The big money was not in the individual fluctuations but in the main movements—that is, not in the reading of the tape but in the sizing up the entire market and its trend."

- Jesse Livermore

I was a believer in the pivots for intraday use for quite some time before I discovered higher timeframe pivot analysis. It took me a while to warm up to the idea for the sheer fact that setups and price-to-pivot behavior take much longer to develop, thus observe, using daily or weekly bars. With intraday trading, however, I was able to quickly and easily observe the effectiveness of pivots and setup follow-through using anywhere from a one-to sixty-minute chart. Therefore, in a matter of minutes, or hours, I was able to gauge the effectiveness of the pivots in real-time trading. Conversely, higher timeframe pivots can take weeks, months, or even years, before you finally see the end result of a trade or setup. However, one chart and an amazing call changed my view on higher timeframe pivot analysis forever.

At the beginning of 2003, I made a bold call in my daily market commentary that the S&P 500 would return to the 1,000 level. If you recall, the market had been in a major three-year correction since topping out in the year 2000, but was beginning to find support at the end of 2002. The index traded lower in the first quarter of 2003, but found both visual and pivot support at about the 800 level, which happened to be the yearly L3 Camarilla support level. As you can see from the chart in Figure 9.1, three separate wick reversal signals fired long at this level, essentially confirming strength at this important pivot level. These elements helped me predict a major reversal in the market, as the S&P 500 rallied to 1,100 to finish the year.

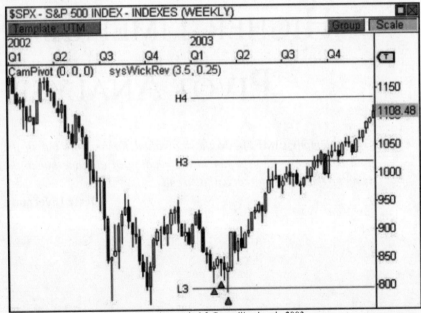

FIGURE 9.1: The S&P 500 reacts to the yearly L3 Camarilla pivot in 2003

Up to this point in my trading and analytical career, it had been quite easy to call bearish moves in the market, as my entire professional career coincided with the stock market bubble of 2000 after the roaring bull market of the 1990s. However, this particular juncture in the charts became my first major public bullish call on the market. There was a heavy confluence of visual and pivot support at the eight hundred level and it was my opinion that the market would rebound significantly, sparking a multi-year recovery. I actively structured the holdings in my 401k retirement account, as well as those of my family and friends, to reflect this long-term bullish outlook and it paid off dearly. Needless to say, I've gotten high-fives from family and friends ever since.

Without a doubt, higher timeframe pivots can be as explosive and reliable as their intraday counterparts. As a matter of fact, the majority of market participants will actually find higher timeframe pivots to be a better fit to their trading style, since this group comprises the majority of players in the market. Aside from the fact that most market participants are long term oriented, many may argue that higher timeframe pivot analysis is much more valuable due to the fact that the resulting moves are vastly larger, thus significantly more profitable. Therefore, instead of capturing multiple intraday moves a day, you could capture just one or two moves a month, or year, and come out far ahead of your intraday trading profits. This approach can add an interesting dimension to your trading regimen.

As you will soon discover, the same concepts that we have covered throughout the book will also apply to higher timeframe pivot analysis. Concepts like pivot trend analysis, pivot width analysis, and important pivot relationships all play a major role in this chapter. In fact, if you are a swing trader, position trader, or investor, you may find a lot more value in this chapter, as the information and the resulting moves will likely complement your trading style.

TYPES OF HIGHER TIMEFRAME PIVOTS

Up to this point in the book, we have been using a prior session's values to calculate the pivots for the upcoming session. However, with higher timeframe pivots, we use the values for a prior period of time to calculate the pivots for the next period of time. The three major types of higher timeframe pivots are yearly, monthly, and weekly pivots. To calculate the yearly pivots, you use the high, low, and close prices of the prior year in order to generate the levels for the upcoming year. For monthly pivots, you use the high, low, and close prices of the prior month in order to see the levels for the following month. Likewise, you would use the high, low, and close prices of the prior week in order to calculate the levels for the next week.

These types of higher timeframe pivots are important because they inspire different types of market participants to enter the market. Namely, weekly pivots inspire swing traders to buy or sell, monthly pivots offer a call to action to position traders, and the yearly pivots trigger investor participation. Understanding this paradigm will help you understand which groups of market participants are influencing price behavior, which allows you to gauge price conviction.

Let's take a closer look at the yearly pivots. Remember, to plot the yearly pivots, take the high, low, and close prices of the prior year and insert these values into the pivot formula. The outcome will be the pivots for the upcoming year. Therefore, taking the high, low, and close of 2008 gives you the pivots for all of 2009, as seen in the weekly chart of the continuous contract of the Mini-Sized Dow futures contract in Figure 9.2. Depending on the trading platform you use, however, the indicators for the Floor Pivots and the Camarilla Equation may not automatically calculate the yearly pivots for you. When I submitted the "spec sheet" for the creation of the pivots for the OmniTrader and VisualTrader platforms, I made sure to include the yearly pivots for these indicators. Therefore, when I flip to a weekly bar chart, the yearly pivots automatically appear when one of these indicators is plotted. Look no further than the weekly chart of the Mini-Sized Dow futures contract for proof that higher timeframe pivots are special.

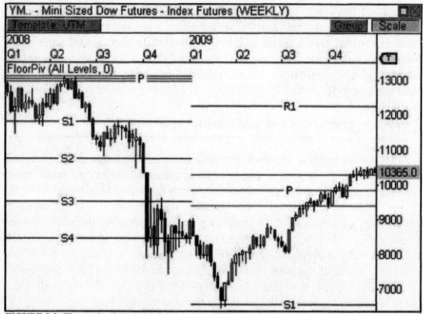

FIGURE 9.2: The yearly pivots helped make sense of 2008 and 2009 in the YM.

Figure 9.2 shows a two-year view of the continuous contract of the YM from 2008 to 2009. As you may recall, 2008 was a year that saw a major collapse in the financial markets. However, despite the chaotic nature of the market during this time, the Floor Pivots show the YM actually traded in a much more orderly manner than most people realize, as price played off these levels quite nicely. Even in a year that saw financial ruin, the pivots were one of the few tools that demonstrated a high level of accuracy.

Of course, the Dow continued to sell off in the first quarter of 2009, but found a major source of support at the yearly S1 pivot level. The Dow rallied sharply from S1 and pushed higher the rest of the year, culminating its move at the central pivot range. It seems the smart money was definitely using the pivots as a guide during this tumultuous time, as the Dow reacted to every pivot level in an orderly, and almost mechanical, manner. In fact, the yearly pivots helped me to identify where the Dow might be headed *much* earlier than the talking heads you are used to seeing on television. The accuracy of the Floor Pivots during this two-year period is simply incredible. Of course, the pivots aren't always this precise, but I'd much rather have them on my charts than without, which would be like driving your car at night without headlights.

The monthly pivots can be equally outstanding and can open the door to very nice profits for swing and position traders. These pivots are calculated in much the same fashion as the yearly pivots, but instead use the prior month's high, low, and close prices to plot the pivots for the upcoming month of trading. While the yearly pivots can inspire long- term traders and investors to enter the market en masse, the monthly pivot levels offer a call to action to position and swing traders, as the resulting moves range anywhere from a week to several months.

Let's take a look at an example. Figure 9.3 shows a two-month view of a daily chart of the Crude Oil futures contract. Two key moves were seen off the Floor Pivots in December, while an amazing reversal occurred off the Cams in January. Every major swing in this chart was a result of price reacting to a pivot in addition to important candlestick signal confirmation. Clearly, major players in the market are watching the pivots and putting money to work when price approaches theses key pivot levels. In this case, Crude Oil turned on a dime after dipping below $70 a barrel near S3 support, as responsive buyers stepped in to push price to higher value. Once price reached H3 resistance in January 2010, however, responsive sellers entered the market and pushed price back to the L4 support level. These were razor sharp reversals that were highly predictable in a commodity that is widely traded by speculators across the world.

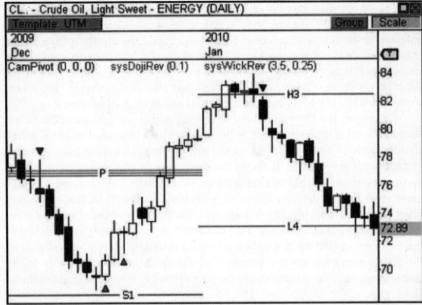

FIGURE 9.3: Crude Oil reacts to the monthly Floor and Camarilla pivots in consecutive months.

What continues to amaze me is the fact that all types of financial markets respond to the pivots, including stocks, commodities, and forex, regardless of the timeframe. This is no more apparent than in the recent Gold boom, where the precious metal experienced an unprecedented rally from $700 an ounce to over $1,200 an ounce by the end of 2009, partially shown in Figure 9.4. Gold found one last push late in 2009 and rallied to over $1,225 per ounce, but the advance stalled right at the monthly H3 pivot level. Price formed a bearish doji reversal pattern at the pivot, which helped to signal a major correction in the price of Gold over the following three weeks. Gold prices dropped back below the $1,100 mark, which was precisely L4 support. Isn't it amazing that price-to-pivot behavior with signal confirmation can help to identify major market reversals? The combination of the pivots and key signal confirmation at these levels never ceases to amaze me.

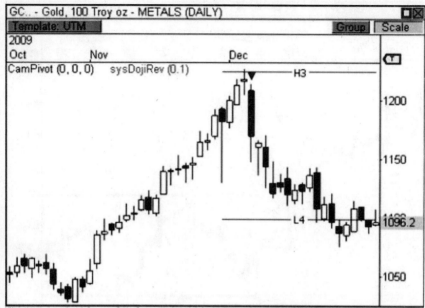

FIGURE 9.4: Gold futures falls from all-time highs in December 2009 after testing monthly H3

While investors and position traders pay attention to the yearly and monthly pivot levels, swing traders usually hone in to the weekly pivots. As you recall, weekly pivots are calculated by using the prior week's high, low, and close prices in order to forecast the pivots for the upcoming week of trading. Therefore, you would use the high, low, and close prices that occurred from Monday to Friday in order to forecast the pivots for the upcoming week, from Monday to Friday, as illustrated in sixty-minute chart of Devon Energy in Figure 9.5. The Camarilla pivots in this chart were derived from price activity that occurred from March 15 through March 19. Since DVN had a wide price range during this week of trading, the pivots for the following week were wider than normal and forecasted trading range behavior. Given the theory of trading range behavior, you will look for price reversals at key Camarilla pivot levels with candlestick confirmation. As it turns out, the wick reversal and extreme reversal setups helped identify key turning points in the charts at both L3 and H3, which offered perfect two- to three-day swing trading opportunities.

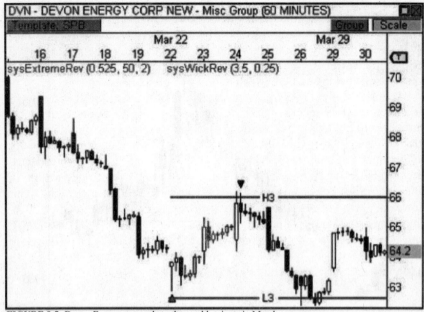

FIGURE 9.5: Devon Energy responds to the weekly pivots in March

As you may recall from Chapter 2, the higher the periodicity of the chart, the more meaningful the candlestick setup will be. Put another way, the longer it takes to form a candlestick setup, the more trader psychology went into creating that pattern, thereby creating more meaning in the market. Two hours of trader psychology went into creating the extreme reversal setup at the H3 pivot level. This setup alone in a sixty-minute chart is trader gold, as this pattern has been mechanically back and forward tested to be highly profitable. However, qualifying this signal with a test at a major pivot level within the right trend is almost unfair, as the results are typically phenomenal. Remember, the code for this setup is in Appendix B. The extreme reversal setup is like a sports car. I have given you the key to the Porsche, all you have to do is turn the key to the ignition and drive responsibly.

LONG-TERM PIVOT WIDTH FORECASTING

As I have illustrated throughout the book, forecasting price movement via pivot width can be a powerful practice. In fact, understanding when a market is likely to trade in a range or explode into a new trend gives you a huge advantage and can be the crystal ball that guides your trading for a typical day, month, or year. If the pivots are abnormally tight, the market has a higher tendency to break out and trend. Conversely, an unusually wide pivot range typically results in a sideways or trading range market. Each result carries with it a certain method for trading the market, so knowing what to expect at the earliest possible time becomes a major advantage.

Coincidentally, the pivot width concept helped me to forecast the 8,385 target for the Dow Jones Industrial Average, which I talked about in the Introduction. Let's take a closer look at the chart of the Dow in Figure 9.6 to analyze what I saw. This three-year view of the Dow displays the yearly pivot ranges for 2006 to 2008. The widths of the pivot ranges gave expected price behavior for each year, which allowed me to forecast price action. In 2006, the range is very tight, which ultimately forecasted a trending year. However, the pivot range for 2007 was noticeably wider than that of 2006. This range essentially helped to forecast a trading range market in 2007, which then led to a tight pivot range for 2008. The narrow pivot range in 2008 was the trigger that caused me to identify a breakout move for the index. However, I was uncertain on direction.

I remember alerting my readership that a move of over two thousand points could be seen in the Dow in the months ahead, but direction still eluded me. Of course, this forecast received a mixed reaction. On the one hand, many traders and investors were happy for the advanced notice. However, others were not so pleased, especially given the indecision about direction. I'm not fortune teller. I used pivot width analysis and basic technical analysis to forecast a calculated price move. However, only the market can decide direction. When the Dow broke below the 13,000 level to begin 2008, we had our direction. I forecasted a move to 10,000, and then readjusted my targets to 8,385 and 6,500 over the course of the following months, using the pivots as a guide. As you recall, the Dow reached the 8,385 level by the end of 2008, and then reached 6,500 early in 2009 after reaching the yearly S1 pivot level, which became the low of the eighteen-month bear market.

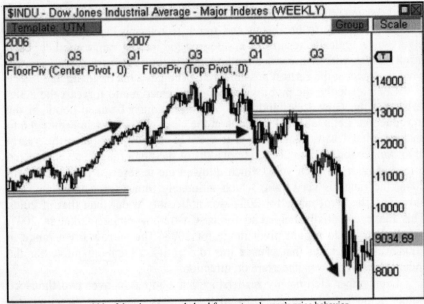

FIGURE 9.6: The width of the pivot ranges helped forecast each year's price behavior.

Forecasting price movement using pivot width analysis isn't something that just began to work recently. As a matter of fact, long-term pivot width analysis helped forecast the technology boom of the 1990s, as seen in the weekly chart of the NASDAQ Composite Index in Figure 9.7. The wide central pivot range in 1994 forecasted a sideways year for the index, which essentially came to fruition. However, the trading range behavior in 1994 paved the way for an extremely tight central pivot range for 1995. The narrow pivot range helped to forecast a powerful trending year for the index, as the NASDAQ ultimately rocketed to new all-time highs. Again, the consolidation of 1994 led to the breakout in 1995, both of which were anticipated through the width of the central pivot range.

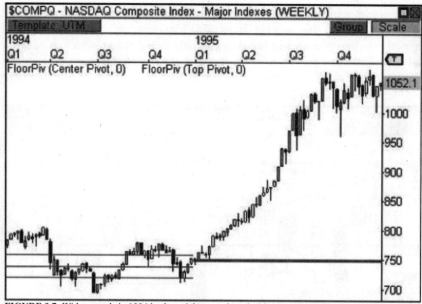

FIGURE 9.7: Wide centrals in 1994 leads to tight centrals and a big move in 1995.

The Money Zone levels also do a fantastic job at forecasting long term price behavior using pivot width analysis. As you may recall from Chapter 4, an abnormally wide or narrow value area gives you a great indication of potential price. Therefore, a wide value area typically indicates a trading range or sideways market, while a narrow value area is indicative of a breakout or trending market. When these relationships occur in a daily timeframe, you are typically able to forecast price behavior for an entire month of trading, which is perfect for investors and position traders eager to enter a market that is poised to move. The best part is the fact that this analysis can be done before the first bar of the new data set is even recorded.

Take a look at Figure 9.8, which shows a daily chart of Crude Oil futures with both the static and developing Money Zone levels plotted. The static Money Zone value area for the month of April is quite wide, which essentially forecasted a sideways trading month in this commodity. Getting advanced notice that a month may be a snoozer helps you prepare for this scenario by trading with tight stops and close profit targets, or by staying out of the market completely, which is sometimes the best course of action. However, since the market traded sideways throughout the month of April, the developing Money Zone indicator forecasted a narrow value area for the month of May, which means trending price behavior could be seen. Moreover, the two-month pivot relationship is an Overlapping Higher Value relationship, which points to a bullish breakout. The stage is now set for big price action, but the market must first demonstrate acceptance of this hypothesis by opening the following month above VAL, which is roughly $48.50. Furthermore, a violation through VAH and the top of the prior month's price range will need to be seen in order to confirm this opportunity.

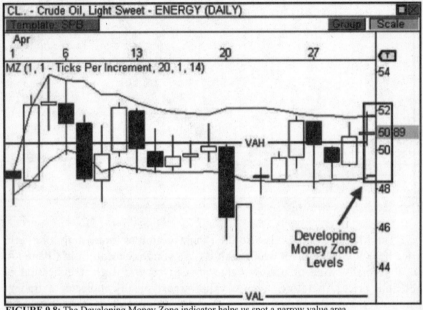

FIGURE 9.8: The Developing Money Zone indicator helps us spot a narrow value area.

Let's take a look at Figure 9.9 to see how price behavior played out. As it turns out, Crude Oil opened the month of May above VAL and proceeded to break through VAH and the prior month's high price en route to a major rally the rest of the month. The prior month's consolidation, coupled with the current month's narrow value area, helped forecast an amazing rally in Crude worth over $15 per barrel! Of course, doing your homework allowed you to forecast this major opportunity. This is a perfect example of planning your trade and trading your plan. Create a plan and then let the market prove or disprove your hypothesis. Approaching the market in this manner significantly increases your chances for success.

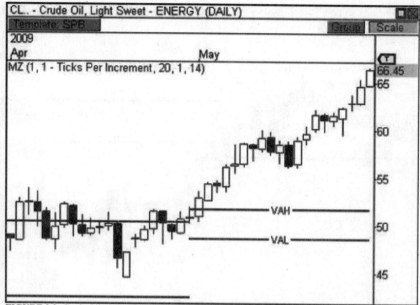

FIGURE 9.9: Crude Oil responds to both wide and narrow Money Zone levels.

A narrow Money Zone value area can be extremely powerful in and of itself. But this concept is improved when it coincides with an Inside Value relationship, as seen in Figure 9.10, which is a daily chart of the GBP/USD forex pair. The Money Zone value area for February 2010 was narrow and also developed within the prior month's value area, which is indicative of a major breakout opportunity. Add to this the fact that this relationship formed in the midst of a downtrend and you have the makings for a bearish breakout opportunity, which the market must now prove. If the market opens the month below VAH and breaks through VAL, a sizeable breakout opportunity could be seen. In this case, price actually opened the month below VAL, which confirmed bearish conviction. A pull-back to VAL or a violation through the prior month's low price can both trigger short entries in this scenario. Regardless of your entry technique, a major decline followed, which was easily forecasted by doing our homework and allowing the market to dictate acceptance or rejection of our hypothesis.

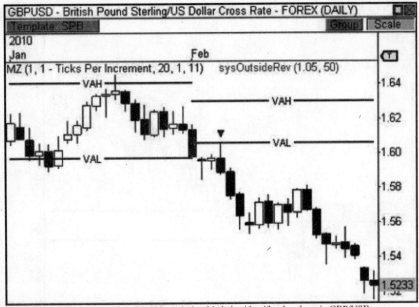

FIGURE 9.10: A two-month Inside Value relationship helps identify a breakout in GBP/USD

As you are now aware, narrow pivots and trending markets usually pave the way for wide pivots and trading range markets. It is extremely important to formulate an opinion on potential price behavior based on this analysis. Knowing that trending behavior will likely lead to trading range price activity allows you to prepare properly for this type of trading environment using the right tools and approach. Having a plan of action gives you a blueprint to trading the market.

Take a look at Figure 9.11, which shows a daily chart of First Solar, Inc. Notice that price trended higher throughout the month of September 2009, which led to a wide third layer of the Camarilla pivots. Given the wide range of price movement in September and the unusually wide nature of the third layer of the pivots forecasted trading range behavior for October, which turned out to be the case. As you recall from Chapter 8, the Camarilla pivots offer perhaps the best method for trading a range market, as the hidden layers of the indicator prove to be extremely useful. Furthermore, drilling down into an intraday timeframe and playing the moves based off the monthly pivot levels gives swing traders a lot of firepower during this type of trading range market.

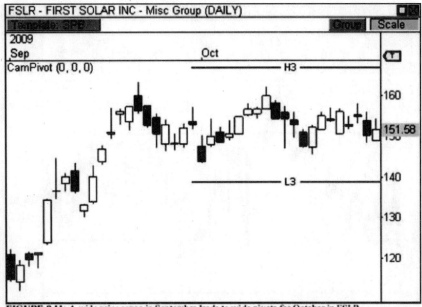

FIGURE 9.11: A wide price range in September leads to wide pivots for October in FSLR.

Figure 9.12 shows a sixty-minute chart of First Solar, Inc. during the month of October. Since the wide nature of the third layer of the Cams indicated trading range behavior during this month, the hidden layers of the indicator have been exposed. Notice that every significant reversal during this month occurred off the hidden layers of the indicator. While H2 and L2 each signaled key reversal points in the chart, H1 and L1 got the bulk of the action. These levels easily helped to forecast two- to three-day moves in the market, which is perfect for swing traders.

This chart also demonstrates an important concept: higher timeframe pivots can be played in all timeframes, not just the originating timeframe. Therefore, yearly pivots can be played in all timeframes from intraday to weekly, while monthly pivots can be used in intraday and daily charts. This concept allows you to drill down and find extremely precise entry points when playing the pivots.

FIGURE 9.12: Dropping down in time frame to play the monthly pivots

Long Term Pivot Trend Analysis

Investors and position traders will find that long-term pivot trend analysis offers amazing opportunities to profit during trending markets, whether you are using Floor Pivots, the Money Zone, or the Camarilla Equation. In an established trend, the pivots act as a police barricade that keeps the crowd moving in a desired direction. That is, once an established trend has formed, the pivots act as support in an uptrend, and resistance in a downtrend, offering excellent opportunities to buy the dips and sell the rips. The pivots help you pinpoint precise pull-back entry zones during these trends, allowing you to enter the market when the smart money does. Important pivot relationships, like Higher Value, Overlapping Higher Value, Lower Value, and Overlapping Lower Value relationships play a huge role in this section.

Let's jump into a few charts to see long-term pivot analysis at work using the various forms of pivots that I've covered. Figure 9.13 shows a daily chart of Cliffs Natural Resources (ticker: CLF) with pivot ranges plotted for each month. The stock formed an established uptrend for the greater part of three months; highlighting two great pull-back opportunities. Notice the narrow pivot range for the month of April helped forecast trending price behavior during this month, which kicked off the bullish uptrend. Once the market established the initial leg of the trend, Higher Value relationships helped you identify pull-back opportunities in each of the two months that followed.

The key to playing these pull-backs lies in price acceptance. If price closes the prior month above the pivot range for the following month, continued trending behavior is likely to occur. However, the opening price for the next month must accept this theory by opening anywhere above the bottom of the pivot range. When these two criteria are met, any pull-back to the pivot range should be seen as a buying opportunity. In this case, CLF closed both April and May above the following month's pivot range, indicating further overall strength. Moreover, price opened both May and June above the pivot ranges for the month, which creates solid buying opportunities at the pivot range when tested. Once price sees a successful bounce off the pivot range, a push to new highs is likely to occur, as was the case in this instance.

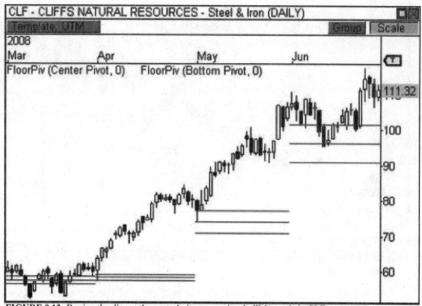

FIGURE 9.13: Buying the dips at the central pivot range in a bullish trends in CLF

In the summer of 2008, Crude Oil made an incredible run to nearly $150 per barrel, which is currently the all-time high for this commodity. Figure 9.14 shows a five-month view of Crude Oil during part of this magnificent run. Crude Oil had already doubled from $50 to $100 per barrel in the prior year, so traders obviously knew the commodity was in the midst of an extremely bullish trend. It takes just seconds to notice a clear pattern of price behavior when the central pivot range is plotted. Notice that throughout the uptrend during this period of time (May, June, and July) traders bought every pull-back to the central pivot range in anticipation of a move to new highs. Furthermore, the Higher Value relationships month over month helped identify the strength of the trend, while providing excellent entry points during the advance.

This, my friends, is "buying the dips" at its best. Every major player in the market knew Crude Oil was headed higher, so once new highs were reached, traders would take profits and wait for a dip to occur so they could re-enter long positions. Once price pulled back to the pivot range, traders pounced at another opportunity to ride the bull to the bank.

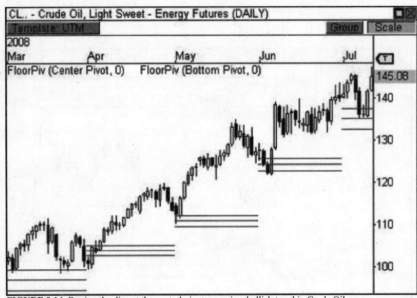

FIGURE 9.14: Buying the dips at the central pivot range in a bullish trend in Crude Oil

As a matter of fact, a mechanical system I created for a managed futures fund fired a long signal at the central pivot range at about $136 per barrel in July. This signal put us in the move to all-time highs in this commodity and gave us a handsome profit in return. Of course, soon after Crude Oil reached all-time highs during the historic rally, it experienced an epic collapse, as the price of Crude dropped from nearly $150 per barrel to under $40 in just six months. Figure 9.15 shows this decline in Crude Oil with the Money Zone levels plotted for each month. Notice that during the free fall, price remained below the top of the Money Zone throughout the sell-off. Moreover, each pull-back to the Money Zone levels offered excellent selling opportunities within the bearish decline. The Point of Control and VAL offered excellent levels to short the market during this time, further illustrating the power of long-term pivot trend analysis.

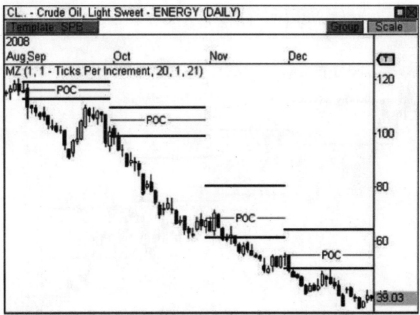

FIGURE 9.15: After Cruds hit all-time high's traders begin to sell the rips using the MZ levels.

Keep in mind that I am not claiming that all traders are watching the pivots for a pull-back to enter positions at optimum levels. There are tens of thousands of traders, which means there are tens of thousands of methods for trading the market. Each trader has his own recipe for deciphering when to pull the trigger on a pull-back opportunity. However, the pivots illuminate these action zones more clearly than any other tool I have come across. Knowing the location of the pivots on your charts certainly puts you ahead of the pack when choosing precise entries during a trending market.

The Camarilla pivots also offer excellent opportunities for pinpointing precise entry points during a trending market. As a matter of fact, using these color-coded pivots to identify pull-back opportunities makes the process fairly easy and straight forward. Take a look at Figure 9.16, which shows a daily chart of Natural Gas futures during a bearish trend. Every pull-back to the monthly H3 pivot level was seen as a prime selling opportunity during this four-month decline. As long as price opens the month below H3, any pull-back to this zone should be a sold, with expectations of price reaching a new low within the trend, which was certainly the case in this scenario. While it didn't happen during this particular trend, if price were to open the month *below* the monthly L3 pivot level, then a pull-back to L3 becomes a selling opportunity.

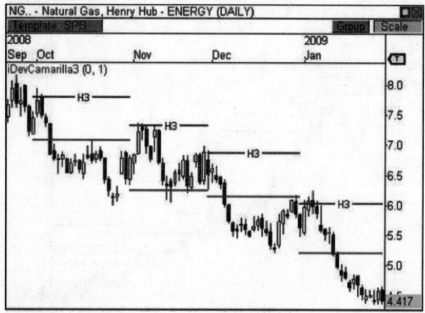

FIGURE 9.16: Selling the rips at H3 in a bearish trend in Natural Gas

As I mentioned earlier, there are many ways to capitalize on identifying pull-back entry points during a trending market. The Volume at Price indicator offers another method for pinpointing these highly profitable opportunities. As a matter of fact, this indicator gives a more visual approach to buying and selling during a trend, since you physically are able to see the price points at which the market is putting money to work.

Figure 9.17 shows a daily chart of Whirlpool Corporation during a bullish advance in the middle of 2009. It is important to note that the two-month Unchanged Value relationship in the Volume Point of Control for May and June provided the initial breakout opportunity that sparked the bullish trend in this stock. After this relationship kicked off the bullish trend, every pull-back to the VPOC provided a buying opportunity. The VPOC visually displays where the majority of market participants have put money to work. Therefore, when price returns to the high volume clusters, responsive buyers enter the market to push price higher. This type of market dynamic allows this indicator to flourish during trending markets.

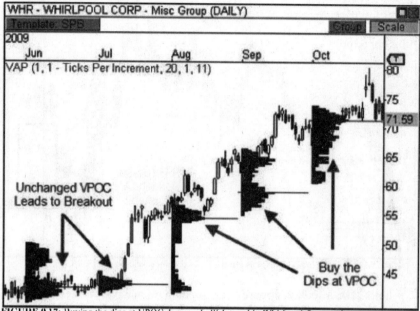

FIGURE 9.17: Buying the dips at VPOC during a bullish trend in Whirlpool Corporation

Remember, the suite of developing pivot indicators that I have introduced in prior chapters allow you to easily anticipate market behavior and plan your trades accordingly. Let's take a look at this process in more detail. Figure 9.18 shows a daily chart of the EUR/USD forex pair with the Developing Pivot Range indicator plotted. This particular cross rate had been trending higher in a predictable manner, but the trend was severely violated in December 2009. As a matter of fact, the developing indicator showed a highly bearish Lower Value relationship for the following month, January 2010, which helped us visualize a plan of action. Given the bearish two-month relationship, it's easy to see that any pull-back to the central pivot range between 1.444 and 1.468 should be seen as a selling opportunity, especially if the right signal confirmation is present. We now have a plan of action, but the market must prove our theory by opening anywhere below the top of the pivot range. If this occurs, market participants will be ready to pounce with sell orders.

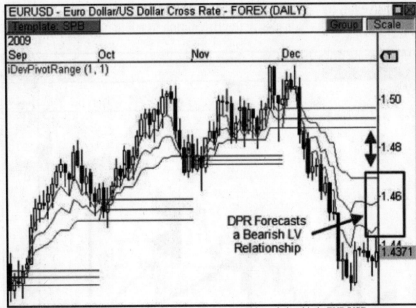

FIGURE 9.18: The DPR indicator helps us identify a Lower Value relationship in EUR/USD.

Let's take a look at Figure 9.19 to see how our plan turned out. Price opened the month of January below the pivot range and pushed cautiously higher into the range until meeting resistance at the central pivot point. Price stalled at this monthly pivot and eventually formed a bearish doji reversal signal, which helped to identify selling pressure in this pair. The Euro then dropped sharply versus the U.S. Dollar and pushed steadily lower the rest of the month, thereby proving our initial plan of action. This is the type of pre-trade analysis that creates wealth in the markets. By identifying major points of interest for the following month using the developing indicator, we were able to create a plan of action for the following month, which proved to be highly profitable. Plan the trade; trade the plan.

FIGURE 9.18: A pull-back to the pivot range proved to be a nice selling point in EUR/USD.

TRADING THE BIG PICTURE

Higher timeframe pivot analysis offers extremely powerful methods for trading longer-term opportunities. The pivot concepts that we have covered span across timeframes, allowing various types of traders to benefit from these highly profitable opportunities. However, concepts like pivot trend analysis, pivot width analysis, and pivot relationships offer much more bang for the buck for long-term traders, as the money made during these opportunities far exceeds typical intraday trading profits. Moreover, planning your trades using the developing suite of indicators creates a sweet recipe for success.

Traders wanting to utilize these concepts simultaneously in both real-time and end-of-day trading can add an interesting dimension to their trading approach. The ability to profit from long-term positions, while benefiting from intraday swings, provides additional income and relieves the day-to-day pressures of intraday trading. Knowing that you have a profitable swing or position trade in your hip pocket can do wonders for your intraday approach, as you are afforded the opportunity to hunker down and cherry pick the best intraday trading opportunities.

CHAPTER 10

MULTIPLE PIVOT
HOT ZONES

"It is good business to take chances when the possible profit is big enough."

- Jesse Livermore

Multiple pivot confirmation is one of the amazing trading secrets that I would not have discovered was it not for automated pivot plotting. It was already too much work to hand plot every single pivot from just one indicator day after day, let alone plotting those from a second or third indicator as well. However, once trading platforms began to automate the process of plotting the Floor Pivots and the Camarilla Equation, a whole new road map began to reveal itself. Add to these the Money Zone suite of indicators, and you have the makings for quite an explosive fireworks show.

I mentioned in the Introduction that individually, the Floor Pivots, the Camarilla Equation, and the Money Zone are like a road map for your charts. However, when you combine these amazing pivots, the road map can be exponentially more precise, akin to how a GPS system is far superior to a paper map. Multiple pivot pairings, like Double Pivot Zones, Golden Pivot Zones, and Multiple Timeframe Hot Zones, illuminate the market in a manner that many traders never thought possible. When used correctly, these multiple streams of pivots can take your trading to the next level.

THE POWER OF CONFLUENCE

The power of confluence can be quite amazing when used in a proper manner, which is why this method of confirmation remains a key part of my trading regimen. *Confluence* occurs when two or more uncorrelated indicators identify the same level, or levels, as key areas of interest. I also call these levels *hot zones*. The key is to use indicators that are not correlated in the way they are calculated. That is, you want to avoid confirming with three types of oscillators, as each is basically calculated in the same way, thus giving you a false sense of confirmation. Instead, separate indicators using completely different formulas should be used to confirm key levels of interest.

When a confluence of pivot levels from different equations are pointing to the same level on the chart, more traders are going to participate in the move when the level is tested. This creates key activity at certain levels that can lead to major moves in the market. For example, let's say that one group of traders using the Floor Pivots has identified a certain support level as a key area of interest. Two other groups of traders have also identified the same level as support, but by using completely different methods; one using the Camarilla Equation, and the other the Money Zone. Eventually, when this level is tested, all three groups of traders are going to respond to this level, thus creating an amazing level of participation that sparks a responsive buying rally.

Any key area of interest can be considered a hot zone, as long as two or more pivots identify the same level. Notice I used the word "pivots" instead of the word "indicators," as the same indicator can identify a hot zone by using multiple timeframe confirmation, which we will discuss later in the chapter. A hot zone can be created by any combination of indicators, pivots, and timeframes, so long as the indicators are not correlated. Therefore, a hot zone can be comprised of S1 support, L3 support, and the volume point of control. Or, the point of control can be matched with the central pivot range to provide a powerful zone of support or resistance, depending on the current trend. Throughout the chapter, I will discuss the major pairings of indicators and levels that create amazing hot zones in your charts. But keep in mind that the process is free flowing and fun, rather than rigid and stressful.

Also, not only are multi-pivot setups phenomenally accurate at times, but recognizing these action zones early in a trading day will allow you to anticipate bigger money-making opportunities. The best traders in the world, and those of prior generations, knew when to "double-down" when the stars aligned. Upping the ante when you have a straight flush is the way to prosper in this game. It's not the quantity of trades, but the quality of the setups and the amount of money you're laying on the line when the stars finally do align. The multiple pivot hot zones ahead, combined with key signals, are the types of setups that can command a bigger bet.

DOUBLE PIVOT HOT ZONES

One of the basic multi-pivot pairings is what I call the Double Pivot Hot Zone. A *Double Pivot Hot Zone (DPZ)* is any support or resistance level that develops when two pivots align to highlight a level as significant. A DPZ can consist of any combination of indicators or timeframes that identifies a level, or zone, as significant. Therefore, the market may see resistance in an area that consists of the R2 and H4 levels. Or, R2 may be paired with a virgin POC from three days ago, which could provide a nice reversal zone as well. If you think about it for a moment, when two completely different mathematical formulas are recognizing the same level as support or resistance, the chances of a reaction at the level will likely increase than if there were no confluence at all. When this occurs, you typically see the market react to these levels in a very obvious manner. That is, these dual pivot zones are strong enough to influence the market time and again, which leads to easily telegraphed reversal opportunities.

Take a look at Figure 10.1, which illustrates a typical double pivot hot zone. Notice that any two pivots can create a hot zone, whether from different indicators or the same indicator using different timeframes. To be clear, both pivots creating the hot zone *do not* have to identify the exact numerical level. Rather, the pivots just have to be close enough that they are in the same vicinity, although sometimes the lines do sit right on top of one another. Lastly, while a double pivot hot zone may indicate a major area of confluence, you still want to see confirmation at this level via one of your candlestick setups, which essentially trigger your entry. In the example, the outside reversal setup triggers the bounces at both extremes. However, the wick, extreme, and doji reversal setups can also trigger entries as well.

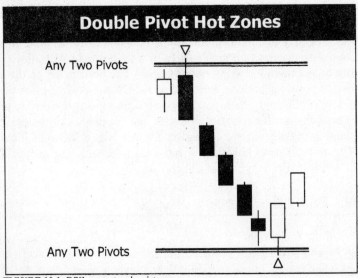

FIGURE 10.1: DPZ support and resistance

Let's take a look at an example. Figure 10.2 is a fascinating chart of Crude Oil futures because it combines visual support with a double pivot hot zone, which consists of S2 and L4. I'm a big fan of visual and pivot confluence, as this tandem allows more market participants to enter the fray. I know it's tough to believe, but not everyone knows about the pivots. Some market participants will trade based off these levels, while others will use classical forms of technical analysis, like support and resistance. More market participants will enter the market at a level when these two powerful forms of confirmation line up.

Looking at the chart, there is clear double pivot support at about $81.15, but the market has also found three-day visual support at about $81. This means that another realm of technical traders will be finding value at or around the $81 level. When the streams of confluence point to a level this precisely, in addition to the highly bullish extreme reversal signal, major market participation is usually the result. In this case, Crude Oil rallied over two points from the $81 level to $83 per barrel—a gain of $2000 per contract traded.

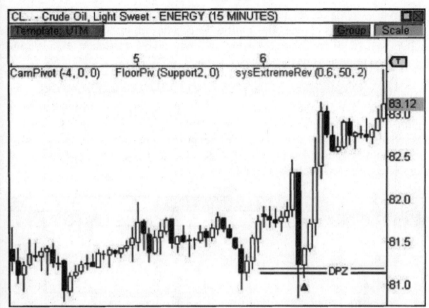

FIGURE 10.2: DPZ support coupled with an extreme reversal signal leads to a rally in Crude

An interesting note about the chart above is the fact that the two pivots are spaced a few cents apart, illustrating a great example of how the pivots *do not* have to be perfectly aligned to signify a great area of support or resistance. Actually, I've never seen support or resistance as a perfect line in a chart, although they can be at times. I've always seen support and resistance as "price zones" to which the market reacts.

When I notice there is strong double pivot support or resistance, I usually check the direction of the overriding trend. As I discussed in prior chapters, the trend can be a major ally when playing the pivots. Any pull-back within an established trend should be seen as a buying or selling opportunity once a hot zone is reached, as responsive market participation is likely to occur.

Take a look at Figure 10.3, which is a fifteen-minute chart of the E-Mini S&P 400 futures contract. The contract had been trending lower over the prior week of trading, making every pull-back a selling opportunity. The contract rallied early in the day on January 29, 2010, but ran into double pivot resistance at the 719 level, where both R1 and H4 resistance identified this area as a hot zone. As you recall, any pull-back during a downtrend gives sellers the advantage above value, as responsive market participants are likely to push price back toward value. Add to this the fact that price formed a bearish extreme reversal setup at the double pivot hot zone, and you have a recipe for success. Given the multitude of confirming factors, responsive sellers easily overwhelmed buyers at dual pivot resistance at 719 and proceeded to push price back toward value.

As always, you can play the move to a prior support level, which is usually a safe bet. However, the fact that this setup occurred in the midst of a highly bearish trend indicated that new lows would likely be reached at some point over the next few hours, or maybe even the next session. Given this knowledge, you can also use a trailing profit stop that trails price with a comfortable cushion. Eventually, the MC closed the day near the lows of the session at 698.7, completing a move of 17.4 points!

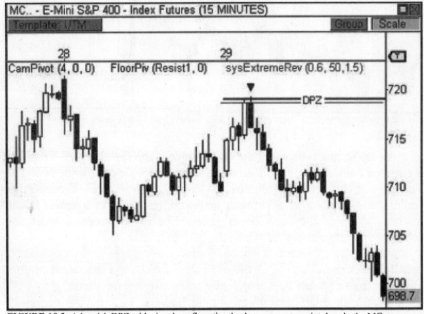

FIGURE 10.3: A bearish DPZ with signal confirmation leads to a twenty-point drop in the MC.

Again, several confirming factors contributed to the successful outcome of this setup. First, the market formed an established trend over the prior week of trading, which should immediately set your focus to selling every qualified pull-back opportunity. Secondly, the morning advance was halted once the double pivot hot zone was reached at 719, indicating that responsive market participants were likely to enter the market at this point. Moreover, the extreme reversal setup confirmed weakness at the session's highs, which ultimately confirmed a potential entry. One more note: price reversed at dual pivot resistance after the first hour of trading locked in the day's initial balance, which left the door open to a potential reversal back toward the initial balance low. Remember, markets will typically reverse at the extremes of the day's initial balance on most sessions, until initiative buyers or sellers overwhelm one of the extremes in order to extend the day's range.

BOSS IN ACTION

One of my favorite DPZ setups occurs when the market opens the day beyond the prior day's range and value, which sets the stage for a major breakout opportunity and a Trend Day scenario. As you may recall from earlier chapters, I use many different tools to help me anticipate when a breakout of this caliber may occur, including pivot width and two-day relationships. The ability to anticipate this pattern will give you the best chance at capturing the biggest moves of the month.

When price opens the day beyond the prior day's range and value, I also want to know if price gapped beyond a double pivot hot zone. If price does indeed open beyond the DPZ, I will watch for a test of this hot zone for signs of a continuation or failure. If price gets a successful test of the hot zone, I will enter the trade with the intention of riding the move as long as I can, which usually means holding the position to the close of the market.

Take a look at Figure 10.4, which is a fifteen-minute chart of the E-Mini S&P 400 futures contract. The MC opened the day with a bullish gap beyond the prior day's range and value, which occurred after two days of sideways movement. When I noticed that the gap also occurred beyond a DPZ, I allowed the first fifteen-minute bar of the day to play out to see if a successful test would occur. Typically, I like to see price test the hot zone and then reverse to close back near high of the bar, which was the case in this instance. A bullish wick reversal signal fired after the test at the hot zone, which was the confirmation that I needed to trigger my long entry at 762.80. I set my fixed loss stop below the day's low and set up a basic 1.5 ATR cushion on my trailing profit stop, which kept me in the trade throughout the session. My trade was automatically liquidated fifteen minutes before the close of the market at 769.60, which gave me a gain of 6.8 points, or $680 per contract traded.

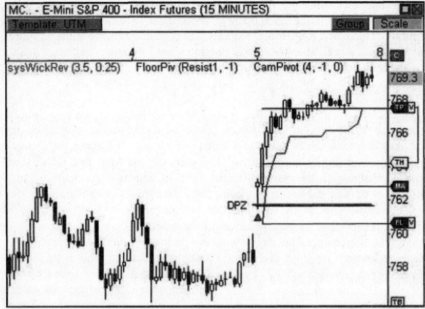

FIGURE 10.4: A breakout beyond range and value is confirmed by a DPZ

THE GOLDEN PIVOT ZONE

In Chapter 6, I wrote about the power and versatility of the central pivot range. This range has a significant influence that both attracts and rejects price in a manner than no other technical tool offers. However, by combining the central pivot range with a pivot level from either the Camarilla Equation or the Money Zone, you can actually amplify its effectiveness in the market. This pivot combination, which I call the *Golden Pivot Zone (GPZ)*, is the most fascinating and powerful pivot combination in trading. It combines the versatility and strength of the centrals, with the precision of the Camarilla Equation and the Money Zone. Basically, the Golden Pivot Zone occurs when *one* of the pivot levels from either the Camarilla Equation or the Money Zone lies within the central pivot range (TC >= MZ/CE <= BC). Therefore, the Camarilla or Money Zone level is either equal to or below the top central pivot (TC) *and* equal to or above the bottom central pivot (BC). When this pattern occurs, oceans are parted and angels sing as you trade. This combination can be simply phenomenal.

What makes this pattern so powerful is the fact that the central pivot range, which in itself is a fantastic tool, is paired with key support or resistance from other price-based indicators that are completely uncorrelated.

Again, two completely different formulas are identifying this zone as a significant area of support or resistance. Instead of just one pivot level identifying support or resistance, you are basically getting a confluence of four lines that identify an entire zone as a key area of significance. When used within the proper context the Golden Pivot Zone can be a game-changer in your trading.

Look at it like this. If you had the football in your hands, would it be harder to break through the line of defense of just one tackler, or that of four defenders? One defender would represent one pivot level, while four would represent the entire Golden Pivot Zone. Trust me, unless you are Earl Campbell, you will be quickly smacked down by four defenders, which is why the GPZ easily rejects moves into the zone and creates great reversal opportunities time and again.

Figure 10.5 illustrates a bearish Golden Pivot Zone. A bearish GPZ occurs when H3 of the Camarilla Equation, or any of the Money Zone levels, is mixed within the central pivot range. Therefore, a GPZ is present if any of the following pivots falls within the boundaries of the central pivot range: H3, VAL, VAH, POC, or VPOC. Any bullish advance that fails at the GPZ typically leads to a drop back toward the next area of pivot support, which is generally S1 or L3.

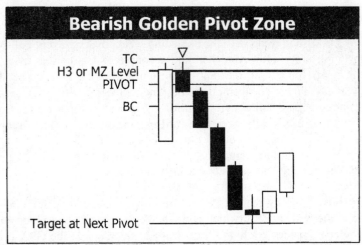

FIGURE 10.5: Bearish Golden Pivot Zone

Along the same lines, Figure 10.6 illustrates a bullish Golden Pivot Zone. A bullish GPZ occurs when L3 of the Camarilla Equation, or any of the Money Zone levels, is mixed within the central pivot range. Therefore, a GPZ is present if any of the following pivots falls within the boundaries of the central pivot range: L3, VAL, VAH, POC, or VPOC. A sell-off or pull-back to a bullish GPZ generally leads to an advance back toward the next area of pivot resistance, which is usually R1 or H3.

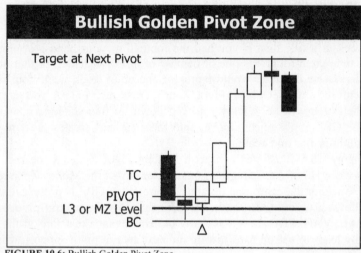

FIGURE 10.6: Bullish Golden Pivot Zone

Take a look at Figure 10.7, which is a fifteen-minute chart of the E-Mini S&P 400 futures contract on February 19, 2010. The MC had been in the midst of a bullish uptrend over the preceding week, making every pull-back a buying opportunity. However, there are a couple of factors that must be in place in order for a "buy the dip" opportunity to exist. First, price should open the day above the central pivot range. Second, the prior session's closing price should fall above the prior day's central pivot range. Both of these criteria are basically geared toward measuring the current strength of the market, while forcing you to remain in tune with the market's current trend. If both of these factors pass the test, the market is likely primed for another "buy the dip" opportunity (reverse for shorts).

Since the MC opened the day above the central pivot range, while closing above the prior day's CPR, we are in good shape to try for a potential bounce at the bullish GPZ, which consists of the central pivot range and the Money Zone's value area high. Price dropped sharply into the GPZ to begin the session, but immediately formed a bullish extreme reversal setup, along with a bullish doji reversal setup. The bullish candlestick setups are the last line of confirmation that essentially tip the tables of probability in your favor, as the MC rallied from about 733 to the 740 level, which happened to be H4 for the day.

While this trade looks simple from the outside looking in, there were many layers of confirmation that allowed this trade to become successful. The established trend, the day's open price, the prior day's close price, the bullish Golden Pivot Zone, and the two candlestick setups all contributed to a high probability trade and a successful outcome.

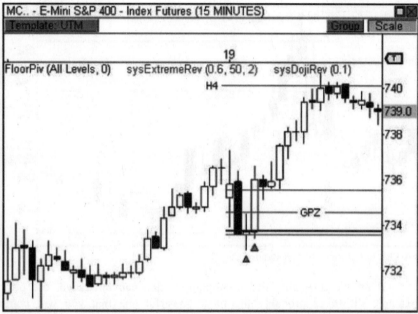

FIGURE 10.7: A bullish reversal at a Golden Pivot Zone in the MC

Let's take a look at an example where the GPZ acts as a major source of resistance. Figure 10.8 shows a five-minute chart of the E-Mini Russell 2000 futures contract on March 6, 2009. The contract had been trending steadily lower over the prior two weeks of trading, making every pull-back a selling opportunity. The TF opened the day with early strength, but immediately found resistance at a bearish GPZ, consisting of the central pivot range and the H3 Cam level. Again, the major candlestick combination that formed at the GPZ was the extreme reversal setup, which is my favorite pattern. As you recall from Chapter 2, this pattern excels when it forms in an established trend. Therefore, the fact that it fired a short signal in a downtrend at a bearish Golden Pivot Zone is very significant. The confirmed short opportunity occurred at about $356, as responsive sellers proceeded to push price back toward perceived value. The TF eventually halted the morning decline right at S1 support for a move of over ten points, which is easily $1000 per contract traded.

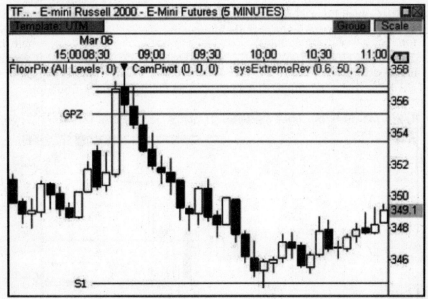

FIGURE 10.8: A bearish GPZ rejects price in the TF

Of all the different GPZ combinations that can be traded, the prior example illustrates probably the most powerful one that you will come across. As you may recall from Chapters 7 and 8, the H3 and L3 Camarilla levels are not just pivots; they are color-coded action levels. That is, when price approaches the H3 pivot level, traders following the Camarilla method are typically looking to sell that level. Therefore, when H3 is mixed within the central pivot range, the GPZ contains more inherent resistance. Likewise, when price approaches L3, traders following the Camarilla method are looking to buy at this level, thereby giving a bullish GPZ with this combination a stronger area of support.

The H3 and L3 combinations are the original Golden Pivot Zones, as these were the first that I discovered to be truly powerful. As I progressed with my research, I also found various other pivots that work fantastically as well, thus the addition of the Money Zone levels to the Golden Pivot family.

Let's take a look at a forex example. Figure 10.9 shows a sixty-minute chart of the USD/GBP forex pair on February 18, 2010. The pair opened the day with early strength at the bullish GPZ, which contained the volume point of control within the central pivot range. However, nothing actionable came of this bounce. Price later returned to the GPZ for another test, however, which turned out to be a great opportunity to buy the Dollar versus the Pound. Notice that price dropped sharply into the GPZ, forming a bullish extreme reversal pattern. Price pushed steadily higher from this zone, confirming the advance with a bullish doji reversal setup as well. Since the forex pair found strength at the GPZ after the prior day's advance, a bullish "buy the dip" opportunity easily presented itself for a gain of nearly one hundred pips. Of course, the bounce off the GPZ was a success since we were able to put the move in context, complete with signal confirmation.

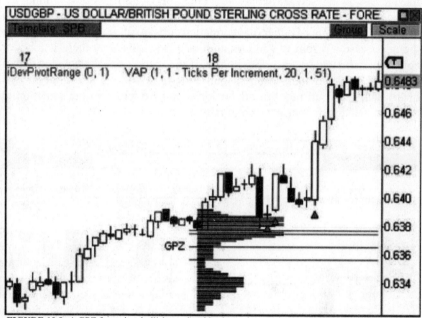

FIGURE 10.9: A GPZ forms in a bullish trend and leads to a bounce in USD/GBP.

BOSS IN ACTION

Since it is my strong belief that the Golden Pivot Zone is a confluence powerhouse, I have set up my trading platform (OmniTrader Professional) to filter through my focus list of stocks and futures automatically to find this relationship in real time. It's a basic scan with a few simple lines of code that looks for the general GPZ criteria that we have covered in this chapter (i.e., TC >= POC >= BC) and automatically assigns each symbol in my list a True or False grade depending on whether the criteria has been met on that particular day. It goes without saying that the symbols that are found by the scan get my immediate attention to begin the day.

However, if you do your homework on the key symbols that you trade the night before, you will have advanced notice that an important pivot setup will form in the upcoming session. Using the developing suite of indicators that we have covered throughout the book, you can see all of the important pivot relationships that I have discussed, from two-day relationships, pivot width relationships, and even multiple pivot hot zones.

Take a look at Figure 10.10, which is a fifteen-minute chart of the E-Mini Russell 2000 futures contract. The Developing Pivot Range and Developing Point of Control indicators reveal a bullish Golden Pivot Zone for the following day, whereby the Point of Control will be within the boundaries of the central pivot range. Also, the pivot range has developed a two-day Overlapping Higher Value relationship, which indicates strength for the next session. From this information, we can gather that there is a heavy confluence of support from 595 to 597. If the market opens above or within this range, we will look to buy a pull-back to this hot zone. If the market opens below 595 all bets are off for longs and we will turn our attention to the short side given the right opportunity.

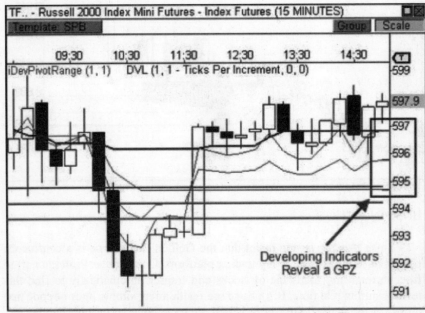

FIGURE 10.10: The developing indicators reveal a GPZ for the next session in the TF.

If we fast forward to the next day, you see that price opened the session with a gap above the day's GPZ, which set up nicely for a bullish play (Figure 10.11). The TF actually performed a beautiful Magnet Trade prior to the test at the bullish GPZ, but I had my sights set on the bounce play. After filling the morning gap, the TF cautiously tested the Golden Pivot Zone at around 596, forming a highly bullish wick reversal setup, which triggered my entry at 598. After the entry, I used a 1.5 ATR trailing profit stop in anticipation of a push to two-week resistance at 606.50, which also corresponded with the H5 Cam level. Ultimately, my trade session boundary stop automatically liquidated my trade just before the close of the market at 605.90, completing a 7.9-point trade worth $790 per contract traded.

FIGURE 10.11: E-Mini Russell 2000 responds to a bullish GPZ

Preparedness led to the successful outcome of this trade. Form an opinion about the upcoming day by doing your homework before the market opens. Without an opinion, or theory, how will you anticipate market behavior? The pivots give you leading information to help you develop your plans before the first tick of the market is recorded. With the use of developing pivot indicators, you can see all of the major relationships that we have covered in this book. These tools and techniques have been vital to my success in trading and price forecasting. It is my firm belief that they can help you achieve another level of trading success as well.

MULTIPLE TIMEFRAME HOT ZONES

Up to this point, I have demonstrated how to combine the Floor Pivots, Camarilla Equation, and the Money Zone to create powerful areas of confluence in your charts. However, by adding higher timeframe pivots to these areas of confluence, you can actually create a more powerful band of support or resistance. These levels, which I call *Multiple Timeframe Hot Zones (MTZ)*, add another dimension of significance to these amazing areas of confluence.

As you may recall from Chapter 10, Higher Timeframe Pivot Analysis, pivot levels from higher timeframes can pack a major punch. In fact, the reactions from these pivots typically lead to bigger moves in the market, mainly because the moves occur over the course of several days, or even weeks. The reason these combinations of pivots work so powerfully is because each level inspires a certain type of trader. There are four main categories of traders when it comes to classifying them alongside the pivots, seen in Table 11.1. When these traders converge to trade the same zones due to high confluence areas, the results can be quite amazing. For example, if a certain price level or range contains a high confluence of pivots, you will see participation from several types of traders, which puts more force behind the move. More participation typically sparks larger and more impressive moves in the market.

The Four Types of Market Participants	
Investors	Yearly Pivots
Position Trader	Monthly Pivots
Swing Trader	Weekly Pivots
Day Trader	Intraday Pivots

TABLE 10.1: The four types of traders and the pivots they trade

Take a look at Figure 10.12, which illustrates the multiple timeframe confluence phenomenon. When price approaches a multiple timeframe hot zone, the yearly, monthly, weekly, and intraday pivots will send a call to action to various types of traders, including Investors, Position Traders, Swing Traders, and Day Traders. When each of these types of market participants puts money to work at the same area of focus, the result is usually widespread participation that leads to key moves in the market. Putting your money to work at a MTZ alongside various groups of market participants will keep you on the right side of the market at points in the chart that have the most significance.

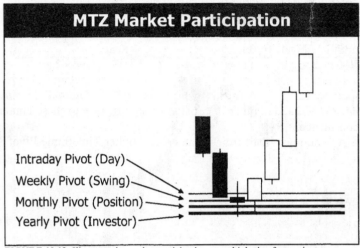

FIGURE 10.12: Illustrates the market participation at multiple timeframe pivots

Let's take a closer look at the MTZ concept. Figure 10.13 shows a daily chart of the E-Mini Russell 2000 futures contract. The contract had been trending steadily lower through the first five weeks of 2010, but approached a major area of higher timeframe confluence in early February. The TF dropped right into this multiple timeframe hot zone, which contained yearly, monthly, and weekly pivots, and immediately began to show strength. Despite the five-week decline, it became quite clear that all major types of market participants had begun to see value at the current area of confluence and began to put money to work. This is evidenced by the fact that the TF formed a highly bullish wick reversal candlestick on the day that it touched all major timeframes of pivots, signaling a potential reversal ahead. When an exaggerated form of this particular candlestick forms in a daily or weekly chart, the potential for a reversal is magnified. There is no need to wait for a new closing high on the following bar. Instead, taking an entry at the close of the wick candlestick, or at the open of the following bar, will usually prove highly profitable over the following five to ten days.

The herd mentality of the major market players sparked a huge advance in the TF that sent the contract soaring from the 580 low to the monthly R1 resistance level at 634, which is a big fifty-four point move worth $5,400 per contract. Again, anytime you have two different equations that mark the same area as support or resistance, you have to take notice. But in this case, two different equations *and* multiple timeframes all marked this band of support as a significant area confluence, which essentially influenced price in a major way.

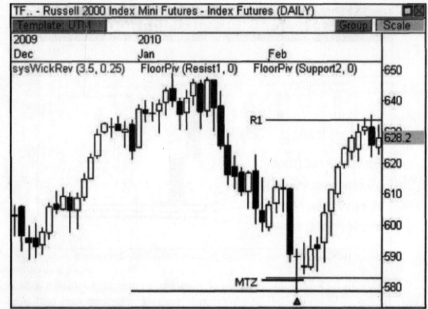

FIGURE 10.13: Clear MTZ support sparks a two-week rally in the TF

Let's take a look at another example of multiple timeframe confluence. Figure 10.14 shows a sixty-minute chart of the Silver futures contract that shows the convergence of major pivot confluence and multiple signal generation. Silver rallied up toward the $19.50 level, but ran right into multiple timeframe pivot resistance, consisting of intraday, monthly, and yearly pivot levels. Add to this the fact that every major signal that I have shared throughout this book fired in a three-day window, and you have the makings of a major market reversal in this commodity.

The chart shows that all four bearish signals (the extreme, outside, doji, and wick reversal setups) fired within a few days of each other, as price tested this major band of pivot confluence. Basically, the market was beginning to see major resistance at the MTZ and price behavior, via candlesticks, began to sound the alarm bells, which ultimately led to a significant drop in price over the following two weeks. A price drop in Silver futures from $19.50 to $17.00 is a major move, but what is more interesting is the fact that price dropped precisely to the next area of pivot confluence, which was a higher timeframe DPZ.

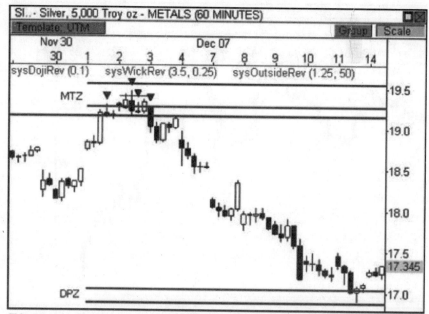

FIGURE 10.14: The Silver futures contract drops away from a major band of MTZ resistance

The next chart I want to share shows a bearish test at a MTZ resistance band that sparks a two-day drop in the E-Mini S&P 500 futures contract. Figure 10.15 shows the ES formed a bearish outside reversal pattern in the sixty-minute chart in late January 2010. This bearish signal was accompanied by intraday, weekly, and monthly pivot resistance from both the Floor Pivot indicator and Camarilla Equation. This bearish mix of factors led to a steady decline of fifty points over the next two sessions, which is quite a move for the ES. Of course, price halted its decline after reaching a higher timeframe DPZ, consisting of monthly S1 and L4 support, which made for a perfectly fine target.

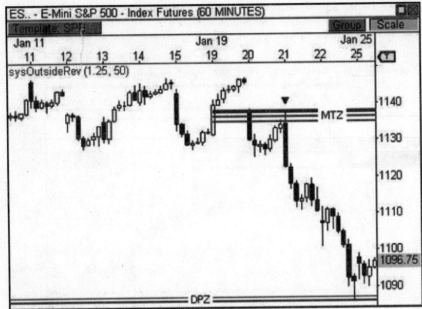

FIGURE 10.15: The ES turns down off MTZ resistance

BOSS IN ACTION

Finding and trading multiple timeframe hot zones can be difficult at first. Actually, the task can be quite overwhelming. For those that are new to pivot-based trading, I usually suggest trading based off one set of pivots and one timeframe until you become comfortable with sorting through all the information that is presented in the charts. I do not like to clutter my charts, so I definitely do not plot every pivot-based indicator with every possible timeframe on my charts. Instead, my trading platform allows me to keep indicator templates where I can store various combinations of indicators, systems, and even chart styles. When the mood strikes, I simply flip to certain templates to see how price is responding to various pivot combinations across timeframes. It's actually an efficient process.

I also have a routine that I follow at the conclusion of each trading session whereby I analyze each of the major instruments that I follow. I will look for major bands of confluence, study pivot relationships, and even identify key chart patterns in the chart, among other things. Therefore, when Apple, Inc. was approaching a monthly GPZ, I knew that a potential bounce could be seen off this MTZ (seen in Figure 10.16). Apple opened the session with early weakness and dropped precisely to monthly and intraday pivot support, consisting of four levels of pivot confluence. Since I knew the monthly GPZ was likely to reject a bearish continuation, I waited for signs of a reversal via any of the key candlestick setups that I have covered. Seventy-five minutes into the trading session, AAPL formed a bullish wick reversal candlestick and a bullish doji reversal, which easily triggered my entry at $205.10. My initial target became double pivot resistance at $209.50, which was reached, but I also kept a trailing profit stop, since there was quite a bit of distance to cover in this trade. Ultimately, the trade delivered a gain of $4.40 off this powerful band of multiple timeframe confluence.

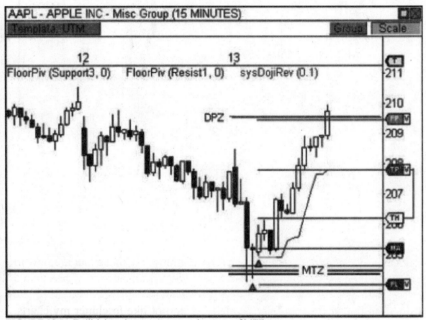

FIGURE 10.16: Bullish intraday response to a clear area of MTZ support

ENGAGING HOT ZONES

Multiple pivot confluence levels carry an amazing ability to influence price. This is due to the fact that they command the attention of multiple types of market players. While trading based off of intraday pivot levels can certainly light the path to profits, combining multiple pivot confluence levels with higher timeframe pivot analysis can easily take your trading to another level of trading success.

The key to trading successfully trading with multiple pivot confirmation, however, lies within the ability to filter out the "noise." While all pivots have a certain amount of significance, not all pivots are created equal. Understanding that the market has been in an uptrend should immediately turn your focus away from any pivot level below S1 support when using the Floor Pivot indicator. Likewise, noticing that L3 support lies within the central pivot range should automatically turn your attention to potential buying opportunities off this highly bullish GPZ. Of course, this will come with practice and patience. The more you engage the information, the more knowledgeable you will become. With knowledge comes power.

CHAPTER 11

PLANNING
FOR SUCCESS

"The courage in a speculator is merely the confidence to act on the decision of his mind."

- Jesse Livermore

The prior chapters have unlocked the door to a world of pivots that only professionals knew existed. This world illuminates the underlying support and resistance levels professionals have been using for decades in every market and timeframe. Now, traders from all backgrounds and levels of experience can enjoy the power of pivots and the many layers of analysis and triggers they offer. I have literally spilled more than a decade of knowledge into the pages of this book and I strongly believe that the content herein will help you achieve a higher level of trading.

While I strongly believe the trading edge the pivots offer is one of the best ways to approach the market in terms of analysis, trade triggers, and trade management, I will not tell you that every chart or every day will offer picture-perfect trading opportunities. Illiquid and irrational markets will not adhere to the pivots in a manner consistent with profitable trading. When a market is not responding to the pivots in a predictable and fluid manner, simply exclude that particular market from your watch list. If you make it a habit to trade only the charts that have a history of responding to the pivots, you will put yourself in a position to consistently profit in the markets.

Oddly enough, while trading profitably is difficult enough to accomplish, it is only a part of what makes a successful trader. The most successful traders are highly prepared and have a planned course of action for every aspect of trading, from selecting setups to deciding which markets to trade. It is this type of preparation that speeds up the learning curve and helps traders progress to the next level of trading success. In the following section, I will walk you through one of the most important routines of my trading regimen, which any aspiring trader should consider adopting.

THE FLIGHT PLAN

If you study the common traits of the most successful traders, you will find they are all highly prepared. They diagnose the current state of the market and create expectations for potential market behavior. They have visualized what the market is likely to do, and can immediately identify when the market has diverged from the anticipated course of action. They prepare for certain types of outcomes and are ready for the expected, and the unexpected.

Many of the most successful traders use what I call a *Flight Plan* to help guide them in the market. In aviation, pilots are generally required to file a flight plan before departure. Flight plans include information such as departure and arrival points, estimated time en route, the amount of fuel on board, the number of people on board, and alternate airports in case of bad weather or an emergency. In essence, flight plans help guide pilots under good conditions and bad, setting a course of action under both circumstances.

Like pilots, the most successful traders create daily flight plans prior to each market day to help guide them in the upcoming trading session. Of course, each trader is different, so plans can differ vastly depending on whose you read. If you have never created a flight plan, it is usually best to view how other traders have formulated their plans in order to incorporate what works best for your particular trading style. I've seen flight plans that make me dizzy trying to decipher what I'm supposed to do for the upcoming session. Many pivot traders will list every single pivot point from many different pivot equations for various markets onto a single sheet of paper, which thoroughly confuses me and exhausts me at the same time. The point of a flight plan is not to see how much information you can fit onto a sheet of paper. Instead, a flight plan is meant to bring the most pertinent information to your attention to guide you in the upcoming session.

I have provided a snippet of a recent flight plan that I created for April 16, 2010, seen in Figure 11.1. You'll notice that I do not include every single pivot point from every indicator for each timeframe. Instead, I include the most pertinent pivots from each of the three indicators that I have discussed in the book. Moreover, instead of just knowing where the pivots will be for the following session, I also want to know important two-day pivot relationships, pivot width characteristics, and their implications for the upcoming day. I also include any virgin Money Zone levels that have yet to be closed and any hot zones that are worth noting. Each piece of information is interrelated and provides me with a game plan for the following session.

Given the vast amount of information that can be gleaned from pivot point analysis, however, there are many ways to organize the information that you will want to view for the upcoming day. For example, position traders or long-term investors may want to include monthly and yearly pivot relationships in their flight plan, while swing traders may want to include daily and weekly relationships. Flight plans are meant to be tailored to your specific trading style so you can flush out the right opportunities for your approach. The flight plan I have provided shows the information that I like to include for intraday trading purposes.

The Pivot Boss Flight Plan
for April 16, 2010

	ES	MC	CL
Previous Price Range			
High	1210.50	832.6	86.24
Low	1204.50	827.1	85.27
Money Zone Levels			
VAH	1209.80	831.2	85.91
POC	1207.25	830.4	85.63
VPOC	1207.25	830.3	85.63
VAL	1206.25	828.4	85.47
Central Pivot Range			
TC	1208.00	829.6	85.75
Central Pivot	1207.75	829.9	85.68
BC	1207.50	829.3	85.60
Camarilla Third Layer			
H3	1209.90	830.6	85.80
L3	1206.60	827.6	85.26
Virgin Money Zone Levels			
POC	1201.25	825.5	83.77
VPOC	1190.75	821.6	83.65
POC		815.8	
VPOC		812.9	
Hot Zones			
Hot Zone High	1208.00	830.6	85.80
Hot Zone Low	1207.25	829.3	85.60
2-Day Relationships			
Money Zone	Higher	Higher	Inside
Expected Outcome	Bullish	Bullish	Breakout
Floor Pivots	Higher	Higher	OL Higher
Expected Outcome	Bullish	Bullish	Bullish
Camarilla	OL Higher	Inside	Inside
Expected Outcome	Bullish	Breakout	Breakout
Pivot Width Relationships			
Money Zone	Narrow	Narrow	Narrow
Expected Outcome	Breakout	Breakout	Breakout
Floor Pivots	Narrow	Narrow	Narrow
Expected Outcome	Breakout	Breakout	Breakout
Camarilla	Narrow	Narrow	Narrow
Expected Outcome	Breakout	Breakout	Breakout

FIGURE 11.1: The flight plan for April 16, 2010

Let's take a closer look at the flight plan for April 16 and walk through how it would have helped us in our trading. When I glaze over a flight plan, I first want to know if any important two-day pivot relationships are present. Relationships like Higher Value, Overlapping Higher Value, Lower Value, and Overlapping Lower Value relationships give you important directional bias for the upcoming session. This bias should steer you in the direction of the current trend, but will also alert you to a change in bias if the opening print doesn't confirm the forecast. Relationships like Inside Value, Outside Value, and Unchanged Value forecast potential trending or sideways scenarios. I also want to know if the market has developed unusually wide or narrow pivots, because these relationships can lead to highly predictable price behavior in the market. When several of these relationships line up perfectly, the market could be on the verge of anticipated price behavior.

Looking over the flight plan for April 16, I notice the E-Mini S&P 400 futures contract has developed potentially explosive pivot relationships, which could lead to a Trend Day scenario—one of my favorite days in the market. The Camarilla Equation has formed a two-day Inside Value relationship, while each of the indicators has formed unusually narrow pivots for the upcoming session. These pivot characteristics are highly indicative of a potential breakout opportunity for the following day. Keep in mind, however, that you must confirm your forecast with actual price behavior the next morning. In this case, an opening print beyond the prior day's price range will confirm breakout behavior, which could progress into a Trend Day. Therefore, we would like to see the MC open the session either above 832.60 or below 827.10 in order to prove our breakout theory.

Let's take a look at Figure 11.2 to see how the E-Mini S&P 400 fared the following session. The MC opened the session with a gap below the prior day's low price of 827.10, which is our first indication of key weakness. The MC then formed a bearish wick reversal candlestick upon testing the L3 pivot level from underneath, which essentially confirmed a short entry in this contract. The MC proceeded to drop the rest of the morning and eventually filled three of the four virgin Money Zone levels that were noted in the day's flight plan. Depending on how you managed the trade, you would have pocketed anywhere from $500 to $1000 for each contract traded, which is nice incentive to do your homework.

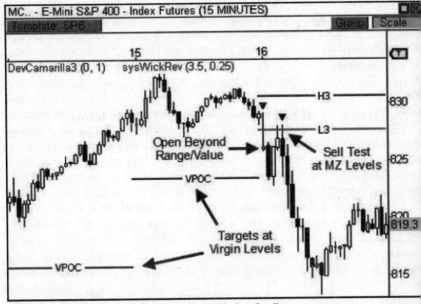

FIGURE 11.2: The flight plan helped us prepare for this day of trading.

I have found it to be extremely beneficial to update my flight plan daily. While it can seem tedious at first, simple spreadsheet calculations can easily streamline the process, which is well worth the effort. And don't forget to tailor your flight plan to suit your trading style. I've covered so many ways to profit with pivots that every trader will gravitate toward different setups and relationships. Finding your niche will be crucial to your success with these concepts.

PREPARATION BREEDS CONFIDENCE

You have embarked on a journey that can truly revolutionize the way you trade. But you must have the confidence to pull the trigger and the fortitude to stick with your plan. A great many failures can be traced back to the times that traders strayed from their game plan. A trader thinks more clearly *before* a trade is placed. Know your entry, target, and stop loss *before* you enter a trade. You must have confidence in your analysis and act quickly upon reaching a conclusion derived from your analysis.

The setups in this book are some of my favorite money-making ideas. These, along with the key pivot behaviors that I have explained, are fabulous methods for picking off winners in the market. However, given the abundance of trading ideas in this book, it is best that you pick and choose a few that you are comfortable trading. After all, even the best money-making ideas will make you zilch if you are not comfortable with the concept. As a matter of fact, being uncomfortable with a trading approach can usually turn a great system into a pitiful loser. Become a master of a few setups, instead of a casual fan of many. Expanding into new setups after mastering a few is usually a prudent approach.

Trading is an endeavor that requires consistent learning. After many years of trading with the pivots, I continue to learn new and interesting techniques to profit in the market using these incredible indicators. Even writing this book allowed me to grow as a trader and as a connoisseur of these fabulous price-based indicators. Trading is about finding an edge in the market. As long as you continue to keep an open mind toward your trading education, you will allow yourself to continue to grow as a trader. The day a trader believes he knows everything about the market is the day that he stops growing and allows the competition to surpass him. This can be one of the most fatal errs in trading.

Continue to polish your use of the concepts and techniques in this book. Over time, I hope that you will continue to draw beneficial nuggets away from these pages. With great pleasure and gratitude, I would like to express my genuine appreciation for reading *Secrets of a Pivot Boss*. It is my sincere hope that this book will be of service to you on your path to trading success.

Good luck in your trading endeavors,
Franklin O. Ochoa, Jr.

APPENDIX A

FLOOR PIVOTS

RESEARCH

"General wisdom is less valuable than specific savvy."

- Jesse Livermore

Learning to understand the pivots and their nuances is usually best done under live fire. There is no substitute for real bullets on the battlefield; neither should there be in the trading field. Aside from learning the pivots with live charts, one of the best ways to understand pivot behavior is to learn what the statistics are telling you. Knowing that the market tests the central pivot 63 percent of the time at some point during the day is a huge advantage. Knowing that on days when the market doesn't touch the central pivot you usually see a highly directional, trending day toward R3 or S3 can make a significant improvement in your trading.

I've compiled and crunched the statistics on eight months of the latest data for the Mini-Sized Dow futures contract, from November 2008 through June 2009. These eight months covered all three market cycles: a sideways period from November through December 2008, a bear period from January through February 2009, and a bull period from March through June 2009 (Figure A.1). This is important when analyzing the data because you do not want one market phase to dominate the data collection phase, which could skew what the data are intending to tell you.

Keep in mind that I gathered these statistics for intraday trading. That is, these figures work for any minute periodicity below a daily chart.

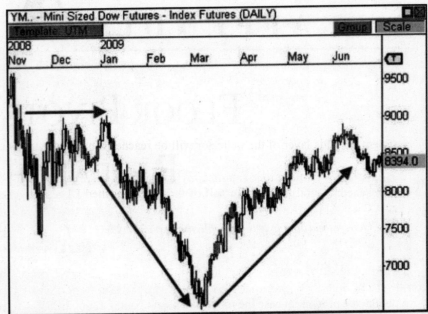

FIGURE A.1: All three market phases were captured in the data collection.

The first major statistics I wanted to collect were basic touches in a day. Anytime the YM merely touched a pivot, it was noted. I wanted to see how often the YM visited certain pivots, which could help to refine both our entries and exits. Keep in mind that I've combined each layer so that L1 means both S1 and R1. Thus, the first layer refers to S1/R1, the second layer refers to S2/R2, and so on (see the table).

Basic Touches at Pivots				
CP	L1	L2	L3	L4
63.0%	73.3%	38.2%	17.6%	5.5%

Each of these percentages tells a story. First, the central pivot was reached 63 percent of the time at some point during the day. I was hoping that this number would be higher, but there are two reasons for this. First, I only used the central pivot for my data collection, not the pivot range (BC and TC). Many times price would test either BC or TC and would simply reverse, which caused the central pivot not to be reached. Secondly, I used the YM for my data collection, which is an instrument that can often gap at the open, which causes price to miss the central pivot completely at times. Still, 63 percent is statistically significant.

What surprised me the most was the fact that the first layer of the indicator (R1 and S1) was reached 73.3 percent of the time. This is in line with our theory from Chapter 1 that traders like to test the first layer of support or resistance early in the day to see what type of market day it may become. Also, this percentage is so high that it allows us to set profit targets at either S1 or R1 when we take positions, since there is a high probability of reaching our target. Therefore, if we get a breakout through the top of the centrals early in the session, we can set our targets to R1 since we can feel confident that this layer of the indicator will be reached a high percentage of the time.

Layers two through four significantly dropped off after either S1 or R1 were reached. Slightly more than half of those that reached L1 also reached L2 (38.2%). Then slightly more than half of those that reached L2 also reached L3 (17.6%). Lastly, the YM only reached L4 5.5 percent of the time; just 9 times out of 165 days. In other words, for a market to reach out to L3 or L4 is quite rare. Therefore, if you are in a trade, you may want to begin liquidating most of your position once you've reached R2 or S2, since this will usually mark the end of the move. Leaving on a tiny portion of your trade may be prudent in case the move extends beyond L2, however.

The next chunk of data I gathered were closes beyond pivots. That is, once a pivot was reached, where did price close. See the table below.

Closes Beyond Pivots				
Within L1	L1	L2	L3	L4
53.4%	24.8%	12.1%	6.7%	3.0%

Looking at the table above shows that after price reaches the first layer of the indicator 73.3 percent of the time, it closes beyond this layer only 46.6 percent of the time. This means that more than half the time (53.4%) after reaching L1, price will close within S1 and R1. Each layer beyond L1 shows a clear half-life, as the percentage of closes beyond each additional level is reduced by half. Moreover, a full 36.9 percent of the 46.6 percent of closers that fell beyond L1 closed below R3. To put it more simply, 79.2 percent of the closings that occurred beyond L1 closed below L3 and L4. This means that four out of every five times that price closes beyond L1, it will close between L1 and L3. This is important to remember.

Another statistic that I wanted to track was the percentage of the time the Central Pivot Forecast worked out. That is, I wanted to track the percentage of the time an open above the central pivot meant a close above the pivot, and the number of times an open below the pivot would mean a close below it. This would give us an advantage right at the open knowing that "X" percent of the time an open above the central pivot means a close above it, and vice versa. Basically, any open above the central pivot would mean having a bullish bias, and any opening below it would mean having a bearish bias. See the results below.

Central Pivot Forecast	
Open > CP = Close Above	Open < CP = Close Below
53.4%	48.8%

It turns out that 53.4 percent of the time that price opened above the central pivot, it also closed above it. While any time price opened below the central pivot, it closed below it 48.8 percent of the time. Keep in mind that this doesn't necessarily mean that price advanced (or declined) the rest of the day; only that it closed above or below the central pivot. For example, price can open above the central pivot by fifty points via a gap in the YM and still close above the central pivot if only by one point. Therefore, the YM actually lost traction after the gap, but our condition was still met.

The symmetry in the percentages between a bullish and bearish forecast are nice. This means that you basically have the same shot of the condition working out despite an opening above or below the central pivot. What these numbers do tell us is that the Central Pivot Forecast will work a little over 50 percent of the time, which can still be statistically significant when used correctly.

One particular statistical category took me by surprise, one that I didn't intend on studying at first. We know that the central pivot is reached 63 percent of the time at some point during the day. Well, what happens the other 37 percent of the time when the central pivot is not reached? The answer: something fascinating.

Days when the central pivot is not reached are usually trending days in the market. Every statistical category increases in percentage beyond L1. This means that touches at pivot levels beyond L1, and closes beyond them all increase significantly due to the trending nature of the market. Interestingly, touches at R1 and S1 decrease from the stellar 73.3 percent clip. See the table below.

Days When Central Pivot is Not Touched				
Basic Touches at Pivots				
CP	L1	L2	L3	L4
0%	67.2%	63.9%	34.4%	11.5%
Compare to Original Percentages				
63%	73.3%	38.2%	17.6%	5.5%
Closes Beyond Pivots				
CP	L1	L2	L3	L4
0%	27.9%	23.0%	16.4%	6.6%
Compare to Original Percentages				
63%	24.8%	12.1%	6.7%	3.0%

The table above shows that touches beyond L1 increased significantly, with most cases doubling their original value from before. R2 and S2 were reached 61.9 percent of the time versus just 38.2 percent before, while touches at L3 and L4 doubled from 17.6 percent to 34.4 percent and 5.5 percent to 11.5 percent, respectively. On days when the central pivot is not reached, the market is trending in one direction or the other, easily reaching beyond the second layer of the indicator (R2 and S2). On these days, it is much more prudent to hold targets at the third layer of the indicator (R3 or S3) instead of just L1 or L2.

The percentages also increased dramatically when measuring closures beyond key pivot levels. The percentage of closures beyond L1 (but below L2) barely increased by just three percentage points, but closures above L2, L3, and L4 all doubled. This indicates that not only is the market trending steadily in one direction, but it also is closing at or near the extremes of the move. This means a vast reduction in the number of reversals we see in the market on these days, thus allowing you to ride the trend comfortably.

I've found that on many of the days where the central pivot is not touched, you see a gap *beyond* the central pivot, and oftentimes beyond L1 (thus the reason its percentage of touches dropped from 73.3% to 67.2%). If the market gaps beyond these two levels, and they hold on a retest, you typically see steady movement in the direction of the gap.

I'll give you one final argument to support the strength of trending days when the central pivot is not touched. The table below shows the original touches at pivots and closures beyond pivots that we discussed at the top of this Appendix. I originally stated that R1 and S1 are the most likely stopping grounds for a typical market, with movement occasionally pushing to the second layer of the indicator. The table below shows that days that do not test the central pivot make up the *vast majority* of touches at pivots and closures beyond pivots.

Percentage of Original Touches & Closures that Occurred when the Central Pivot was Not Touched				
Basic Touches at Pivots				
CP	L1	L2	L3	L4
0%	33.9%	61.9%	72.4%	77.8%
Original Percentages				
63%	73.3%	38.2%	17.6%	5.5%
Closes Beyond Pivots				
CP	L1	L2	L3	L4
0%	41.5%	70.0%	90.9%	80.0%
Original Percentages				
63%	24.8%	12.1%	6.7%	3.0%

A full 61.9 percent of touches at L2 occurred on days when the central pivot was not touched, while 72.4 percent and 77.8 percent of touches at L3 and L4, respectively, occurred on these days. Moreover, only 33.9 percent of touches at L1 came on days when the central pivot was not touched. This proves our theory that the market was typically gapping through L1 and trending in the direction of the gap the rest of the day.

Most impressive, however, are the closures figures. A hefty 70 percent of closures that occurred beyond L2 (but within L3) occurred when the central pivot was not tested. That figure increases to 90.9 percent and 80 percent when calculating closures beyond L3 and L4. Given this information, we know that when the central pivot is not tested during the day, there is a 73.8 percent chance that the market will close beyond the first layer of the indicator, S1 or R1. Compare that whopping percentage to the original 46.6 percent. This means that on days when the market zooms through the first layer of pivots, with total disregard for the central pivot, three out of four days will result in a close beyond S1 or R1. This is a significant advantage.

The Abbreviated Version:

1. This study was conducted on intraday data ranging from November 2008 through June 2009 on the Mini-Sized Dow futures contract.
2. The central pivot is reached 63 percent of the time at some point during the day.
3. L1 was reached 73.3 percent of the time, as traders want to test the first level of support or resistance on most days. Setting profit targets at this layer is prudent on most sessions.
4. Fifty-three percent of the time the market will open *above* the central pivot and close above it; 48.8 percent of the time the market open *below* the central pivot and close below it.
5. Price closed within R1 and S1 53.4 percent of the time; only 46.6 percent of the time will it close outside this range.
6. Of the times that price actually closed *outside* R1 and S2, 79.2 percent of these cases closed below R3 and above S3.
7. Once a pivot is reached, the chances of reaching the next pivot significantly reduces by half.
8. You usually see trending movement beyond L2 on the days when the central pivot point is not touched.
9. When the central pivot is not touched, the instances of touches beyond L1 increase significantly, doubling in most cases.
10. When the central pivot is not touched, the instances of closures beyond L1 increase significantly, more than doubling in every case.
11. When the central pivot is not touched, touches at L1 and closures beyond this level decrease, signifying an extended move beyond this layer.
12. Of the touches that occurred beyond L1, 61.9 percent of the L2 touches occurred when the central pivot was not touched on the day. Likewise, 72.4 percent of the tests at L3, and 77.8 percent of the touches at L4 occurred when the central pivot was not reached.

13. Of the closures that occurred beyond L1, 70 percent of closures beyond L2 (but below L3) occurred when the central pivot was not touched on the day. Likewise, 90.9 percent of the closures beyond L3 (but below L4) and 80 percent of the closures beyond L4 occurred when the central pivot was not reached.

14. Touches of L1 significantly dropped on the days when the central pivot was not touched, falling to 33.9 percent (down from 73.3 percent). This indicates the market is gapping past L1 on most occasions and continuing to push toward higher pivot levels.

15. Most importantly, on days when the central pivot is not tested, there is a 73.8 percent chance that the market will close *beyond* L1. This is up from the original 46.6 percent.

APPENDIX **B**

CUSTOM CODE
LIBRARY

For those of you that trade with OmniTrader Professional or VisualTrader Professional, I am including the exact VBA code of the various signals, stops, and indicators that I have covered throughout the book. While these scripts will allow you to see the same opportunities that I have covered, they also give you the ability to create incredibly powerful mechanical strategies. If you do not trade with these platforms, the easy language syntax is fairly close to that of other trading programs, so assimilating the information should be fairly easy.

SYSTEMS
Wick Reversal System
File Name: sysWickRev

```
#System

#PARAM "Wick_Multiplier", 2.5, .5, 20
#PARAM "Body_Percentage", .25, .1, 1

If C > O _
AND (O - L) >= ((C - O) * Wick_Multiplier) _
AND (H - C) <= ((H - L) * Body_Percentage) _
OR C < O _
AND (C - L) >= ((O - C) * Wick_Multiplier) _
AND (H - C) <= ((H - L) * Body_Percentage) _
OR C = O AND NOT C = H _
AND (H - L) >= ((H - C) * Wick_Multiplier) _
AND (H - C) <= ((H - L) * Body_Percentage) _
OR O = H AND C = H _
AND H - L >= AVG(H-L, 50) Then
      Signal = LongSignal

ElseIf C < O _
AND (H - O) >= ((O - C) * Wick_Multiplier) _
AND (C - L) <= ((H - L) * Body_Percentage) _
OR C > O _
AND (H - C) >= ((C - O) * Wick_Multiplier) _
AND (C - L) <= ((H - L) * Body_Percentage) _
OR C = O AND NOT C = L _
AND (H - L) >= ((C - L) * Wick_Multiplier) _
AND (C - L) <= ((H - L) * Body_Percentage) _
OR O = L AND C = L _
AND H - L >= AVG(H-L, 50) Then
      Signal = ShortSignal

End If
```

Extreme Reversal System
File Name: sysExtremeRev

```
#System

#PARAM "BodySize", .525, .05, 1
#PARAM "BarsBack", 50, 1, 50
#PARAM "BodyMultiplier", 2, .25, 5

Dim AverageBody          As Single
Dim myBodySize           As Single
Dim myCandleSize         As Single
Dim AverageCandle        As Single

myBodySize = ABS(C - O)
AverageBody = Average(myBodySize,BarsBack)
myCandleSize = (H - L)
AverageCandle = Average(myCandleSize,BarsBack)

If ((O[1] - C[1]) >= (BodySize * (H[1] - L[1]))) AND _
((H[1] - L[1]) > (AverageCandle * BodyMultiplier)) AND _
((O[1] - C[1]) > AverageBody) AND _
(C > O) Then
     Signal = LongSignal

ElseIf ((C[1] - O[1]) >= BodySize * (H[1] - L[1])) AND _
((H[1] - L[1]) > (AverageCandle * BodyMultiplier)) AND _
((C[1] - O[1]) > AverageBody) AND _
(O > C) Then
     Signal = ShortSignal

End If
```

Outside Reversal System
File Name: sysOutsideRev

```
#System

#PARAM "BarMultiplier", 1.25, .05, 3.5
#PARAM "BarsBack", 50, 1, 250

Dim AverageCandle        As Single
Dim myCandleSize         As Single

myCandleSize = (H - L)
AverageCandle = Average(myCandleSize,BarsBack)

If L < L[1] AND C > H[1] AND _
((H - L) >= (AverageCandle * BarMultiplier)) Then
        Signal = LongSignal

ElseIf H > H[1] AND C < L[1] AND _
((H - L) >= (AverageCandle * BarMultiplier)) Then
        Signal = ShortSignal

End If
```

Doji Reversal System
File Name: sysDojiRev

```
#System

#PARAM "Percentage", .10

Dim    fRangeHL    As Single
Dim    fRangeCO    As Single

fRangeHL = H[1] - L[1]
fRangeCO = ABS(C[1] - O[1])

If fRangeCO <= fRangeHL * Percentage _
AND C < L[1] _
AND L[1] > SMA(10) _
AND C < O _
OR C < L[2] AND NOT C[1] < L[2] _
AND fRangeCO[1] <= fRangeHL[1] * Percentage _
AND C < O _
AND L[2] > SMA(10) Then
     Signal = ShortSignal

ElseIf fRangeCO <= fRangeHL * Percentage _
AND C > H[1] _
AND H[1] < SMA(10) _
AND C > O _
OR C > H[2] AND NOT C[1] > H[2] _
AND fRangeCO[1] <= fRangeHL[1] * Percentage _
AND C > O _
AND H[2] < SMA(10) Then
     Signal = LongSignal

End If
```

INDICATORS
Central Pivot Range Indicator
File Name: iCentralPivotRange

```
#Indicator

#PARAM "Show_Current_Only", 1, 0, 1
#PARAM "Show_Level", 0, 0, 3

Dim fHigh, fLow, fClose         As Single
Dim fPP, fBC, fTC               As Single
Dim nBreakBar                   As Integer
Dim bBreakBar                   As Boolean = False

If Periodicity = 1 Then
     bBreakBar = Not BarDayOfYear() = BarDayOfYear()[1]
ElseIf Periodicity = 2 Then
     bBreakBar = Not BarMonth() = BarMonth()[1]
Else
     bBreakBar = False
End If

If Bar = SymbolData.NumRec - 1 Then
     bBreakBar = True
End If

If Bar = 0 then
    fHigh = H
    fLow = L
    nBreakBar = 0
Else
    fPP = fPP[1]
    fTC = fTC[1]
    fBC = fBC[1]

    fHigh = fHigh[1]
    fLow = fLow[1]
    nBreakBar = nBreakBar[1]

    If bBreakBar Then
        If Bar = SymbolData.NumRec - 1 Then
            If Show_Level = 1 Or Show_Level = 0 Then
                    PlotPriceTrendLine("PP",
nBreakBar, fPP, Bar, fPP, fuchsia)
```

```
            End If
            If Show_Level = 2 Or Show_Level = 0 Then
                      PlotPriceTrendLine("BC",
nBreakBar, fBC, Bar, fBC, fuchsia)
            End If
            If Show_Level = 3 Or Show_Level = 0 Then
                      PlotPriceTrendLine("TC",
nBreakBar, fTC, Bar, fTC, fuchsia)
            End If
        ElseIf nBreakBar > 0 And Show_Current_Only = 0
Then
            If Show_Level = 1 Or Show_Level = 0 then
                      PlotPriceTrendLine("PP",
nBreakBar, fPP, Bar - 1, fPP, fuchsia)
            End If
            If Show_Level = 2 Or Show_Level = 0 then
                      PlotPriceTrendLine("BC",
nBreakBar, fBC, Bar - 1, fBC, fuchsia)
            End If
            If Show_Level = 3 Or Show_Level = 0 then
                      PlotPriceTrendLine("TC",
nBreakBar, fTC, Bar - 1, fTC, fuchsia)
            End If
        End If

        fClose = C[1]

        fPP = ((fHigh + fLow + fClose) / 3)
        fBC = ((fHigh + fLow) / 2)
        fTC = ((fPP - fBC) + fPP)

        fHigh = H
        fLow = L
        nBreakBar = Bar
    End If

    If H > fHigh Then ' If we found a higher high
          fHigh = H ' Record new high
    End If
    If L < fLow Then ' If we found a lower low
          fLow = L ' Record new low
    End If

End If

Return 0
```

Developing Pivot Range Indicator
File Name: iDevPivotRange

```
#Indicator

#PARAM "Plot_Developing", 1, 0, 1
#PARAM "Plot_Pivots", 1, 0, 1

Dim fHigh, fLow, fClose        As Single
Dim fPP, fBC, fTC              As Single
Dim nBreakBar, nLastBar        As Integer
Dim bBreakBar                  As Boolean = False

If Periodicity = 1 Then
      bBreakBar = Not BarDayOfYear() = BarDayOfYear()[1]
ElseIf Periodicity = 2 Then
      bBreakBar = Not BarMonth() = BarMonth()[1]
Else
      bBreakBar = False
End If

If Plot_Pivots = 1 And (bBreakBar Or Bar =
SymbolData.NumRec - 1) Then
      If Bar = SymbolData.NumRec - 1 Then
            nLastBar = Bar
      Else
            nLastBar = Bar - 1
      End If

      PlotPriceTrendLine("Central Pivot", nBreakBar-1,
fPP[Bar - nBreakBar + 1], nLastBar, fPP[Bar - nBreakBar
+ 1], fuchsia)
      PlotPriceTrendLine("Top Pivot", nBreakBar-1,
fTC[Bar - nBreakBar + 1], nLastBar, fTC[Bar - nBreakBar
+ 1], fuchsia)
      PlotPriceTrendLine("Bottom Pivot", nBreakBar-1,
fBC[Bar - nBreakBar + 1], nLastBar, fBC[Bar - nBreakBar
+ 1], fuchsia)
End If

If Bar = 0 Or bBreakBar then
    fHigh = H
    fLow = L
    nBreakBar = Bar
```

```
Else
      If H > fHigh Then
             fHigh = H
      End If
      If L < fLow Then
             fLow = L
      End If
End If

fPP = ((fHigh + fLow + C) / 3)
fBC = ((fHigh + fLow) / 2)
fTC = ((fPP - fBC) + fPP)

If Plot_Developing = 1 Then
      PlotPrice("Developing Central Pivot", fPP,
fuchsia)
      PlotPrice("Developing Top Pivot", fTC, fuchsia)
      PlotPrice("Developing Bottom Pivot", fBC, fuchsia)
End If

Return 0
```

Developing Camarilla 3 Indicator
File Name: iDevCamarilla3

```
#Indicator

#PARAM "Plot_Developing", 1, 0, 1
#PARAM "Plot_Pivots", 1, 0, 1

Dim fHigh, fLow, fClose        As Single
Dim fH3, fL3                   As Single
Dim nBreakBar, nLastBar        As Integer
Dim bBreakBar                  As Boolean = False

If Periodicity = 1 Then '
      bBreakBar = Not BarDayOfYear() = BarDayOfYear()[1]
ElseIf Periodicity = 2 Then
      bBreakBar = Not BarMonth() = BarMonth()[1]
Else
      bBreakBar = False
End If

If Plot_Pivots = 1 And (bBreakBar Or Bar =
SymbolData.NumRec - 1) Then
      If Bar = SymbolData.NumRec - 1 Then
            nLastBar = Bar
      Else
            nLastBar = Bar - 1
      End If

      PlotPriceTrendLine("H3", nBreakBar-1, fH3[Bar -
nBreakBar + 1], nLastBar, fH3[Bar - nBreakBar + 1], red)
      PlotPriceTrendLine("L3", nBreakBar-1, fL3[Bar -
nBreakBar + 1], nLastBar, fL3[Bar - nBreakBar + 1],
green)
End If

If Bar = 0 Or bBreakBar then
    fHigh = H
    fLow = L
    nBreakBar = Bar
Else
      If H > fHigh Then
            fHigh = H
      End If
    End If
```

```
    If L < fLow Then
            fLow = L
    End If
End If

fClose = C

fH3 = ((fHigh - fLow) * (1.1 / 4)) + fClose
fL3 = fClose - (fHigh - fLow) * (1.1 / 4)

If Plot_Developing = 1 Then
     PlotPrice("Developing H3", fH3, red)
     PlotPrice("Developing L3", fL3, green)
End If

Return 0
```

Pivot Range Histogram
File Name: iPivotRangeHIST

```
#Indicator

#PARAM "UpperMarker", .75
#PARAM "LowerMarker", .25

Dim fPivotRange          As Single

fPivotRange = ((FLOOR_PIV(1) - FLOOR_PIV(-
1))/FLOOR_PIV(0)) * 100

PlotHIST("PRHIST", fPivotRange, .5, red, 3)
PlotLabel(UpperMarker)
PlotLabel(LowerMarker)

SetScales(0, 1)

Return 0
```

STOPS
Trailing Centrals Stop
File Name: stoTrailingCentralsStop

```
#Stop

Dim fTCS      As Single

If Signal = LongSignal Then
      fTCS = FLOOR_PIV(-1)
      if L <= fTCS Then
      Signal = ExitSignal
      end if

      PlotPrice("TCS",fTCS,red)

ElseIf Signal = ShortSignal Then
      fTCS = FLOOR_PIV(1)
      if H >= fTCS Then
      Signal = ExitSignal
      end if

      PlotPrice("TCS",fTCS,red)

End if
```

Summary:
Creates a trailing stop based off the central pivot range. The top central pivot is the trailing stop for Shorts, and the bottom central pivot is the stop for Longs.

INDEX